CONTEMPORARY SC

General Editor: ANTHON

This series aims to create a forum for debate between different theoretical and philosophical traditions in the social sciences. As well as covering broad schools of thought, the series will also concentrate upon the work of particular thinkers whose ideas have had a major impact on social science (these books appear under the sub-series title of 'Theoretical Traditions in the Social Sciences'). The series is not limited to abstract theoretical discussion – it will also include more substantive works on contemporary capitalism, the state, politics and other subject areas.

Published titles

Tony Bilton, Kevin Bonnett, Philip Jones, Ken Sheard, Michelle Stanworth and Andrew Webster, *Introductory Sociology*
Simon Clarke, *Marx, Marginalism and Modern Sociology*
Emile Durkheim, *The Rules of Sociological Method* (ed. Steven Lukes, trans. W. D. Halls)
Anthony Giddens, *A Contemporary Critique of Historical Materialism*
Anthony Giddens, *Central Problems in Social Theory*
Anthony Giddens, *Profiles and Critiques in Social Theory*
Anthony Giddens and David Held (eds), *Classes, Power and Conflict*
Jorge Larrain, *Marxism and Ideology*
Ali Rattansi, *Marx and the Division of Labour*
Gerry Rose, *Deciphering Sociological Research*
John Scott, *The Upper Classes: Property and Privilege in Britain*
Steve Taylor, *Durkheim and the Study of Suicide*
John B. Thompson and David Held (eds), *Habermas: Critical Debates*
John Urry, *The Anatomy of Capitalist Societies*

Forthcoming titles

Martin Albrow, *Weber and the Construction of Social Theory*
Clive Ashworth, Chris Dandeker and Terry Johnson, *Theoretical Sociology*
David Brown and Michael Harrison, *Industrial Sociology*
Emile Durkheim, *The Division of Labour in Society* (trans. W. D. Halls)
Boris Frankel, *Beyond the State*
Anthony Giddens, *Between Capitalism and Socialism*
David Held, *Bureaucracy, Democracy and Socialism*
Geoffrey Ingham, *Capitalism Divided*
Claus Offe, *Structural Problems of the Capitalist State*
Ali Rattansi and Dominic Strinati, *Marx and the Sociology of Class*
Michelle Stanworth, *Gender and Class*
John B. Thompson, *Language and Ideology*

CONTEMPORARY SOCIAL THEORY

General Editor: ANTHONY GIDDENS

Theoretical Traditions in the Social Sciences

This series introduces the work of major figures in social science to students beyond their immediate specialisms.

Published titles

Barry Barnes, *T. S. Kuhn and Social Science*
Julian Roberts, *Walter Benjamin*
Dennis Smith, *Barrington Moore: Violence, Morality and Political Change*

Forthcoming titles

Ted Benton, *Althusser and the Althusserians*
David Bloor, *Wittgenstein and Social Science*
Chris Bryant, *Positivism in Social Theory*
John Forrester, *Jacques Lacan*
John Heritage, *Garfinkel and Ethnomethodology*
Athar Hussain, *Foucault*
Bob Jessop, *Nicos Poulantzas*
James Schmidt, *Maurice Merleau-Ponty and Social Theory*
Robin Williams, *Erving Goffman*

Marxism and Ideology

Jorge Larrain

Lecturer in Sociology, University of Birmingham

First published 1983 by
THE MACMILLAN PRESS LTD
London and Basingstoke
Companies and representatives throughout the world

ISBN 0 333 30542 6 (hard cover)
ISBN 0 333 30543 4 (paper cover)

Typeset in Great Britain by
Furlonger Phototext Limited
Bournemouth

Printed in Hong Kong

To Caroline

Acknowledgements

I am greatly indebted to Anthony Giddens, who constantly encouraged and assisted me while I was writing the book and who also read through the manuscript in detail, suggesting many improvements which proved very valuable. I should also like to thank very specially Bill Schwarz for his useful comments and his help with my idiosyncratic English. However, the numerous deficiencies in content and style which the reader will, no doubt, still find remain my own responsibility. Doreen Taylor deserves my gratitude for generously helping with the typing of the manuscript. Finally, I owe a particular debt to Mercedes, my wife, whose unflagging support and understanding, amid difficult circumstances for her, made the writing of this book possible.

July 1982 JORGE LARRAIN

Contents

Introduction

In writing a book on the Marxist conception of ideology one has the feeling of embarking upon a very risky undertaking. The reason for this is not just because ideology is one of those highly complex and elusive concepts which resist any easy definition, but also because there is no single Marxist conception of ideology or agreement as to which version should be considered the properly Marxist one. Divisions in this field are deep and entrenched to the point that, in comparison, Marxist economics or Marxist politics appear as relatively harmonious fields of inquiry. A glance at the various studies on the subject will immediately reveal not only an enormous variety of viewpoints, but also the fact that ideology seems to be considered a privileged terrain of struggle between different interpretations of Marx. The central place which ideology occupies in the competing theories of authors like Lukács, Gramsci and Althusser clearly illustrates this point. In particular, the Althusserian conception has become widely influential explicitly describing the field of ideology in terms of an irreconcilable opposition between structuralism and historicism, and appears to leave no room for other options.

In a sense it is just as well that Marxism should not be a body of received truths, the contents and scope of which are predefined and settled. Since Marx's death, Marxism has developed and become enriched by a series of different interpretations, traditions and perspectives, despite demands from certain quarters laying claim to the true position, as opposed to 'deviations' and 'revisions'. There is no question, therefore, of aspiring to the uniquely correct Marxist conception of ideology. In this area, like in others, Marxism is an active and expanding body of thought which challenges all attempts to fix its meaning once and for all. Yet in another sense the controversy between various interpretations results in some problems for Marxist discussions of ideology. Two effects seem particularly relevant. First, Marx's own specific contribution has increasingly been eclipsed. Second, the development of an overall assessment of the concept of ideology within

Marxism has not been attempted by any Marxist able to produce both sufficient generality and also the necessary historical perspective. These two facts suggest why this book seems worth while. Let us examine these points in order.

(1) It has become increasingly common to discuss Marx's position at second hand, or via the interpretation of an 'authority'. But little attempt is made to assess directly Marx's own contribution. This can be justified by the fact that many authors want only to use a Marxist concept of ideology in order to carry out concrete analyses of social reality. But often because they cannot find a systematic exposition in Marx, nor is it reasonable to indulge in lengthy theoretical discussion, they assume an interpretation already worked out by someone else. In other cases this can be the result of theoretical difficulties involved in analysing Marx's own conception. Thus the propositions of some analysts are attributed to Marx without further examination and, what is worse, some of the shortcomings of the interpreters are also attributed to Marx. For instance, a common occurrence among authors influenced by Marxist structuralism (for example, Paul Hirst, Ernesto Laclau, Rosalind Coward and John Ellis) is the fact that they attempt to deal with a Marxist theory of ideology by referring to Althusser's writings without ever sufficiently considering Marx's own conception – or, at least, without adequately examining whether there exists a worthwhile conception in Marx. This situation leads to confusions and does little justice to Marx's own position.

One of the purposes of my discussion is therefore to reassess Marx's contribution and to provide an interpretation which, in the main, challenges the major interpretations currently available. In particular, I want to distance myself from the Althusserian conception of the problem which primarily defines the issue as an opposition between structuralism and historicism. My impression is that these trends somehow resemble, and rekindle, elements of an unhistorical materialism and an idealism – the two extremes which Marx fought against in order to establish his own original position. It is necessary to rescue Marx's specific contributions from their reduction to any of these one-sided positions. But this is not all. I am far from believing that one could exhaust the Marxist problematic of ideology by merely going back to a more appropriate understanding of Marx. This may be necessary but it can never be sufficient. I believe that we must advance beyond the point at which Marx left the discussion, and that it is necessary to deal with more recent authors and perspectives – especially because Marx left unresolved a number of key conceptual issues.

This is important if one is to avoid a common pitfall. The complexity of some of the problems which must be faced within the Marxist conception of ideology demands a serious effort of interpretation and reconstruction. Sometimes this can be too readily substituted for a discussion of the validity of the assertions involved. It is very easy to confuse a correct interpretation with the truth of its argument. Although it may be difficult in practice, it seems important to keep these two aspects firmly distinguished. Thus in an effort to reconstruct a Marxist theory of ideology, the more radical questioning of its tenets must not be overlooked. It is impossible within the limits of this book to take into account all the criticisms which have been levelled against Marxist theories of ideology. However, these constraints have not prevented me from selecting and analysing the most important difficulties which derive from the Marxist position – some of which have been highlighted by critics such as Karl Mannheim, Martin Seliger, Barry Hindess and Paul Hirst. Nevertheless, it is important to stress that, despite the ambiguities which Marx's concept of ideology presents, this book intends to demonstrate that, on the whole, there is a coherent conception of ideology in Marx which provides a valuable analytic tool for a contemporary critical social science.

(2) The division of the field into the various entrenched positions has seemed to prevent Marxist authors from delivering an adequately total account of the role and significance which the concept of ideology has contributed to the Marxist tradition. Most authors side with either one conception or the other, or develop their own theories; but they rarely assess, in a more general fashion, the possible contributions of different versions. Still less do they try to explain the causes of the existence and evolution of the various conceptions within what, after all, is the same theoretical tradition. It is paradoxical that one of the few – if not the only – overall survey of the Marxist concept of ideology should have been written by someone who is not only totally lacking in sympathy with Marxism, but also grossly misunderstands its basic tenets. Thus Martin Seliger's book on *The Marxist Conception of Ideology*[1] starts from the premise that Marx's theory equates ideology with false consciousness and that, because this idea is

inherently dogmatic, his successors necessarily have to abandon it. However mistaken this account may be – and this I hope to show in Chapters 2 and 3 – it does at least raise a point which has eluded many Marxist authors who desperately search for *the* Marxist concept of ideology. This is the fact that after the death of Marx and Engels a major shift in the conception of ideology took place which completely altered the meaning of the concept.

None the less, Seliger's explanation of this change in the meaning of ideology cannot be accepted. Nor does this transformation in meaning necessarily invalidate Marx's contribution. It is therefore a further important objective of this book to explore this transformation, and its causes and consequences for the study of ideology. Whatever the ultimate causes of this shift, it seems to have been particularly difficult for Marxist authors to come to terms with it. Its existence is hardly ever recognised by Marxists, and most of the time they tend to stick to the belief that there exist only variations on the same theory, which seemingly underlies the Marxist tradition from Marx to Althusser. If there are versions which present an alternative picture, then these are condemned as misinterpretations of the true notion of ideology. I shall argue that there are, at least, two broad and basically opposed Marxist conceptions of ideology: one negative (which refers to a kind of distorted thought), and one positive (which refers to the totality of forms of social consciousness or to the political ideas of social classes). Within each of these broad conceptions various versions are possible, and this has provoked many equivocations and confusions. In spite of this, some valuable contributions have been made by both conceptions.

Nevertheless, this book will emphasise the importance of one of these conceptions – the negative one – for a critical social science. Following from this, my third objective is to explore the interconnections between a critical concept of ideology and other central issues of Marxist analysis. It is not surprising that mainstream social science should find it difficult to accept a critical concept of ideology. Geertz, for instance, proposes to 'defuse' the concept. He wonders

> what such an egregiously loaded concept is doing among the analytic tools of a social science that, on the basis of a claim to cold-blooded objectivity, advances its theoretical interpreta-

> tions as 'undistorted' and therefore normative visions of social reality. If the critical power of the social sciences stem from their disinterestedness, is not this power compromised when the analysis of political thought is governed by such a concept . . . ?[2]

This view raises many interesting points which will be tackled in the book. But one thing is clear. The critical power of social science does not stem from an alleged – and certainly illusory – disinterestedness. Rather, the power of a social science derives from the use of critical concepts (such as ideology) which are capable of passing judgements upon social realities which are deemed undesirable or unjust.

The first three chapters of the book follow a loose historical sequence. Chapter 1 seeks to ascertain the specific character of Marx's own contribution to the problem. Chapters 2 and 3 deal with the change in the meaning of the concept of ideology, from its original negative connotation to a positive sense, and examine various theories and controversies about these two meanings. The last three chapters are more analytical. They are concerned with the examination of some basic notions and implicit assumptions of Marxist analysis which are connected with a critical concept of ideology. Chapter 4 deals with the difficult concepts of contradiction and inversion, concepts which lie at the heart of Marx's understanding of ideology. Chapter 5 examines critically the relation of ideology to the spatial image of base and superstructure, and attempts to reappraise the notion of determination. Finally, Chapter 6 deals with some objections to the allegedly dogmatic character of a critical concept of ideology, and discusses some problems involved in the notions of critique of ideology and the end of ideology.

1

On the Character of Ideology: The Interpretation of Marx

Some methodological problems

Most discussions of the Marxist concept of ideology overlook the historical emergence of the concept, particularly its relations to the class struggles which resulted in the formation of capitalist societies. It is often thought that a merely synchronic investigation of the works of Marx himself, or of his followers, is sufficient to provide an explanation of the problem of ideology. But this is to ignore the intellectual tradition in which Marx himself was formed. Two problems can follow from this predominantly unhistorical approach. First, the relation of the concept of ideology – as a critical category – to the emergent capitalist mode of production is drastically underestimated. Second, the major object of investigation is elevated to that of the concept of ideology in general, a concept applicable in the same fashion to all historical periods.

I cannot go here into a detailed analysis of the historical threads which lead to the development of the concept of ideology.[1] Nevertheless, it is at least worth mentioning the two strands of intellectual development in the eighteenth century which were the immediate antecedents of the concept of ideology: French materialism and the German philosophy of consciousness. They shared a common critical attitude, the former primarily against religion and metaphysics, the latter mainly against the traditional epistemology. These two strands reflected the concerns and interests of the emergent bourgeoisie in its struggle against feudal society. This was the historical ground upon which the concept of ideology was born. The critical outlook which characterised early bourgeois thought was to prove crucial in the determination of the character of the concept of ideology.

However, bourgeois critiques were not exempt from serious

problems. They tended to be one-sided and were unable to grasp the connection between the criticised object and its social basis. The bourgeois structure of thought regarded former historical stages merely as steps leading to its own emergence, and therefore tended one-sidedly to conceive their historical specificity as contingent or self-alienating. Thus it was compelled to foist on to the past elements which belonged solely to the present. On the other hand, the critique of religion was based upon imputations of prejudice or priestly conspiracies and could not identify the basis of religion in the particular social structure. Similarly in the field of economy, bourgeois critiques were unable to perceive the social basis of feudal institutions and believed that such institutions were 'artificial' in contrast to bourgeois institutions which were supposed to be 'natural'.

Despite these limitations, Marx was able to incorporate many elements of bourgeois critiques in his own concept of ideology. But he went further. The decisive new fact, of which Marx's work was but a major theoretical expression, was the manifestation of the contradictions of the capitalist mode of production in creating new and revolutionary forms of class struggle. When the contradictions of capitalism became manifest, it was no longer possible to criticise the past from the perspective of a system which purported to be beyond criticism itself. Then, and only then, was it possible to discover the one-sidedness of the bourgeois critique of the past. And this is itself the result of the realisation that bourgeois forms of theorisation are themselves open to criticism precisely because of their inability to account for these contradictions. This new critical consciousness lay at the centre of Marx's concept of ideology.

However, the task of ascertaining the specific, critical character of ideology in Marx confronts the particular difficulty that there is no general definition or systematic treatment of the concept in his writings which provides a definitive version. Of course, Marx gives numerous clues by using the concept in a certain way and by describing some of its essential features in the context of concrete analyses. But on the whole it is necessary to accept that the concept of ideology is not satisfactorily elaborated in Marx's writings and that in consequence it must be reconstructed and theoretically elaborated from the various scattered elements provided by the texts. This is a difficult task, for two reasons.

First, there are a number of ambiguities in Marx's treatment of the concept which lend themselves to different interpretations. By attempting to reconstruct a coherent version of Marx's concept one can easily be accused of covering up those ambiguities, and of trying to attribute more consistency to Marx than is warranted. None the less, it is worth while to attempt a systematic interpretation. This makes sense only if one assumes that ultimately, despite the ambiguities, it is possible to arrive at a reasonably coherent picture. Additionally, this task inevitably demands, in the first instance, an emphasis on those aspects which show some consistency and, as in any reconstruction, the pulling together and rearrangement of elements which are dispersed or disconnected. An interpretative effort of this nature is bound to introduce in the final picture the organising focus of the interpreter and is likely to go beyond what Marx strictly said. However, in order not to give a misleading impression of absolute consistency, Marx's ambiguities must also be recognised; I suggest this especially in the first sections of Chapters 2 and 5.

Second, the references to ideology are very unevenly distributed in writings of different periods, in such a way that the importance of their contribution to the concept is not always matched by a similar degree of elaboration. Some texts relevant for understanding the *theory* of ideology hardly use the *term*. For instance, Marx's early philosophical critique of Hegel and religion is important for the production of the concept despite the fact that the term *ideology* itself is absent. Equally, Marx's detailed analysis of the capitalist mode of production and, in particular, of the fetishism of commodities is crucial for understanding the specific workings of capitalist ideology, despite the fact that the term ideology has all but disappeared from *Capital*. This elusive and patchy appearance of the concept of ideology in Marx's texts make its interpretation dependent upon understanding the different contexts and stages of Marx's intellectual development. The question arises whether Marx held the same conception throughout his career or whether he radically changed his conception at certain points. One could even legitimately wonder whether, from 1859 onwards, the concept of ideology loses all importance for Marx, so few are the occasions on which he uses it.

With regard to these questions two main methodological positions are often proposed. The first suggests that it is possible to conceive such a fundamental theoretical unit in Marx's writings that any change in perspective or evolution is deemed irrelevant for our understanding of the concept of ideology. In this view all the texts have the same status, and a complete coherence in Marx's approach is assumed to exist from the beginning to the end of his intellectual development. Most attempts to describe Marx's concept of ideology implicitly take these premises as their starting-point and pay little attention to the evolution of his thought. The second approach is best identified with Althusser, who has put forward the idea of an 'epistemological break' which separates the 'pre-Marxist problematic' from the 'Marxist problematic' in Marx's own writings, so that an essential discontinuity is seen to affect the development of Marx's ideas. The texts from the first period, including *The German Ideology*, are perceived as insufficient, ambiguous and still 'ideological' in contrast to the scientific maturity expressed in *Capital*. In Althusser's own terms the thesis of *The German Ideology* is 'positivist and historicist'; it offers us 'an explicit theory of ideology, but . . . it is not Marxist'.[2] According to this view, Marx radically transformed his conception of ideology in his mature writings.

In contrast to these two extreme positions, I follow an intermediate path; this acknowledges the need to consider the concept of ideology within the whole context of Marx's intellectual development, and takes into account the existence of well-demarcated stages in that evolution. At the same time, however, it recognises a basic coherence and unity which rules out any dramatic break. In other words, the basic unity of the concept of ideology is not static, nor is it uniformly elaborated and presented at each stage. Changes and new perspectives are introduced, but these do not amount to 'epistemological breaks' or totally new 'problematics'. Rather, it is the same basic nucleus which acquires new dimensions and expressions as Marx develops his position and tackles new issues. In this way it is possible to determine the various elements which constitute the essential features of the concept and the different stages at which Marx elaborates them.

The stages of Marx's intellectual development

Marx's intellectual development follows a logical pattern in which three periods stand out. During the first stage Marx was very much involved in a philosophical debate and critique in which the main theoretical references were Hegel and Feuerbach. There is an element of truth in Althusser's contention that the 'problematic' of this stage was not 'Marxist'. But this can only mean that the main parameters of the discussion were set by Hegel and Feuerbach and that Marx's most original contributions were yet to be produced. This does not mean that there occurred an 'epistemological break', for it was precisely this philosophical debate that led Marx to the next stage.[3] The second period was dominated by the construction of historical materialism. Here Marx elaborated the main general premises of his approach to society and history and definitely abandoned the Feuerbachian perspectives of the first stage. It was at this point that the concept of ideology was first produced. The establishment of the general premises of historical materialism set Marx new tasks: instead of starting from ideas or their philosophical critique it became necessary, as Marx saw it, to study material practice. But this could not be adequately formulated in the abstract; if materialism were to be historical, material practice must be examined in the context of a specific mode of production. A third stage opened, therefore, when Marx began his detailed analysis of capitalist social relations. It is not my intention to dwell on the stages of Marx's intellectual development, or give a detailed account of their characteristics. This has been done by others.[4] My interest will be limited to analysing the connections between these broad stages and the construction of the concept of ideology. If we roughly follow the dates proposed by Rafael Echeverría, the first philosophical stage comprises Marx's early writings and continues until 1844. The second stage begins with the break with Feuerbach in 1845, which finds its most coherent expression in the 'Theses on Feuerbach' and *The German Ideology*, and lasts until 1857. The start of the third stage is marked by Marx's re-reading of Hegel's *Science of Logic* in 1858 and encompasses his mature writings from the *Grundrisse* onward.[5]

Ideology and philosophical critique

Two things must be clarified at the outset. First, the extent of Feuerbach's influence on the young Marx is the subject of a very complex debate, the result of which is by no means clear. However, even those who challenge the exaggeration of this influence still accept it exists. It cannot be otherwise because Marx himself acknowledged its importance.[6] But, as Colletti has rightly pointed out, this is no argument for underrating the early writings, nor does it mean that Marx entirely espoused Feuerbach's anthropology.[7] In fact, Marx progressively separated himself from the Feuerbachian problematic, a process which, although still ambiguous, was already apparent in the *Economic and Philosophical Manuscripts*. Second, at this stage the term ideology still does not appear, nor even is the notion of ideology clearly elaborated under different terms. However, the material elements of the future concept are already present and these are crucial for understanding the critical character which the concept later assumes.

In effect, the negative content of ideology is anticipated in Marx's critique of religion and of the Hegelian conception of the state. In both cases Marx attempted to prove that the decisive problem was the inversion in thought which concealed the real nature of things. Hegel identified being and thought and this led him to follow the history of the abstract Idea as if it were 'the real', while real human practice was transformed into a mere manifestation, a finite phase, of this Idea. By means of this inversion, human activity 'necessarily appears as the activity and product of something other than itself', and this led Hegel 'to convert the subjective into the objective and the objective into the subjective'.[8] From this perspective, any empirical reality assumes the character of being the real truth of the Idea. This is what took place in Hegel's treatment of the Prussian state: by starting from the assumption that the Idea necessarily manifests itself in the empirical world, Hegel's contemporary state institutions were bound to appear as the self-realisation of the Idea. The mechanism of ideology is thus anticipated, for what Hegel did was to justify the Prussian state as the incarnation of God's will. As Marx put it, 'as the whole point of the exercise is to create an *allegory*, to confer on some empirically existent thing or other the *significance* of the realised Idea, it is obvious that these vessels will have fulfilled their function as soon as they have become a determinate incarnation of a moment of the life of the Idea'.[9]

Hence Marx scorned the conservative overtones of Hegel's analysis of the Prussian state and showed them to be the necessary consequence of his idealist philosophy. But there appeared also a second inversion in Hegel's conception of the state. Having recognised the contradictory character of modern bourgeois society, Hegel assigned to the state the task of overcoming its contradictions. But in order to do so, he had to assume that the separation between civil society and political society could be bridged by retrieving the form of the medieval estates which were supposed to compensate for bourgeois individualism and the contradictory nature of private interests. Marx objected to this mediation by insisting that Hegel 'wants the "absolute universal", the political state, to determine civil society instead of being determined by it. He resuscitates the form of the medieval Estates but reverses their meaning by causing them to be determined by the political state.'[10] What Hegel did not realise was that the estates, instead of mediating between the people and the executive, represented no more than 'the organised *political* antagonism of civil society'.[11] So the identity between political society and civil society was in fact only an appearance. As Marx claimed, 'Hegel's chief error is that he regards *contradiction in the phenomenal world as unity in its essence, in the Idea*. There is, however, a profounder reality involved, namely an *essential contradiction*.'[12] So, by covering up this contradiction, Hegel inverted reality; the unity of the political state appeared to determine the divisions of civil society, and the abstract seemed to determine the empirical.

It is interesting to note that Marx did not accuse Hegel of 'inventing' anything. If his point of view was abstract it was because 'the "abstraction" is that of the political state.'[13] The origin of the Hegelian inversion was in reality itself: the bourgeois state itself is an abstraction separate from civil society. That is why, according to Marx, 'Hegel should not be blamed for describing the essence of the modern state as it is, but for identifying what is with the essence of the state'.[14] This is very important because it shows that even in his very early writings Marx was quite aware that the theoretical distortions he criticises – which he will later call ideology – were not mere illusions, in the sense of purely logical or cognitive errors, but have a basis in reality itself. As he puts it, 'the "point of view" cannot be concrete when its *object* is "abstract"'.[15] The implicit consequence was that no criticism can abolish the real inversion which lies at the bottom of the ideological inversion. This is a theme which runs throughout Marx's intellectual development and which was at the origin of his interest in the concept of practice – for the real inversion can only be reversed by practical means.

Marx elaborated these ideas in his critique of religion. It is in this area that critics find Feuerbach's influence most decisive. For Feuerbach, religion was an illusion, the result of an objectivation of man's own essence which becomes separated and projected into a new self-sufficient being which is called God. The idea of God was nothing more than the projected image of all that was good in man. Hence religion involved a basic inversion: God being a creature of man became the creator, and man who was the producer of God became a product. But man could liberate himself from this alienation by discovering its true nature. That was the role of philosophical critique. Indeed, one can find in the young Marx many traces of Feuerbach's critique of religious alienation. The following, for example, is a typically Feuerbachian formulation: 'The foundation of irreligious criticism is: *Man makes religion*, religion does not make man. Religion is indeed the self-consciousness and self-esteem of man who has either not yet won through to himself or has already lost himself again.'[16]

Yet Marx goes further than Feuerbach. For Marx, man is no abstract being outside society, and for this reason philosophical critique cannot suffice. The only way for man to rid himself of this illusion is to destroy the social world that produces it. As Marx proposes, '*religious* suffering is at one and the same time the *expression* of real suffering and a protest against real suffering. Religion is the sign of the oppressed creature.'[17] So the struggle against religion is necessarily a struggle against that world 'whose spiritual *aroma* is religion'. It is in this context that religion can appear as the 'opium of the people'.[18] Here Marx anticipates one of the crucial elements of his concept of ideology, namely that religion compensates in the mind for a deficient reality; it reconstitutes in the imagination a coherent solution which goes beyond the real world in an attempt to resolve the contradictions of the real world. So Marx confirms his conviction that the ideological inversion responds to and derives from a real inversion. As he suggests, 'this state and this society produce religion, which is an *inverted consciousness of the world*, because they are an *inverted world*'.[19]

So for Marx the critique of religion and theology must turn into a critique of law and politics. However, he is quite aware that 'the criticism of the speculative philosophy of law finds its progression not within itself but in *tasks* which can only be solved in one way – through *practice*'.[20] For the first time Marx recognises the inadequacy of criticism and the necessity for practice: 'the weapon of criticism cannot replace the criticism of weapons, and material force must be overthrown by material force'.[21] This does not underrate the importance of philosophical critique, for 'theory also becomes a material force once it has gripped the masses'.[22] Hence theoretical emancipation is supposed to have practical significance. But there remains a problem. Any revolution in the real world needs a material basis. In the case of Germany, Marx finds it in the proletariat; and so, for the first time, Marx entrusts the proletariat with the task of realising, practically, the criticism of German philosophy.

Here one can still detect the influence of Feuerbach, for the relationship between philosophy and practice is conceived as the relationship between the active theory and the passive, material basis. It seems as if the real subject is in fact philosophy, which is 'realised in a people'. In Marx's words, 'just as philosophy finds its *material* weapons in the proletariat, so the proletariat finds its *intellectual* weapons in philosophy . . . The *head* of this emancipation is philosophy, its *heart* the *proletariat*.'[23] The distinction between the head and the heart of revolution is clearly Feuerbachian in origin[24] and seems to propound a somewhat idealist relationship between theory and practice. In effect, the revolutionary character of the proletariat appears to be founded upon philosophy, which somehow sets for history a rational goal which must be realised through the struggle of a particular class. In this view, practice depends on theory and theory itself seems quite independent. The balance is redressed later when Marx encounters the real working-class movement in Paris. At that point his view changes: he no longer needs to justify the proletariat's revolutionary potential through philosophy, but on the contrary he sees the need for understanding its real practice and its concrete revolutionary impulses.

Whatever the problems of this stage, it is clear that Marx advanced a great deal in setting up the bases of his future concept of ideology. The theoretical context from which the concept emerged was that of a critique of certain distorted forms of consciousness, which Marx equated with inversions. But these inverted forms of consciousness were not seen as empty illusions or misrecognitions without any social basis; they spring from real inversions in society, from social contradictions. The role of the cognitive inversion is to compensate at the level of consciousness for the inversion at the level of social reality. Thus religion makes up for real sufferings, while the idealist conception of the state compensates for the basic separation between civil society and political society which capitalism intensifies. In short, in all but name, the concept of ideology is anticipated in Marx's early writings as a *critical* notion. However, in order for the concept of ideology to be produced as such, a more fully elaborated theoretical framework was needed, developing an integral conception of society and history in order to constitute a firmer basis to support its critical character. This is why the final production of the concept of ideology is inextricably linked with the construction of historical materialism during Marx's next stage of intellectual work.

Ideology and the construction of historical materialism

This stage opened in 1845 with the writing of the 'Theses on Feuerbach' and *The German Ideology*. The theses brilliantly sketch some of the crucial ideas which were to be developed in the first chapter of *The German Ideology*. In this latter work, Marx first presented an integral account of historical materialism and also, for the first time, introduced the concept of ideology. These two features alone justify the importance of the work. However, this is not evident to a number of authors who take a more critical view of *The German Ideology*. Some, like Lucien Goldmann,[25] base their judgement on Marx's and Engels's own opinions about this work. In the famous 1859 'Preface' Marx announced that 'we abandoned the manuscript to the gnawing criticism of the mice all the more willingly as we had achieved our main purpose – self-clarification'.[26] Engels's 1888 foreword to his *Ludwig Feuerbach and the End of Classical German Philosophy* is even more disillusioned: 'Before sending these lines to press I have once again ferreted out and looked over the old manuscript of 1945–46. The section dealing with Feuerbach is not completed. The finished portion consists of an exposition of the materialist conception of history which proves only how incomplete our knowledge of economic history still was at that time.'[27] As Goldmann has pointed out, in 1888 Engels could have perfectly well published the manuscript if he had found it of real interest. But he chose not to. This attitude condemned *The German Ideology* to oblivion for another four decades.

Others, such as Echeverría, go beyond these arguments to indicate that *The German Ideology* is a conceptually problematic text because of the absence of three key concepts: relations of production, private ownership of the means of production and labour-power. Furthermore, the absence of a historical analysis of material production within the specifically capitalist mode contradicts the very principle which claims that such specific analysis is necessary in order to explain ideological phenomena, and prevents Marx from adopting a more adequate resolution to the problem.[28] In so far as the concept of ideology itself is concerned, McCarney has pointed to the polemical character of *The German Ideology* such that it 'should not be viewed as primarily a "theoretical" work, but rather as a "chapter of cultural history"'. Thus one has 'to deny that it is concerned to develop a theoretical account of ideology' as is shown by 'the failure to provide a definition of what is presumably the key term in the analysis'.[29] John Mepham, in his turn, seizes upon Marx's *camera obscura* metaphor and tries to demonstrate its inadequacy: to him it suggests that 'each idea is the distorted representation of some one "thing" in reality' and that by inverting the thing in reality 'representations are in some sense "mere illusions" . . . and "mere epiphenomena"'.[30] So, he concludes, the theory of ideology has to be sought in *Capital* rather than in *The German Ideology*. This position echoes Althusser's belief that the theory of ideology present in *The German Ideology* is positivist rather than Marxist, for, as he puts it, 'ideology is conceived as a pure illusion, a pure dream, i.e. as nothingness. All its reality is external to it.'[31]

There can be little doubt that *The German Ideology* is only a first formulation of the materialist conception of history. However, it is hardly disputable that its main conclusions constituted the theoretical basis of, and a programme for, future work. The importance of this achievement should not be underestimated. Apart from the 1859 'Preface', *The German Ideology* is the only place where one can find a general exposition of Marx's principal ideas about society and history. True, the brilliancy and precision of the Preface cannot be matched by *The German Ideology*, but they are certainly compensated by a more detailed account and elaboration of themes which the Preface (a condensed summation of Marx's work) can only mention in passing. It is well known that the necessary brevity of the Preface is the source of a number of misunderstandings and ambiguities. One must not give too much weight to Engels's hard assessment of *The German Ideology*, for on the one hand his disappointment can be explained by the fact that he did not find in it useful material for his book on Feuerbach, and on the other, it is not unnatural to be wary of something one wrote forty years previously. But this cannot hide the seminal character of this first breakthrough. A work which for Marx achieved the purpose of self-clarification, and which he intended for publication, cannot be lightly dismissed.

It is true that in *The German Ideology* some important concepts, like 'relations of production', are replaced by more ambiguous formulae such as 'forms of intercourse'. But the difference lies in the degree of precision, and not in the fundamental meaning of these concepts. It is also true that Marx proposed to elucidate ideology by analysing material production, and yet he attempted no specific analysis of capitalist production. But this is no contradiction, for in order to reach the latter, he had first to arrive at a general theoretical conclusion that this was necessary. Of course, the specific analysis carried out in *Capital* was to clarify the origins and functions of ideology, particularly within the capitalist societies. But this was the development and not the abandonment of the ideas sketched in *The German Ideology*. Certainly this text is polemical and one does not find in it a formal definition of ideology. But this does not deprive it of its theoretical character nor of its importance for the concept of ideology. For a start, nowhere else in Marx's writings can one find a formal definition or a systematic treatment of ideology. Or to put it in negative terms, what would have happened to the concept if *The German Ideology* had never been published? Can it be reasonably argued that the scattered and rare references to the term in other works would have sufficed to develop the concept? I do not think so. Indeed, many of Marx's metaphors are ambiguous and difficult to interpret. However, Marx cannot be accused of presenting a concept of ideology as pure illusion as Mepham and Althusser suggest. We have already seen that even before *The German Ideology*, Marx emphasised that inversions in consciousness necessarily correspond with inversion in reality. This is only confirmed by Marx at this stage in his work.

This is not to deny that *The German Ideology* is problematic and very difficult to interpret. Being a polemical work, Marx and Engels contend with positions on two separate fronts against mechanical materialism and idealism. This often results in one-sided formulations. As Alfred Schmidt has put it, 'Marx argued against the old materialism in idealist fashion, and against idealism in materialist fashion'.[32] This is the origin of the one-sidedness of some metaphors. If one takes separately metaphors like '*camera obscura*', 'phantoms', 'inversions on the retina',[33] one may gain the impression that the ideological distortion is an empty illusion, a mere cognitive problem. Yet if one isolates metaphors like 'reflexes', 'echoes', 'sublimates',[34] it appears that ideology is, on the contrary, a mere epiphenomenon, a passive reflection of external reality. So in interpreting *The German Ideology* it is especially important not to get bogged down in particular metaphors, but to consider carefully the overall context. As C. J. Arthur has pointed out, it is not adequate to select and amplify isolated expressions only employed by Marx and Engels to contrast their own conception to the various positions of German philosophy.[35] Marx wanted to assert his conviction that consciousness is not independent of material conditions, against idealism, and that consciousness is not a passive reflection of external reality, against the old materialism.

This point is most forcefully and clearly made in the first thesis on Feuerbach. Feuerbach's understanding of the world is confined to mere contemplation of it. He does not conceive reality '*as sensuous human activity, practice*'. Idealism had developed the active side of the subject, but abstractly. It did 'not know real, sensuous activity as such'.[36] Hence, while idealism reduces practice to 'intellectual activity', Feuerbach's materialism does not conceive practice as objective activity. So the break with Feuerbach and the old materialism was very much about the relationship between theory and practice, and the eclipse of the latter. But the practice Marx referred to is no longer the activity of consciousness or philosophy; it is sensuous activity, the ability to change the world. At this stage Marx no longer talked of the 'realisation of philosophy', but rather he became critical of the distortions and inversions of German philosophy in general. His point is, precisely, that German philosophers 'descend from heaven to earth', that they do not 'inquire into the connection of German philosophy with German reality' and that they explain practice from the formation of ideas instead of explaining ideas from practice.[37]

The 'inversion' Marx criticised is at this point more general in scope. In the first stage he had criticised the inversions contained in religion and in Hegel's conception of the state. But so too had the young Hegelians. Marx realised now that their critique was profoundly dependent on the same Hegelian categories because they had accepted that the problem was fundamentally a mistaken consciousness, which could be changed by a new interpretation of that world. So they fought against ideas in the hope of liberating men from them. 'They forget, however, that to these phrases they themselves are only opposing other phrases, and that they are in no way combating the real existing world.'[38] This inversion was common to both old and young Hegelians and consisted in starting from consciousness instead of from material reality, whereas Marx affirmed, on the contrary, that the real problems of mankind are not mistaken ideas, but real social contradictions, and that the former are a consequence of the latter.

This is the immediate context within which the concept of ideology is produced. Three important elements of this context must be underlined. First, the elaboration of the concept of ideology is part of a wider theory about the 'formation of ideas'. Second, the concept of ideology emerges from the critique of the inversions of German philosophy and from the attempt to link them to real inversions. Third, the concept of practice plays a crucial role for understanding the formation of ideas and therefore of ideology. If ideas in general are to be explained from practice, then the distorted or inverted ideas of German philosophers should also be referred to material practice. The importance of practice for the production of ideas derives from the more basic assumption that social reality itself should be conceived as practice. It is therefore necessary briefly to elucidate what Marx means by practice.

We have already seen that Marx's main objection to the old materialism was that reality could not be conceived as practice, whereas for historical materialism all social life is essentially practical. This means that social reality cannot be taken as given once and for all but it is the product of 'unceasing sensuous labour and creation'.[39] Social reality is permanently in the process of being produced, reproduced and transformed by the activity of men. As Marx writes, 'What is society, whatever its form may be? The product of men's reciprocal action.'[40] There are three steps leading to this conclusion. First, men must satisfy their basic material needs and so the first form of practice is the production of the means to achieve this. Second, the satisfaction of the first need leads to further needs and new forms of practice follow in order to satisfy them. Third, in the process of human reproduction family relations emerge. Marx's conclusion is that 'the production of life, both of one's own in labour and of fresh life in procreation, now appears as a double relationship: on the one hand as a natural, on the other as a social relationship. By social we understand the co-operation of several individuals.'[41] If one puts together the various elements present in the 'three aspects of social activity' as described by Marx, one may say, therefore, that practice is men's conscious and sensuous activity whereby they produce their material existence and the social relations within which they live, thus transforming nature, society and themselves.

As practice is necessarily social, that is to say, as it entails a certain mode of co-operation, 'there develop various divisions among the individuals co-operating in definite kinds of labour'.[42] But this division of labour is not normally chosen by those individuals. Men and women do not co-operate voluntarily but have a definite activity forced upon them, they are subsumed under a division of labour that they do not control and are divided into classes which exist independently of their will. As Marx commented, as long 'as activity is not voluntarily, but naturally, divided, man's own deed becomes an alien power opposed to him, instead of being controlled by him. For as soon as the distribution of labour comes into being, each man has a particular, exclusive sphere of activity, which is forced upon him and from which he cannot escape.'[43] This means, in other words, that although material conditions and social institutions have been produced in human practice, they have acquired an independence over and above individuals, constituting an 'objective power' which dominates men and women.

The paradox of human activity is that it crystallises into objective institutions and social relations which, despite being produced by men and women themselves, escape their control. So one dimension of practice is to reproduce social relations as alien to individuals. This 'objective power' produced by human practice expresses itself in a specific division of labour; it renders a great mass of humanity 'propertyless' in a world of wealth and culture; and it opposes the ruling class to the direct producers. However, practice may also have *another* dimension which transforms social relations and places them under the conscious control of individuals. This is a practice which aims at dissolving that 'objective power' and abolishing the division of labour which it entails. Hence practice assumes a double dimension in Marx's view. It reproduces material life within certain unquestioned social relations, and is labour; it transforms social relations, thus changing the conditions of labour, and is revolutionary practice.

We may now come back to the concept of ideology. I indicated that the construction of the concept of ideology was part of a wider elaboration about the formation of ideas. This means that ideology is a particular case, a specific mode of being of certain ideas. Yet ideology is by no means a mere equivalent of ideas as such. This is to say that whereas all ideology is made of ideas, not all ideas are ideological. In order to clarify this point it is necessary to analyse Marx's understanding of the origin and function of ideas. This can be summarised in three principles which Marx expresses as follows: (i) historical materialism 'explains the formation of ideas from material practice';[44] (ii) 'The ideas of the ruling class are in every epoch the ruling ideas';[45] (iii) 'Consciousness must be explained . . . from the contradictions of material life.'[46] As not all ideas or forms of consciousness are ideological, there must be a special relationship between ideology on the one hand and practice, the ruling class and contradictions on the other. In other words, it is necessary to identify the specific way in which certain ideas assume the character of ideology and are related to practice, to the dominant class and to contradictions. But first let us examine more closely these three principles.

The importance of practice for the formation of ideas derives from the more basic assumption that reality itself should be conceived as practice. If reality is not conceived 'in the form of the object', as an already given and external world, but is produced by men's practice, then men and women can only form ideas and acquire knowledge about the world inasmuch as this reality is practically constituted. It is by practically producing and transforming reality that human beings come to know it. They do not contemplate it as already formed; they represent it as they construct it. Hence all forms of consciousness emerge from and are closely connected to social practices. Marx expressed this as follows:

> The production of ideas, of conceptions, of consciousness, is at first directly interwoven with the material activity and the material intercourse of men, the language of real life. Conceiving, thinking, the mental intercourse of men, appear at this stage as the direct efflux of their material behaviour. The same applies to mental production as expressed in the language of politics, laws, morality, religion, metaphysics, etc., of a people . . . consciousness can never be anything else than conscious existence, and the existence of men is their actual life-process . . . men, developing their material production and their material intercourse, alter, along with this their actual world, also their thinking and the products of their thinking.[47]

Marx developed this view in opposition to both idealism and the old materialism. For the former, 'the "idea", the "conception" of the people in question about their real practice, is transformed into the sole determining, active force, which controls and determines their practice'.[48] In other words, in idealist thought the idea becomes constitutive of reality. The Feuerbachian materialism rejects this view by proposing the primacy of reality over the idea. But according to Marx, Feuerbach 'does not see how the sensuous world around him is, not a thing given direct from all eternity, remaining ever the same, but the product of industry and of the state of society; and, indeed, in the sense that it is an historical product, the result of the activity of a whole succession of generations'.[49] When Feuerbach mentions the seemingly independent and contemplative approach of natural sciences which alone can disclose elements of reality which others cannot see, Marx retorts, 'where would natural science be without industry and commerce? Even this "pure" natural science is provided with an aim, as with its material, only through trade and industry, through the sensuous activity of men.'[50]

The determination of consciousness by practice is therefore a universal principle which applies to all ideas, whatever their adequacy or degree of abstraction. Marx is quite aware that this is not always easily seen, and that certain disciplines like theology, philosophy and ethics appear to be independent. From the moment of their formation 'consciousness *can* really flatter itself that it is something other than consciousness of existing practice'.[51] Yet even these abstract forms can only emerge as a consequence of the division of labour, and in particular as a consequence of the division between mental and manual labour. Ideology is no exception to this rule. What, then, is the difference between ideas in general and ideology? Marx hints at the distinction when he maintains that men's 'ideas are the conscious expression – real or illusory – of their real relations and activities, of their production, of their intercourse, of their social and political conduct'.[52] By stating that ideas can be a *real or illusory* expression of practice Marx introduces a criterion of distinction which is based upon the adequacy of that expression. Ideology is to do with those ideas which express practice inadequately. The reason for this is not a faulty cognitive process but the limitations of practice itself. For Marx, 'if the conscious expression of the real relations of these individuals is illusory, if in their imagination they turn reality upside-down, then this in its turn is the result of their *limited material mode of activity* and their limited social relations arising from it'.[53]

This 'limited material mode of activity' refers to a practice which reproduces the 'objective power' in opposition to the labourer, a practice which reproduces the contradictory nature of social relations. It entails the dispossession of the labourer from both the means of subsistence and the products of his or her labour, eliminating the worker's creative self-expression. To this extent a 'limited practice' can be conceived as 'alienated labour'. Marx describes this condition under capitalism in his mature writings as the fact

> that social wealth confronts labour in more powerful portions as an alien and dominant power. The emphasis comes to be placed not on the state of being *objectified*, but on the state of being *alienated*, dispossessed, sold; on the condition that the monstrous objective power which social labour itself erected opposite itself as one of its moments belongs not to the worker, but to the personified conditions of production, i.e. to capital.[54]

Of course, the results of this 'limited practice' mainly affect the workers, but they also affect the ruling class. According to Marx, both 'the propertied class and the class of the proletariat present the same human self-estrangement. But the former class feels at ease and strengthened in this self-estrangement, it recognises estrangement as its own power and has in it the semblance of a human existence.'[55]

We may now turn to the second principle, which states that the ruling ideas are the ideas of the ruling class. It is necessary to emphasise that the text does not say that the ruling ideology is the ideology of the ruling class, for this is perhaps one of the most frequent misconceptions one finds in the literature. Here Marx and Engels speak of ideas in general and not of ideology. The expression 'ruling ideology' may be misleading because it can give the impression that opposed to it one can find a 'dominated ideology' understood as a different set of ideas connected with the dominated class. In fact this is not the way Marx constructs the concept of ideology, as will become clear further below. The real sense of the general principle is that 'the class which is the ruling *material* force of society, is at the same time its ruling intellectual force. The class which has the means of material production at its disposal, has control at the same time over the means of mental production, so that thereby, generally speaking, the ideas of those who lack the means of mental production are subject to it.'[56]

This means that the relationship between ideas and the ruling class can be conceived in at least two ways. The first and obvious relationship is genetic; that is to say, the most accepted ideas are produced by the ruling class because it controls the means of intellectual production and because those ideas express the dominant material relationships. So in the case of the ruling class a second relationship arises which normally links the ideas produced by the class with the real interests of the class. In fact, both these aspects cannot adequately be distinguished in the case of the ruling class. However, the ideas produced by dominated classes do not necessarily serve the real interests of those classes. As they lack the means of mental production and are immersed in production relations which they do not control, they tend to produce ideas which are subject to the interests of the ruling class; in other words, they reproduce ideas which express the dominant material relationship. So in the case of dominated classes the production of ideas does not necessarily express the real interests of these classes, but usually expresses the interests of the ruling class. Hence, the relationship between ideas and the interests of the ruling class may or may not entail a genetic relationship between those ideas and the ruling class.

That this should be so is essential for the domination of the ruling class. As Marx puts it, the ruling class 'is compelled, merely in order to carry through its aim, to represent its interests as the common interest of all the members of society, that is, expressed in ideal form: it has to give its ideas the form of universality, and represent them as the only rational, universally valid ones'.[57] In the beginning, in order to achieve this, a dominant class does not need elaborate deceptions or arguments, for when a ruling class is about to take power

> its interest really is as yet mostly connected with the common interest of all other non-ruling classes, because under the pressure of hitherto existing conditions its interest has not yet been able to develop as the particular interest of a particular class. Its victory, therefore, benefits also many individuals of other classes which are not winning a dominant position.[58]

This prompts Marx to say that at the beginning the 'illusion' of the common interests is true. This 'illusion' can be shattered as soon as the ruling class develops its particular interests in opposition to the dominated classes. Yet even in this situation it is very difficult for the dominated classes fully to develop forms of autonomous thinking because of their lack of means of intellectual production and the general constraints imposed upon them by the dominant social relations.

All we have said so far applies to ideas in general. What is the relationship that characterises ideology in particular? The character of ideology is given by its relation to the interests of the ruling class and not by a genetic relation to the class from which it originates. That is to say, ideology necessarily serves the interests of the ruling class even if it has not been produced by that class. This means that, by definition, there cannot be an *ideology* which serves the interests of dominated classes, whereas there are *ideas* which may serve those interests. But Marx never calls these ideas 'ideology'. Despite the dominance of ruling ideas Marx is quite aware that revolutionary ideas may emerge, particularly as the result of the appearance of contradictions which prompt a section of the ruling class to cut itself adrift and join the revolutionary class. In capitalism, for instance, a group of bourgeois ideologists can raise themselves 'to the level of comprehending theoretically the historical movement as a whole'.[59] Presumably Marx was also thinking of intellectuals like himself when he wrote this. Yet it is important to emphasise that he never described his own thought either as ideological or as the ideology of the proletariat.

The fact that ideology necessarily serves the interests of the ruling class does not mean that all ideas that serve the ruling class are ideological, nor does it mean that only this class can produce ideology. As I have already argued, the fact that the ideas of the ruling class are the ruling ideas does not make them all ideological. The same sort of relation applies to the first principle. That is to say, ideology is the result of a limited practice, but not all the products of a limited practice are ideological. This means that neither principle on its own can identify the specific character of ideology. We have to turn, therefore, to the third principle, which proposes that ideas should be explained from the contradictions of material life. Although this principle is best expressed in the 1859 'Preface', Marx had already developed it in *The German Ideology*, where he maintained that political antagonisms, conflicts between different intellectual systems and contradictions in consciousness are the expression of basic material contradictions. These contradictions emerge from a particular division of labour which separates men and women into classes, and which creates an opposition between the interest of the individual and the interest of the community. Out of these contradictions the state emerges as an independent form, but 'all struggles within the State, the struggle between democracy, aristocracy, and monarchy, the struggle for the franchise, etc., etc., are merely the illusory forms in which the real struggles of the different classes are fought out among one another'.[60]

Marx attacked the 'inversions' of the German philosophers precisely because they reduced social problems to conflicts within consciousness and did not have 'the faintest inkling' about the existence of real contradictions which form the basis of those conflicts. On the contrary, Marx asserted that 'where speculation ends – in real life – there real, positive science begins: the representation of the practical activity, of the practical process of development of men. Empty talk about consciousness ceases, and real knowledge has to take its place.'[61] It is possible to infer from this that if one links ideas to contradictions one may find two basic results: either ideas provide an adequate representation of material contradictions or they distort them. Ideology is a particular form of consciousness which gives an inadequate and distorted picture of contradictions, either by ignoring them, or by misrepresenting them. This specific manner of relating to contradictions is the distinctive and typical character of ideological ideas. Marx gives an example of this relation when he criticised Stirner (whom he names Saint Sancho Panza for his defence of egoism) for transforming 'real collisions' into 'ideal collisions'. According to Marx, Stirner

> separates the ideal reflection of real collisions from these collisions and turns the reflection into something existing independently. The real contradictions in which the individual finds himself, are transformed into contradictions of the individual with his idea or, as Saint Sancho also expresses it more simply, into contradictions with the ideas *as such*, with the holy. Thus he manages to transform the real collision, the prototype of its ideal copy, into the consequence of this ideological pretence.[62]

The objective result of such procedure is, according to Marx, 'the canonisation of the world', which, in other words, reproduces the status quo and serves the interest of the ruling class.

Hence, if we put together the various elements contained in the analysis of the three principles, it is possible to see that ideology refers to a limited material practice which generates ideas that misrepresent social contradictions in the interest of the ruling class. The question arises as to what are the relations between a 'limited material mode of activity', the interests of the ruling class and social contradictions. The clue to this relationship is provided by Marx when he refers to the task which material conditions set for men and women. We have already seen that material conditions have been produced by human practice but also that they have acquired an independence over and above individuals. As Marx puts it, these conditions constitute an 'objective power' which dominates human beings. Instead of co-operating voluntarily men and women 'have a definite activity forced upon them' and are divided into classes which exist independently of their will. Marx believed that the general domination of material conditions over individuals – of dead labour over living labour – and the contradictions thus generated had reached their sharpest and most universal form in his time: 'this fixation of social activity, this consolidation of what we ourselves produce into an objective power above us, growing out of our control, thwarting our expectations, bringing to nought our calculations, is one of the chief factors in historical development up till now'.[63]

Yet this very suppression of individuality sets individuals a definite task, for 'it has set them the task of replacing the domination of circumstances and of chance over individuals by the domination of individuals over chance and circumstances'.[64] In so far as men and women in their daily practice reproduce this objective power and its contradictions, and so long as they do not set about destroying them by means of a revolutionary practice, their conscious account of these contradictions is bound to be distorted. The close relationship between consciousness and practice determines that men and women can only solve in consciousness what they can solve in practice. As long as individuals, because of their limited material mode of activity, are unable to solve these contradictions in practice, they will project them in ideological forms of consciousness. Ideology, therefore, is a solution at the level of social consciousness to contradictions which have not been solved in practice. The specific effect of these distorted solutions is the concealment or misrepresentation of the very existence or character of these contradictions.

For Marx, therefore, ideology does not arise as a gratuitous invention of consciousness which purposefully misrepresents reality, nor is it the result of a conspiracy of the ruling class to deceive the dominated classes. The distortion which ideology entails is not the exclusive patrimony of any class in particular, though ideology serves only the interests of the ruling class. That all classes can produce ideology is the consequence of the universality of the 'limited material mode of activity'. That ideology can only serve the interests of the dominant class is the objective result of the fact that the negation or concealment of contradictions plays a major role in the reproduction of those contradictions: it is only through the reproduction of contradictions that the ruling class can reproduce itself as the ruling class. To this extent, the reproduction of contradictions can only serve the interests of the ruling class. So the role of ideology is not defined by its class origin but by the objective concealment of contradictions. This is achieved by trying to reconstitute in consciousness a world of unity and cohesion. The position of the French newspaper, *La Réforme*, which represented the petty-bourgeoisie, is a good example analysed by Marx in 1848. The journal strove to remind the bourgeoisie and the proletariat of their common struggle against feudalism, by invoking patriotic and national sentiments. In criticising this attempt to veil their different interests Marx commented: 'the *Réforme* knows no better way of changing and abolishing these contradictions than to disregard their real basis, that is, these very material conditions, and to withdraw into the hazy blue heaven of republican ideology'.[65]

This example also shows that Marx considered ideology as a historical phenomenon which necessarily changes with the development of social contradictions. The *Réforme*'s appeal to a common struggle during the French Revolution demonstrated its lack of grasp of the historical character of contradictions. According to Marx, when the bourgeoisie and the proletariat struggled together against feudalism in 1789 'their real contradictions were not yet developed. What at that time was an adequate expression of the real position, is today merely an escape from the existing situation. What had substance then, is today just a relic.'[66] This complements what Marx had said in *The German Ideology*: namely that initially the interests of the ruling class were connected with the common interest of all the dominated classes. Hence the leading and progressive ideas generated in the French Revolution were not ideological in 1789, even if they served the interest of the bourgeoisie, for at that time they also advanced the cause of the proletariat or, as Marx suggests, they were 'an adequate expression of the real position'. Nevertheless, once new social contradictions emerged these same ideas became ideological: they could only conceal the existence of those new contradictions and thus they formed 'an escape from the existing situation'.

In sum, during this stage in his work and as a continuation of the philosophical critique initiated in the earlier intellectual period, Marx produced a concept of ideology which is negative and restricted. It is negative because it involves a distortion, a misrepresentation of contradictions. It is restricted because it does not include all kinds of errors and distortions. The relationship between ideological and non-ideological ideas cannot be interpreted as the general relationship between falsity and truth. This is why the structuralist positions which made science the antithesis to ideology are mistaken. Ideology is not a pre-scientific error which disappears when science steps in; ideology is a specific kind of distortion which conceals contradictions and stems from their existence. Hence it can only disappear when the contradictions which gave rise to it are resolved in practice. As Marx stated, 'The removal of these notions from the consciousness of men, will . . . be effected by altered circumstances, not by theoretical deductions.'[67]

The paradox in this stage of Marx's work is that Marx has concluded, theoretically, that it is necessary to set out from practice in order to explain ideas and ideology, and yet he had not yet carried out any concrete analysis of capitalist societies. I have already pointed out that this is not a contradiction, for it was necessary for Marx to arrive at this conclusion before he could embark on any detailed analysis. None the less, this fact explains why, at this stage, he was primarily concerned with ideology as philosophy and not with the characteristically capitalist ideologies deriving from capitalist economic forms. In effect, philosophical ideology is characteristic of a society like eighteenth-century Germany, which, in Marx's view, was materially backward and had only managed to 'think' what the French and the English had 'done'. As he puts it, 'German philosophy is a consequence of German petty-bourgeois conditions'.[68] While the French bourgeoisie carried out its revolution and while the English bourgeoisie revolutionised industry

> the impotent German burghers did not get any further than 'good will' . . . Kant's good will fully corresponds to the impotence, depression and wretchedness of the German burghers, whose petty interests were never capable of developing into the common, national interests of a class and who were, therefore, constantly exploited by the bourgeois of all other nations.[69]

Thus Marx proposes a two-dimensional relationship between philosophical ideology and material practice. On the one hand, there exists the negative relationship between philosophy and the petty-bourgeois conditions and economic backwardness of Germany. On the other hand, there exists the positive relationship between philosophy and the bourgeois achievements and intellectual production of France and England. The result of this combination is that the German petty-bourgeoisie appreciated French and English ideas not 'as the expression and the product of a real movement but as purely theoretical writings which have been evolved . . . by a process of "pure thought"'.[70] In other words, they developed as a philosophy of abstract ideas and principles ideas which elsewhere were the product of capitalist relations of production. The analysis of these advanced forms of capitalist relations, particularly in Britain, was later to provide Marx with examples of fully developed capitalist ideological forms. But as this had yet to be carried out, the conceptualisation of the relation between ideology and material capitalist conditions and contradictions could only be outlined in general.

Ideology and capitalist social relations

The third stage of Marx's intellectual development began with the writing of the *Grundrisse* in 1858 and culminated in *Capital*. Henri Lefebvre, Alfred Schmidt and, more recently, Rafael Echeverría, have shown that this period is profoundly influenced by Marx's re-reading of Hegel's *Logic*,[71] an influence which is especially manifested in the distinction between two levels of reality: the level of appearances or phenomenal forms, and the level of real relations or the essence. This crucial distinction is the key with which Marx analyses in detail the character of capitalist economic relations. In his earlier stage Marx had arrived at the general conclusion that human reproductive practice led to the domination of material conditions over individuals and that a revolutionary practice was necessary in order to transform these circumstances. It is in this new stage that Marx studied the concrete and specific forms of the material conditions in developed capitalism. In *The German Ideology* Marx proposed that ideas could only be understood in relation to material practice. But this was a general statement which needed greater specification. By analysing in detail the structure of the capitalist economy, Marx arrived at the conclusion that capitalist material practices are not simple and that they are not revealed as they are, in their totality. It is here that the Hegelian distinction between two levels of reality is crucial and allows Marx to distinguish two spheres of capitalist material practice – the sphere of circulation, or exchange, and the sphere of production.

The original principle that ideas must be explained from practice is upheld but in a more complex context in which the real character of practice is shown to be concealed by appearances. So the relationship between ideas and practice must take into account the double character of practice itself. Marx had already arrived at the conclusion that if ideas distorted or 'inverted' reality it was because reality itself was upside down. This had been conceived as a direct relationship. By this later stage Marx propounded the idea that this relationship is mediated and complexified by a level of appearances constitutive of reality itself. Thus the basic capitalist 'inversion', namely the fact that past labour dominates living labour, 'necessarily produces certain correspondingly inverted conceptions, a transposed consciousness which is further developed by the metamorphoses and modifications of the actual circulation process'.[72] So ideology conceals the contradictory essential relations, not only by inverting in consciousness an already inverted reality, but also because it is based on a sphere of reality which reveals the contrary to its essential relations. This sphere of phenomenal forms is constituted by the operation of the market and competition in capitalist society. The circulation of commodities appears as that which is immediately present on the surface of bourgeois society from which the apparent equality of exchange relations is visible for all to see.

At the level of the market relations it appears that 'the cost-price of a commodity constitutes its actual value, and that surplus-value springs from selling the product above its value'.[73] From this perspective the circulation of commodities is the source of surplus-value, and profit appears as the difference between the selling price of a commodity and its cost-price. Similarly, on the surface the wage form appears as the equivalent value of a whole working day, as the price of labour which is fixed by the laws of supply and demand. But all these appearances fostered by the market are merely the outward phenomena of a process which operates 'behind' them: the production process. It is at this level that value is created by labour. However, the problem is that production is not merely manifested through, but it is also concealed by, the phenomenal forms. Thus the idea of profit which is generated in the market conceals the appropriation of labour-time by the capitalist, a process which occurs at the level of production. The concept of a fair wage conceals the division of the working day into necessary labour and surplus-labour, and the fact that the latter is unpaid.

As Marx puts it,

> *everything appears reversed in competition*. The final pattern of economic relations as seen on the surface, in their real existence and consequently in the conceptions by which the bearers and agents of these relations seek to understand them, is very much different from, and indeed quite the reverse of, their inner but concealed essential pattern and the conception corresponding to it.[74]

Four main ideas can be drawn from this statement. First, ideology appears as the conceptions of the active participants in economic relations: that is to say, Marx is no longer merely concerned with philosophical and theoretical forms of ideology, but turns his attention to ideological forms which arise in the spontaneous consciousness of men and women as a result of their daily practice. Even more, many theoretical forms of ideology derive from the basic distortions which are spontaneously reproduced in the consciousness of those involved in economic life. Thus, for instance, Marx contends that 'the vulgar economist does practically no more than translate the singular concepts of the capitalists, who are in the thrall of competition, into a seemingly more theoretical and generalised language, and attempt to substantiate the justice of those conceptions'.[75]

Second, ideological conceptions are the reverse of the inner essential pattern, they invert and conceal the real relations. In so far as the real relations are themselves contradictory, or as Marx puts it, 'twisted and inverted',[76] then the ideological conceptions conceal their contradictory character. Thus the function of ideology is still conceived as the reproduction of contradictory social relations.

Third, although ideology is the reverse of, and conceals, the essential relations, it is not an illusion, without any social basis. If the agents of economic relations adhere to these ideological conceptions, it is because these economic relations are surface appearances and can be seen in their real existence as different from the inner relations. As Marx comments while criticising those who think of mere illusions, 'Hodgskin regards this as a pure subjective illusion which conceals the deceit and the interests of the exploiting classes. He does not see that the way of looking at things arises out of the actual relationship itself.'[77]

Fourth, Marx's formulation contains the possibility of a conception which corresponds to the inner relations. He accepts that a non-ideological consciousness may exist. It is true that the inverted world of phenomenal forms induces ideological forms of consciousness. But this cannot be taken as an absolute necessity whereby external reality deceives the passive consciousness of subjects. This is the mistake of some structuralist interpretations which over emphasise the 'opacity' of social reality. Appearances are reproduced in consciousness, not as an unavoidable result, but as an outcome of a 'limited material mode of activity'. Both 'practical capitalist' and labourers in their daily practice are 'blinded by competition' and become 'incapable of penetrating its phenomena'.[78] Yet by conceiving the possibility of a revolutionary practice, Marx asserts that those appearances can be overcome. Marx's analysis of economic appearances is not meant to portray the definitive domination of circumstances over individuals, but on the contrary it seeks to show the possibility of transforming these circumstances. And in this the agency of the working class is crucial. Oppression and exploitation can be the result of capitalism, 'but with this too grows the revolt of the working-class, a class always increasing in number, and disciplined, united, organised by the very mechanism of the process of capitalist production itself'.[79]

It is important to emphasise that it is in this revolutionary practice that Marx sees the possibility for overcoming ideology, and not merely in the development of theory or science. True, Marx conceives of science as that conception which corresponds to the inner relations, in opposition to those conceptions which remain trapped in the outer appearances. As he claims, 'all science would be superfluous if the outward appearance and the essence of things directly coincided'.[80] Yet this does not mean that science can overcome ideology, for it cannot resolve its basic source, namely the inverted social relations. Marx is quite aware of this fact when he points out that

> the recent scientific discovery, that the products of labour, so far as they are values, are but material expressions of the human labour spent in their production, marks, indeed, an epoch in the history of the development of the human race, but, by no means, dissipates the mist through which the social character of labour appears to us to be an objective character of the products themselves . . . This fact appears to the producers, notwithstanding the discovery above referred to, to be just as real and final, as the fact, that, after the discovery by science of the component gases of air, the atmosphere itself remained unaltered.[81]

Once more Marx ratifies the idea that ideology can only be overcome by practically changing the contradictory relations that give rise to it. Science contributes to the 'theoretical collapse' of ideology but cannot by itself bring about its collapse in practice.[82]

The world of appearances produced by the exchange of commodities does not only generate economic forms of ideology. At the same time the operation of the market posits a series of principles which are implicit in all exchange. In every exchange, Marx contends, each exchanger 'has the same social relation towards the other that the other has towards him. As subjects of exchange, their relation is therefore that of *equality*',[83] and the values that they exchange are equivalent. Besides, as neither of the exchangers appropriates the commodity of the other by force, 'they recognise one another reciprocally as proprietors'.[84] They want to exchange their commodities voluntarily and so they are *free* to do so. Furthermore, in each exchange the exchangers pursue their private interests and, by doing so, their mutual interest is served. In other words, the market works by the realisation of equality, freedom, property and self-interest. These are the regulatory principles which allow exchange to take place. This is why Marx concludes that the sphere of circulation of commodities

> is in fact a very Eden of the innate rights of man. There alone rule Freedom, Equality, Property and Bentham. Freedom, because both buyer and seller of a commodity, say of labour-power, are constrained only by their own free will. They con-

> tract as free agents and the agreement they come to is but the form in which they give legal expression to their common will. Equality, because each enters into relation with the other, as with a simple owner of commodities, and they exchange equivalent for equivalent. Property, because each disposes only of what is his own. And Bentham, because each looks only to himself.[85]

These form the bases of bourgeois political ideology and of the main ideological forms of the capitalist mode of production. Marx wants to assert that these elements, too, arise from the phenomenal forms of the capitalist market and that they are thus the product of market relations, and not an incarnation of pure ideas. As he puts it,

> equality and freedom are thus not only respected in exchange based on exchange values but, also, the exchange of exchange values is the productive, real basis of all *equality* and *freedom*. As pure ideas they are merely the idealised expressions of this basis; as developed in juridical, political, social relations they are merely this basis to a higher power.[86]

As in all ideology, political ideologies in capitalism conceal what goes on beneath the surface process where 'this apparent individual equality and liberty disappear' and 'prove to be inequality and unfreedom'.[87] At the level of exchange of commodities, for instance of labour-power (to take Marx's own example), there exists an equivalence of exchange-values; but at the level of production that equality disappears; for the capitalist appropriates the surplus-value produced by the labourer without paying for it. On the surface the worker is free to enter into any agreement with an employer which is suited to his or her own interest. But the reality behind this appearance is that workers are forced to sell their labour-power if they want to survive precisely because they have been deprived of their means of production. The independence of the worker, Marx notes, 'is at bottom merely an illusion'.[88]

It is important to understand that if the sphere of circulation is the source of ideological forms of consciousness, this can be so only as a result of the existence of specific inverted relations in the sphere of production. It would be mistaken to believe that appearances only conceal the real relations; they are also a necessary manifestation, even though distorted, of the real relations. Appearances are not arbitrary; they depend on the form of inversion that exists at the level of production. As Echeverría has pointed out, the appearance of freedom and equality which is propagated in the capitalist mode of production is the result of the very oppression and inequality which characterises its relations of production.[89] If the labourers were not deprived of the means of production and if they were not forced to sell their labour-power, the market would not be the final regulatory instance of economic activity, and if this were so it could not generate surface appearances in this way. This can be demonstrated historically. In other modes of production restrictions on the free market account for totally different connotations being attributed to equality and freedom. As Marx wrote, equality and freedom in the capitalist world

> are exactly the opposite of the freedom and equality in the world of antiquity, where developed exchange-value was not their basis, but where, rather, the development of that basis destroyed them. Equality and freedom presuppose relations of production as yet unrealised in the ancient world and in the Middle Ages. Direct forced labour is the foundation of the ancient world; the community rests on this as its foundation; labour itself as a 'privilege', as still particularised, not yet generally producing exchange-values, is the basis of the world of the Middle Ages.[90]

Hence by clarifying the basis of capitalist ideology, Marx was also able to throw light on to ideological forms of the past. He showed that in former modes of production a different order of appearances operated. Until the emergence of capitalism all modes of production were based upon relations of personal dependence, whereas in capitalism these relations are dissolved into a general form. Relations of personal dependence induce the appearance that relationships among individuals are more personal. In fact, however, individuals 'enter into connection with one another only as individuals imprisoned within a certain definition, as feudal lord and vassal, landlord and serf, etc., or as members of a caste, etc., or as members of an estate, etc.'[91] With the introduction and generalisation of exchange-value under the capitalist mode of production these ties of personal dependence are destroyed and a new appearance emerges in which individuals seem independent and free. But, as we have already seen, this is an illusion based on the operation of the market; the reality is that personal dependence was replaced by an objective dependency.

The difference between the two orders of appearances accounts for the difference in the respective ideological perspectives. In relations of personal dependence the social relations between individuals are not disguised in the shape of social relations between things; they appear as mutual personal relations. Men and women appear bound to 'natural' superiors within a hierarchy of estates. These relations may *appear* as more personal, but *dependence* is in no way hidden. In the ancient modes of production the juridical subordination of some people to others can be seen for what it is. Ideology, therefore, has to justify those relations of domination which are open and visible. This is why it has to have recourse to a transcendent sphere which is beyond the contingency of material life. Ideology therefore assumes a religious form; the justification of personal dependence is found in a sacred order which is revealed by God and which consequently cannot be altered by man. Personal dependence upon, and loyalty to, the landlord is spontaneously expressed in the ideological submission to God, from which all subordination is modelled.

Opposed to such systems of personal and juridical dependence, ideologically justified by religion, the bourgeoisie fought for a free market and its political discourse, emphasised political liberties, the rule of law, the liberal state and human rights. As Engels recorded,

> the Middle Ages . . . knew no other form of ideology than precisely religion and theology. But when the bourgeoisie of the eighteenth century was strengthened enough likewise to possess an ideology of its own, suited to its own class standpoint, it made its great and conclusive revolution, the French, appealing exclusively to juristic and political issues.[92]

This discourse is not entirely ideological in the beginning, for it aimed to overcome, in practice, the contradictions which riddled the feudal mode of production. In order for an economy of free exchange to be established, the system of personal dependence needed to be replaced by a society in which personal freedom was dominant. Only under the rule of a free market could the productive forces continue to expand. To this extent capitalism is a higher stage of social development. But even in the earliest forms of bourgois production one can see that 'already the simple forms of exchange value and of money latently contain the opposition between labour and capital'.[93] These exchange forms develop to higher forms when the potential contradictions between labour and capital become actual, and this is the moment in which the political discourse of the bourgeoisie, based upon these forms, becomes ideological by objectively concealing those contradictions.

Thus bourgeois political discourse begins by expressing the solution to medieval contradictions but ends up concealing the new capitalist contradictions. However, the way in which political ideology conceals contradictions is different from the way in which this was achieved within religious ideologies. While religion justified a system of domination based on personal subordination – that is, a system which was not disguised as the system of natural relations between things – bourgeois political ideology dissolved the system of domination into equality and freedom as they are effectively posited in the commodity exchange. Religious ideology justified a social hierarchy, acknowledged the necessity of social differences. Bourgeois political ideology, on the contrary, negated the very existence of domination.

In its most general form the effect of ideology can be described in terms of the concealment of contradictions. I shall examine the concept of contradiction at length in Chapter 4. Without pre-empting that discussion it can be said that there are various specific ways in which the ideological concealment is achieved. Throughout his writings Marx constantly referred to them, and in his continuing critique of ideology he described several forms of the same mechanism. Without being exhaustive we can mention at least four different forms: *denial* of contradictions, *misunderstanding* of contradictions, *displacement* of contradictions and *dilution* of contradictions. In its simplest form, ideology denies the existence of contradictions. Several forms of political ideology which base themselves on the concepts of freedom, equality and human rights belong to this category. This was also the main error of the vulgar economists and apologists whom Marx systematically criticised. These apologetics, Marx observed, 'consist in the falsification of the simplest economic relations, and particularly in clinging to the concept of unity in the face of contradiction'.[94] He also remarked that vulgar economy 'makes strenuous attempts to talk out of existence the ideas which contain the contradictions'.[95]

The misunderstanding of contradictions is a more subtle and powerful form. It presupposes the recognition of the contradiction, but by misunderstanding its nature it denies the possibilities of a resolution. The best example can be found in Sismondi, who for Marx 'is profoundly conscious of the contradictions in capitalist production . . . He forcefully criticises the contradictions of bourgeois production but does not understand them, and consequently does not understand the process whereby they can be resolved.'[96] Something similar is said of the left-wing critics of Ricardo: 'Just as little as he [Ricardo] understands the identity of *capital* and *labour* in his own system, do they understand the contradiction they describe.'[97]

A special form of misunderstanding is that which displaces the real contradiction by a different conflict which again precludes any resolution. Marx criticised Ravenstone because the latter perceived the problem of capitalism as lying in the existence and development of machinery, luxury products, natural science, art, etc., which depend on capital and are therefore produced in opposition to the workers. Of him and others Marx writes that

> they share the narrow-mindedness of the economists (although from a diametrically opposite position) for they confuse the *contradictory* form of this development with its *content*. The latter wish to perpetuate the contradiction on account of its results. The former are determined to sacrifice the fruits which have developed within the antagonistic form, in order to get rid of the contradiction.[98]

This was also the weakness in the Luddite movement, which showed a clear-cut example of early working-class ideology. According to Marx, 'it took both time and experience before the work-people learnt to distinguish between machinery and its employment by capital, and to direct their attacks, not against the material instruments of production, but against the mode in which they are used'.[99]

Finally, the dilution of contradictions also presupposes a certain form of awareness of social antagonism, but its dilution allows a resolution which attempts, through amelioration or conciliation, to *weaken* the fundamental social contradiction. This was the case of the utopian socialists, who understood the social contradictions of the time but endeavoured 'to deaden the class struggle and to reconcile the class antagonisms'.[100] Marx also saw this form as the epitome of social democracy and petty-bourgeois ideology. Its peculiar character in France was shown by the fact that 'democratic-republican institutions are demanded as a means, not of doing away with two extremes, capital and wage labour, but of weakening their antagonism and transforming it into harmony'.[101] The so-called German or 'true socialism' is another example. These theorists used a phraseology which undercut the sharpness of the opposition between private property and communism. Marx warned the communist movement in Germany against them and urged them 'to resist all phrases which obscure and dilute still further the realisation that communism is totally opposed to the existing world order'.[102]

Marx's concept of ideology in perspective

Although the elements of Marx's concept of ideology are scattered, are not systematically elaborated and are sometimes ambiguously presented, there is a remarkable continuity and consistency in Marx's treatment. Certain basic themes and ideas run throughout Marx's intellectual development, from the early critique of religion and of Hegel's conception of the state, to the unmasking of mystified economic appearances and of the seemingly liberal political principles of bourgeois political philosophy. Of course, there was also a clear evolution in which the concept was elaborated with increasing precision and with new dimensions added. The three stages which were distinguished contain specific contributions which correspond to well-demarcated moments of Marx's thought. But as far as the concept of ideology is concerned, these perspectives are complementary and progressively complex, not contradictory.

Even before using the term 'ideology' Marx had already described its content by referring to the 'inverted consciousness of the world' which corresponded to an 'inverted world'. This basic idea of a double inversion in consciousness and in reality is not only retained but also expanded and developed during the next stage, pinpointing the exact economic mechanisms in which this inversion originates and by which it is concealed. The effect of the ideological inversions was also grasped from the very beginning when religion was described by Marx as compensating in the mind for the deficiencies of the world. This idea was developed at length in the next stages – which depicted the specific contradictions and shortcomings of capitalist social relations which are hidden 'behind' the ideological world of liberty and equality. Thus the critical and negative connotations of the concept of ideology are maintained throughout. But also, and most important, this negative dimension is always utilised for the critique of a specific kind of error which is connected in one way or another with the concealment or distortion of a contradictory and inverted reality. It is in this sense both a restricted and historical concept: restricted because it does not encompass all kinds of errors and because not all the ruling ideas are affected by it; historical because it depends on the evolution of contradictions. Ideology is not an immanent attribute of certain forms of consciousness. It only emerges when ideas are related to changing contradictions in specific ways. So non-ideological ideas may become ideological and vice versa.

The question arises whether this interpretation of Marx, by connecting ideological distortions with the concealment and reproduction of contradictions, is too functionalist an explanation. I do not believe so. In order to argue this I rely on G. A. Cohen's distinction between 'attributing a function' and 'providing a functional explanation'.[103] A functional explanation of ideology maintains that ideology arises *because* contradictions must be concealed. In other words, the effect of ideology explains *why* ideology exists. This is not what I propose. In saying that the effect of ideology is to conceal contradictions I am only 'attributing a function'. Such a statement carries no implication that ideology exists *because* it conceals contradictions. It simply establishes *what* the effect of ideology is. This does not entail a functionalist position. I should add that Cohen distinguishes between functionalism and functional explanations. While he rejects the former, he proposes an interpretation of Marx in terms of the latter. However, even if one were to accept that functionalism is defined by functional explanations, this would not affect my position because I have not attempted a functional explanation.

The variety of elements present in Marx's analyses make ideology an extraordinarily rich and versatile concept. However, there are also a series of problems and unresolved questions which stem from Marx's treatment of the concept and which deserve attention if the concept is to be of any use. I shall mention the most important of them. First, if as I have tried to show, Marx developed a critical and negative concept of ideology, the question arises as to how it is possible that, with few exceptions, the most important Marxist theoreticians have held a positive and neutral conception which conceives various ideologies existing in terms of the interests of opposed classes. This situation has not only introduced a great deal of confusion into the discussion but has also undercut the centrality of the concept of ideology in the social sciences. Whether one should aim at an unequivocal definition or not, it remains crucial to explore historically and confront these two opposite conceptions so that, at least, one understands why the change in the meaning of the concept occurred and what heuristic possibilities each of them provides. However, such an analysis is complicated by the fact that there are several versions of these positions. The broad distinction between negative and positive conceptions is a simplication useful for didactic purposes, but it necessarily subsumes a series of gradations and more or less subtle differences within each pole. This situation also leads to confusions, for sometimes the whole of the negative or positive conception is reduced to a single particular theory. This happens, for instance, when some authors mistake the particular notion of false consciousness for the general idea of a critical concept of ideology. By showing the flaws in the theory of false consciousness they erroneously think that they have done away with the whole notion of a critical and negative conception of ideology.

Second, the central position which the concepts of contradiction and 'inversion' occupy in discussions of Marx's concept of ideology cannot have gone unnoticed. Nevertheless, they do not seem to be clearly defined, and moreover they are often used in such a wide variety of contexts as to make them equivocal. There is also the question as to what the connection is, if any, between inversions and contradictions. Similarly, the relationship between contradictions and class struggle needs to be clarified. The importance of these concepts for ideology makes their elaboration imperative. Yet this is an area which, apart from a few valuable attempts, has remained largely unexplored. As a result, a great deal of ambiguity surrounds these concepts, and this greatly affects the usefulness of the concept of ideology by obscuring the possibilities for applying it in practice.

Third, ideology has been shown to be part of a wider conception about the origin and determination of ideas, or, in other terms, ideology is the modality of certain ideas within what Marx calls 'the forms of social consciousness' which itself is sometimes rendered as the 'ideological' or 'idealistic' superstructure. The question arises as to how one is to understand this superstructure, what are its component parts and how one can conceive of its determination by the base. Is the base–superstructure metaphor adequate? Is it a form of reductionism to maintain that all ideas have a class character? Is it possible to hold a negative concept of ideology and at the same time to accept the existence of an ideological superstructure understood as an objective level of society which encompasses all forms of consciousness? Despite the fact that Marx provided many elements for answering these questions, he did not solve all these problems and much further work remains to be done.

Fourth, ideology was conceived by Marx as a critical instrument with which he could pass judgement upon other conceptions and theories. We must ask whether the fundamentals upon which this critique is based are sufficiently coherent so as not to be, in their turn, criticised as ideological. Is there a vantage-point which guarantees a true critique of ideology? Is not a critical concept of ideology necessarily dogmatic and self-defeating? These questions are at the centre of many objections to Marx's theory of ideology and have to be dealt with if one is to avoid dogmatism. Finally, the idea is implicit in Marx's theory that ideology will disappear in the communist mode of production. This is the logical result of the practical solution of social contradictions. If contradictions are eliminated, then ideology loses its social basis and can no longer exist. Is not the 'end of ideology' a dangerous illusion which may contribute to the concealment of real contradictions in situations where, it is argued, they are supposed not to exist? What is the connection between the claim of those authors who believe that within capitalism ideology is dead and the claim of some socialist governments that their countries have already overcome class contradictions?

These are some of the questions and problems which arise in connection with Marx's theory of ideology. They are not easy to solve, but must be tackled if a critical concept of ideology is to have any chance of being accepted and used.

2

The Change in the Meaning of Ideology: From Marx to Gramsci

Towards a positive meaning: the origins

Soon after Marx's death the concept of ideology began to acquire new meanings. It did not necessarily lose its original negative connotation, but a tendency arose which displaced its critical aspect to a secondary significance. These new meanings had to do with both the idea of ideology as the totality of forms of social consciousness – a meaning best expressed by the concept of 'ideological superstructure' – and the idea of different class ideologies in conflict. The evolution towards these meanings was a complex process which is not easy to trace. For a start, there did not occur a systematic reworking of the concept, in some precise direction. The first generations of Marxists were mainly concerned with the economic analysis of the new imperialist phase of capitalism and with working out a Marxist political theory. Ideology did not constitute a major focus of attention as a theoretical concept. Plekhanov was perhaps the prime exception. As Anderson has shown[1], the preoccupation with ideology and the superstructures is a feature which emerged with the resurgence of Western Marxism in the 1920s. Nevertheless, despite this early lack of concern with ideology, a change in the meaning of the concept began to appear very early on in the writings of the first generation of Marxists.

The recognition of the historical change in the concept of ideology is crucial in order to understand the specificity of later contributions. The first set of causes in the transformation of the connotations in the term *ideology* must be sought in some formulations of Marx and Engels themselves. This does not contradict what I have been maintaining up to now about the importance for Marx and Engels of a negative concept of ideology. For despite a basic thrust in that direction their writings were not exempt from ambiguities, unbalanced statements and unclear formulations, and these ambiguities influenced later interpretations.

As there is no elaborated definition of ideology in the work of Marx with which to contrast isolated utterances, any statement can carry weight and can be considered as providing the essential feature of ideology. This also makes it difficult to contest any such interpretation. In this way ambiguous or unclear statements can be isolated in order to form the basis for a positive interpretation which defines ideology as the totality of forms of consciousness or the political ideas of all classes. The 1859 Preface, because of its importance as a general summary and because it is extremely succinct, is perhaps the greatest source for this. Here Marx argues that

> a distinction should always be made between the material transformation of the economic conditions of production, which can be determined with the precision of natural science, and the legal, political, religious, aesthetic or philosophic – in short, ideological forms in which men become conscious of this conflict and fight it out.[2]

This passage has sometimes been hailed as the moment in which Marx moved towards a broader conception of ideology.[3] Ideology seems to become the superstructural sphere in which men and women reach consciousness and fight the basic contradiction of society. This interpretation, which was to be crucial for Gramsci, is incompatible with a negative concept if it is read as a general statement which excludes no individual: all men and women and all classes would become conscious of the conflict in ideology. I believe that this is not an inclusive statement in so far as Marx begins the passage by tracing a distinction between the scientific theorising of the conflict and its ideological forms. That the ideological consciousness is mistaken is also confirmed by the next passages, which maintain that we cannot 'judge of such a period of transformation by its own consciousness', and that 'we resolved to work out in common the opposition of our view to the ideological view of German philosophy'. However, one has to agree that the schematic formulations of the Preface are not altogether clear.

Another source of positive interpretation is Marx's and Engels's repeated use of expressions such as 'ideologists', 'ideological representatives', 'ideological strata' and 'ideological classes' to refer to the intellectuals and thinkers of social classes.[4] These expressions are taken to have a universal meaning which applies to every class, such that the ideologists are supposed to elaborate the ideologies of all classes, without exception. From this viewpoint, in the case of the proletariat this task would have to be carried out by a 'portion of the bourgeois ideologists' which 'cuts itself adrift, and joins the revolutionary class'.[5] But this cannot be accepted. For a start there is a clear-cut definition of 'ideologist' given by Marx and Engels. In analysing the ruling class they say: 'inside *this* class one part appears as the thinkers of the class (its active, conceptive ideologists, who make the perfecting of *the illusion of the class* about itself their chief source of livelihood)'.[6] Two remarks are necessary here. First, the definition is given in the context of the ruling class and for the ruling class. Second, the negative sense of ideology is clarified by the definition itself, for the role of the ideologist is described as perfecting the *illusion* of the dominant class.

Engels confirmed this in the *Peasant War in Germany*. Referring to the German philosophers he wrote: 'These ideologists are gullible enough to accept unquestioningly all the illusions that an epoch makes about itself, or that ideologists of some epoch make about that epoch.'[7] But then what shall we make of the bourgeois ideologists who shifted their allegiance to the working class? In my view they cease to be ideologists. This can be inferred from Marx's own account of them as those 'who have raised themselves to the level of comprehending theoretically the historical movement as a whole'.[8] Indeed they have left behind them the illusions typical of the ideologists. Apart from this, it is symptomatic that *not once* is the term 'ideologist' or 'ideological' used by Marx or Engels to refer to the working class or to its intellectual representatives. Still, the use of these terms to refer to all the other classes can easily lead one to think that they apply to the proletariat too, particularly if one is not clear about the negative character of ideology. We shall see later some objective reasons why the first generations of Marxists were not clear on this point.

A third factor which may be the source for further confusion about the meaning of ideology is the fact that sometimes Marx and

Engels treated the phenomenon of ideology in conjunction with the principle of the social determination of consciousness, without explicitly examining the differences. Even more, they shifted from one to the other without adequately signalling the distinct levels of generality. A classical formulation in *The German Ideology*, for instance, opens with a general comment on determination – 'Consciousness can never be anything else than conscious existence, and the existence of men is their actual life-process' – and is immediately followed by a more particular comment on ideology: 'If in all ideology men and their circumstances appear upside-down', and so on.[9] One can easily conclude from this that 'consciousness' and 'ideology' are coextensive and interchangeable. In contrast to this, the 'Preface' proceeds more carefully; first, the general statement on determination proposes that it is social being that determines the consciousness of men and women, but then, before examining ideology specifically, Marx introduced a crucial distinction between the scientifically understandable material transformations and the ideological forms which are unable to account for these transformations. However, many authors consider these ideological forms in which individuals become conscious of the conflict as equivalent to the totality of forms of consciousness of a society. So the formulation in *The German Ideology* is even more open to that interpretation.

Engels's contribution

As far as Engels's writings are concerned, there is no doubt that on the whole they support and expand the negative concept of ideology which had originally been elaborated in conjunction with Marx. In fact, the mature Engels devoted far more attention to the specific concept of ideology than the mature Marx. Yet, in contrast to Marx in his later years, who was no longer specifically concerned with analysing philosophy and who shifted his attention to the economic forms of capitalism, Engels kept returning to the issues raised by German idealist philosophy, even after Marx's death. His later elaborations on ideology remained basically within this same context and he made no attempt to develop further the implications of Marx's economic analyses for the understanding of the ideological phenomena in capitalist societies.

Engels's *Ludwig Feuerbach and the End of Classical German Philosophy*, for instance, represents an attempt comprehensively to revisit the 'problematic' of *The German Ideology*. As Engels put it, 'since then more than forty years have elapsed and Marx died without either of us having had an opportunity of returning to the subject'.[10] The occasion prompted him to look again over the old unpublished manuscript. It is not surprising, therefore, that in this and other 'revisits' to the subject many of the old formulae used in *The German Ideology* came up again. This was true even when he was dealing with Dühring's brand of positivism, which he also criticised as ideological.

In his critique of Dühring, Engels claimed that he 'dare not designate thought as being human, and so he has to sever it from the only real foundation on which we find it, namely, man and nature; and with that he tumbles hopelessly into an ideology which reveals him as the epigone of the "epigone" Hegel'.[11] Dühring's philosophy is ideology because it deduces reality from the concept. This 'ideological' or *a priori* method 'consists in ascertaining the properties of an object, by logical deduction from the concept of the object, instead of from the object itself'.[12] The idea of an ideological 'inversion' appears once more but now in relation to Dühring's construction of a universal morality and legality. According to Engels, 'he is in fact only fashioning an image of the conservative or revolutionary tendencies of his day – an image which is distorted because it has been torn from its real basis and, like a reflection in a concave mirror, is standing on its head'.[13] Dühring is an 'ideologist' because he 'proceeds from principles instead of facts', he must fill in the gaps of his system with '*figments of his own imagination*, i.e. engage in *irrational* fancies, ideologise'.[14]

These familiar themes appeared again in Engels's *Ludwig Feuerbach and the End of Classical German Philosophy*, in which Hegel's conception of the movement of nature and history as a reflection of the self-movement of the concept is called an 'ideological perversion'.[15] Ideology, like in so many of the formulations of *The German Ideology*, appears as 'occupation with thoughts as with independent entities, developing independently and subject only to their own laws'.[16] What makes ideology possible is the fact that the material determination of the thought process remains necessarily unknown to the persons concerned. Engels presented a sort of hierarchy of ideological phenomena whereby the higher the ideology, the more difficult it is to ascertain the connection with material conditions. The basis of this hierarchy is the state, which 'presents itself to us as the first ideological power over man.'[17] This is because the state appears as independent *vis-à-vis* society, thus concealing its relation to economic relations and also concealing the fact that it is an institution of the dominant class. Once the state has become independent it produces the law, a further extension of ideology which appears as even more detached and independent. Finally in the hierarchy there comes philosophy and religion, the highest forms of ideology, in which the connection to material conditions is even more obscure.

Engels's famous letters of the 1890s confirm the same ideas. The jurist 'imagines he is operating with *a priori* propositions, whereas they are really only economic reflections; everything is therefore upside down. And it seems to me obvious that this inversion . . . so long as it remains unrecognised, forms what we call *ideological outlook*.'[18] Ideology, he maintained in another letter, entails a conscious thinker but with a false consciousness. The real motive forces must be unknown to this thinker, otherwise ideology would not exist. As he or she cannot know the real motive forces, the thinker imagines 'false or illusory' ones.[19] This concept of ideology may perhaps be unspecific, and different to the earlier elaborations; but even if this is true, it is still a negative concept. Thus there is a remarkable consistency in the way in which Engels returns, time and again, to the same ideas which closely follow the original formulations of *The German Ideology*. From this point of view, therefore, Engels's writings affirm the critical meaning of the concept and cannot be separated from Marx's.

However, the historical and intellectual context in which Engels developed his later writings on ideology had radically changed from the times of *The German Ideology*. In 1845 the development of the materialist conception of history, although still incomplete, constituted a radical departure from and a profound critique of German idealism, the predominant intellectual current of the time. This meant that in general terms Marx and Engels had to emphasise the materialist side and insist on the determination of consciousness by material reality. The intellectual climate of the 1880s was quite different. Historical materialism was becoming increasingly known and many Marxist parties began to emerge in the main European countries. German idealism was no longer the principal adversary of Marxism. As Gareth Stedman Jones shows, 'The new danger came from the positivism of Dühring and Buckle, and the monism of Haeckel – all of which, filtered into historical materialism, tended to reduce it to a mechanistic economic determinism, in which the superstructures became a virtually automatic reflex of the base.'[20]

Quite naturally, therefore, Engels's concern with ideology in the 1880s was shaped by the need to combat those mechanistic positions. Hence his insistence on clarifying his belief that, although the economic base was the ultimate determining factor, it was not the only one.[21] According to Engels, the superstructures could react on the base as secondary causes,[22] and thus have a real effect upon history.[23] He conceives an interaction among the various superstructural elements, and between them and the base, taking place 'on the basis of economic necessity, which *ultimately* always asserts itself'.[24] Engels clearly hoped to reconcile the determinant role of the economy with a relatively independent causal efficacy of the superstructures. However, his solution has been criticised for unwittingly transposing into the base–superstructure relationship Hegel's conception of the nature–notion relationship.[25] The interaction among various superstructural elements results in an 'endless host of accidents',[26] just as for Hegel contingency and chance were apparent on the surface of nature; but at the same time, amid the superstructural accidents, economic necessity ultimately asserts itself, just as for Hegel the apparent contingency on the surface of nature is founded on the necessity of the notion.

Be that as it may, the point which needs emphasising here is that the terrain of this particular debate is that of the general relationships between base and superstructure and of the character of determination. Engels's mature approach to ideology is consequently contextualised by these issues. I have already suggested that, although the concept of ideology is closely connected to the concept of determination and to the base–superstructure relationship, it is not to be identified with them as if they were the same thing. Ideology as a negative concept is necessarily a particular element within a greater ensemble of phenomena which have to do with consciousness. I have also pointed out that one of the factors which may have contributed to the emergence of the concept of ideology as universal and positive is the fact that Marx and Engels did not always adequately present it distinct from the more general theory of determination. It is not surprising, therefore, to find that the general context of the debate in which Engels was involved after Marx's death does not particularly clarify the issues. Hence, in spite of Engels's clear statements about the negative character of ideology, the number of ambiguous formulations which offer an alternative interpretation increases.

For a start, there are three places in which Engels referred to the 'ideological superstructure', the 'ideological spheres' and the 'ideological domain' with sufficient generality to make it at least possible to believe that they cover the totality of forms of consciousness. In one he alluded to 'the political, religious, philosophical or some other ideological domain'.[27] In another he mentioned the 'ideological superstructure in the shape of philosophy, religion, art, etc.'[28] In the last he referred to 'the various ideological spheres which play a part in history'.[29] The open-ended enumeration of forms of thought in the first two quotations and the use of the inclusive plural in the latter may indeed suggest the universality of ideological forms. This is of course directly related to a positive and neutral concept of ideology, for if the whole world of consciousness and culture can be called ideological, it cannot make sense to think of it as entirely distorted. To this ambiguity one must add a rather more explicit reference to the connection between ideology and class, which may be interpreted as describing ideology in terms of the world-view of a class. Engels proposed that the Middle Ages 'knew no other form of ideology than precisely religion and theology. But when the bourgeoisie of the eighteenth century was strengthened enough likewise to possess an ideology of its own, suited to its own class standpoint, it made its great and conclusive revolution.'[30]

Of course, none of these quotations necessarily leads to a positive conception, for they can be interpreted perfectly well in a restrictive sense. Besides, there is the weight of the majority of Engels's statements which, as I have already shown, are remarkably consistent in supporting a negative concept of ideology. None the less, the elements which might sustain a positive interpretation are present in some of the ambiguous statements I have quoted, and they certainly increased after Marx's death. This is not to say that on their own these few ambivalent formulae can account for the change in the meaning of ideology. They are only the seeds, the few elements in Marx and Engels which were to provide a minimal Marxist legitimacy for the positive meaning which was later to emerge. For one must not forget that both Marx's and Engels's writings massively support a critical concept of ideology and that during their lifetime this meaning was neither challenged nor changed by their followers.

A significant absence

Perhaps the most crucial factor in the evolution towards a positive concept of ideology is the fact that the first two generations of Marxist thinkers after Marx's death did not have access to *The German Ideology*. It is necessary to bear in mind that chapter 1, 'Feuerbach' (by far the most important, particularly in respect of the concept of ideology), was first published in Russian in 1924 and in German in 1926.[31] Labriola, Mehring, Kautsky, Plekhanov and, most significantly, Lenin, Gramsci and the Lukács of *History and Class Consciousness* were not acquainted with Marx's and Engels's most forceful thesis in favour of a negative concept of ideology. Even if one recognises *The German Ideology* as a problematic text, there can be little doubt as to its overall significance for the concept of ideology. Other texts are even less systematic and certainly no single one deals with ideology as fully as *The German Ideology*.

It is no exaggeration to maintain that the absence of this text until 1926 had an important bearing upon the evolution of the theory of ideology. The effect of this absence was compounded by the fact that during the first decades after the deaths of Marx and Engels, historical materialism was systematised and codified by the next generations of Marxists. The interpretation of this generation became established and respected and served as the touchstone of orthodoxy. And yet they had no access to the crucial first formulation of historical materialism as an integral theory. This is not so decisive for the most general concepts of historical materialism because Marx and Engels repeated, reformulated and completed their approach in subsequent writings. But it is certainly more important in the case of ideology, for there was to be no further or extensive treatment of the subject again, at least not by Marx.

In these circumstances the elements which the first generation of Marxists had to rely on for their understanding of ideology were rather restricted. In the absence of *The German Ideology* the two most influential texts for discussion of the concept were Marx's 1859 Preface and Engels's *Anti-Dühring*. Both of them were very frequently quoted by the new generations of Marxists, particularly in the context of the relation between ideology and superstructures. As we have seen, these two texts contain significant ambiguities and make no adequate distinction between the base–superstructure relation and ideological phenomena. In the absence of *The German Ideology* these texts confirmed the theory of an ideological superstructure. This in turn implicitly supports a positive conception of ideology, and so, little by little, a new meaning of the concept began to emerge. This process was far from being a conscious one. Neither Labriola nor Plekhanov, Mehring nor Kautsky were aware of the existence of a problem in this area. Nor did they entirely abandon a negative conception. But one can certainly find in their writings an increasing number of occasions in which this new meaning is either implicit or is directly present.

This is not to say that this generation of Marxists followed a single theoretical path. While Labriola and Plekhanov continued Engels's struggle against positivistic and deterministic versions of Marxism and strived to demonstrate the efficacy of superstructures as irreducible parts of social reality, Kautsky and Mehring were more inclined to emphasise the direct determination of consciousness by the economic structure. Yet Labriola and Mehring were more consistent in their use of the term ideology in a negative sense, whereas Kautsky and Plekhanov were more ambiguous in their formulations, drawing up first elements of a positive conception. Thus the change in the meaning of ideology was not necessarily connected with either a positivistic version or a historicist version of Marxism. It occurred simultaneously in both.

In his 1893 pamphlet *On Historical Materialism*[32] Mehring sought to defend Marxism against its critics, particularly Paul Barth and others who criticised Marxism for economism. But instead of arguing in favour of a more dialectical understanding of determination Mehring attempted to show how economic elements lie at the basis of ideas, religion, and so on. This pamphlet prompted Engels's famous letter in which he emphasised the efficacy of the 'ideological spheres' and their ability to 'react' on the economy. Nevertheless, Mehring's utilisation of the terms 'ideology' or 'ideological' was still consistently critical. In fact he contrasted historical materialism with 'ideological conceptions' such as historical idealism and the materialism of the natural sciences. The latter sees human beings as a product of nature but 'does not study how the consciousness of man is determined within human society. So when it ventures into the field of history, it turns into its sharpest opposite, into the most extreme idealism. It believes in the spiritual magic force of great men.'[33] However, Mehring's implicit concept of ideology lacked specificity. Referring to Feuerbach, he asserted that 'he considered the "arrival at truth" still as a purely ideological process. But Marx and Engels did not "arrive at" historical materialism in this way.'[34] 'Ideological' seems to substitute for 'ideal' or 'mental', or rather for 'an invention conjured up out of empty fantasy'.[35]

Mehring's specific concern with the concept of ideology was very limited. This is also true of Kautsky, who rarely used the term. Yet he wrote several books in which he concretely analysed various aspects of the superstructures. The most important was his *Ethics and the Materialist Conception of History*, a history of ethical doctrines written against neo-Kantian Marxism. Kautsky's conception of consciousness is deterministic and influenced by social Darwinism; he tended to conceive human history as an extension of natural history and therefore human consciousness, like animal consciousness, as having a predetermined role which contributes to a necessary movement of society. In particular, he believed moral ideals are not merely connected with class struggles but also with 'social instincts'. As he put it, morality has an 'animal origin' and its changes in human society 'are conditioned by mutations' which occur 'under the impulse of technical development'.[36] Thus moral ideals are not ends but weapons in the social struggle for existence.[37]

Kolakowski has argued that Kautsky's naturalistic position does not necessarily entail underrating the role of consciousness.[38] This is a point that Mehring underlined in a highly appreciative review of Kautsky's book. He pointed out that those who affirm that historical materialism excludes ethics as an effective historical force have not understood Marx and Engels. According to Mehring, Kautsky showed that 'moral consciousness is extraordinarily active in the modern working-class movement and has big tasks to accomplish in the proletarian class struggle'.[39] Yet while Mehring consistently contrasted Marxism with 'ideological' conceptions, thus keeping a critical notion of ideology, Kautsky's use of the concept of ideology was far more ambiguous. He repeatedly used expressions such as 'ideological institutions',[40] 'ideological factors',[41] and 'ideological superstructure' in a general and inclusive sense which seems to indicate an extension of the meaning of ideology. For instance, he maintained that 'with moral canons occurs the same as with the rest of the complex ideological superstructure which raises upon the mode of production. It can separate from its basis and lead for a while an independent existence.'[42] But in such a case it becomes an obstacle to progress. 'Ideological factors' favour economic development when they adapt themselves to the particular characteristics of the society that produces them.

Ideology in this broader sense can be adequate or inadequate, it can favour or become an obstacle to the existence of a mode of production. The impression that Kautsky is speaking of the totality of forms of consciousness is confirmed when he draws a distinction between ideological facts and concrete facts. Arguing against Bernstein he says 'Value is not then *a fact of purely ideological nature*, but a concrete fact . . . What is *of purely ideological nature* and particular to Marx and Jevons, is not value itself, but the theory of value.'[43] Here Kautsky seems to identify 'ideological' with ideas. However, he never called Marxism or socialism 'ideological', which indicates that the extension of the meaning of ideology was not the result of a theoretically conscious decision. On the contrary, he emphasised the autonomous and scientific character of Marxism. And he stressed the need for it to be introduced into the spontaneous consciousness of the working class 'from the outside', precisely because working-class consciousness is restricted to an expression of 'social instincts' but is unable to elaborate a science of its own. Scientific socialism alone can recognise socialism as the necessary result of economic development; the spontaneous working-class movement can only hold it as a moral ideal.

Opposed to the scientistic interpretation of Marxism, Labriola developed a conception of ideology which basically kept its critical character. Yet he approached the problem from a peculiar angle for a non-positivist. Implicitly drawing on Bacon, the tradition of the French Enlightenment and Durkheim, he maintained that in the study of human reality passions, interests, and prejudices of a religious, sectarian or class nature 'conceal the real things'.[44] Historical materialism has to abolish these prejudices and unmask the real trends. As he observed,

> to oppose this mirage of uncritical ideas, these idols of imagination, these effects of literary artifice, this conventionalism, and then substitute for them the real subjects or the forces which act positively, that is to say, men in varying and conditioned social circumstaces – this is the revolutionary enterprise and the scientific goal of the new doctrine which *objectivises* and, I would say, *naturalises* the explanation of historical processes.[45]

These prejudices, or idols of the imagination, constitute the ideological consciousness which conceals real historical causes. Hence historical materialism is born in opposition to various ideologies.

The paradox of these opening statements is obvious. The conception of ideology as prejudice, idols or preconceptions which form an obstacle to scientific inquiry is the hallmark of the positivist tradition from Bacon to Durkheim and Carnap.[46] However, Labriola introduced two provisos which changed the picture. First, he was aware of the difficulty involved in understanding ideology in the same way as Mehring as 'an invention conjured up out of empty fantasy'. According to Labriola, 'As we place ourselves in a perspective which is beyond the ideological views in which the historical actors have consciousness of their activity . . . we can falsely believe that these ideological views are pure appearance, a simple artifice, a mere illusion in the vulgar sense of the word.'[47] In fact, Labriola argues, these views are essential component parts of historical phenomena and cannot be conceived as accidental elements, nor can explanations of history be limited to analysing the economic moment alone.

Second, Labriola was also aware that what he called the naturalisation of history allegedly indicated by Marxism lends itself to misunderstandings, e.g. he referred to social and political Darwinism, which 'has invaded, like an epidemic, for long years the spirit of more than one thinker'.[48] Contrary to Kautsky's approach, Labriola insisted that if it is true that history depends upon the development of technology, it is equally true that technology is an effect of reason and that men and women produce themselves. Of course, human beings are conditioned, but they are not robots who ineluctably realise a predetermined plan. So the social determination proposed by Marxism has nothing to do with the natural determination of the struggle for life. It is no good replacing the ideological voluntarism of idealism by a new ideological automatism. Labriola believed that as historical materialism had fought against the ideologists and rationalists who were ignorant of the real fundamentals of history, it provided an especially propitious terrain 'for building up a new ideology, and for drawing from it a new systematic philosophy of history, that is to say, schematic, tendentious and predetermined'.[49]

Following Engels's struggle against economic determinism, Labriola elaborated a conception which distinguished between the *economic factor* and the *economic structure*. The former isolates a level of society as if it were a separate instance from which derive, in a simple process and as automatic effects, other factors such as ideologies, legal institutions, thoughts, and so on. The latter does not conceive the economy as a separate sphere but as the centre of gravity, the unity and connection of all the spheres of society. The economic structure determines in the first place and directly the practical activities of men and women, but only secondarily and indirectly the objects of imagination and thought.[50] Determination does not mean that these objects are mere vanishing 'reflections' of material interests. As he put it, 'there is no historical fact which does not recall, by its origin, the conditions of the underlying economic structure; but there is no historical fact which is not preceded, accompanied and followed by determined forms of consciousness'.[51] So, these forms are an objective part of history and their connection to the economic structure is not simple, but mediated and complex.

Plekhanov, who was himself influenced by Labriola's writings, continued the struggle against crude economic determinism, but his utilisation of the concept of ideology was not nearly as consistent as Labriola's. In effect, his writings show the increasing importance of elements of the positive conception of ideology. In particular, his extensive use of the expression 'ideological superstructure' indicates the beginnings of a more fundamental change of perspective. One can find this expression as early as 1891 in an article highly praised by Engels.[52] Furthermore, in many places

Plekhanov used this formulation to paraphrase Marx's statements, thus suggesting that Marx himself frequently used it, which is inaccurate. The formulations of the 1859 Preface are in the background to such statements of Plekhanov as 'Marx himself says that economy is the real foundation on which arise the ideological superstructure' or 'on the given *economic foundation* there rises up fatally the *ideological superstructure* appropriate to it'.[53] Elsewhere he glosses that passage in *The Eighteenth Brumaire of Louis Bonaparte* which refers to the superstructure of sentiments, illusions and so on created by a class by proclaiming that 'the process by which the ideological superstructure arises takes place *unnoticed by Men*'.[54] Yet neither the Preface nor *The Eighteenth Brumaire* employs the expression 'ideological superstructure'.

There is an implicit connection between this formulation of Plekhanov's and a positive concept of ideology: if the 'ideological superstructure' includes all forms of consciousness, it is difficult to conceive all of them as distorted. But there is no need to have recourse to a logical inference in Plekhanov's case. He is explicit in extending the meaning of ideology to cover the totality of forms of consciousness. In order to distinguish two kinds of ideology, low and high, he says that the law of property is 'undoubtedly the same ideology we have been concerned with, but ideology of the first or, so to speak, lower sort. How are we to understand the view of Marx regarding ideology of the higher sort – science, philosophy, the arts, etc.?'[55] For the first time one can see here in practical terms how the idea of an 'ideological superstructure' directly leads to a new meaning of ideology. According to this 1895 version, not just the law but also science and art appear as ideology. This is confirmed in all his subsequent writings. Furthermore, Plekhanov analysed the role of class struggle in the development of ideology which, for him, determines in the final analysis the existence of different class ideologies. As he noted, class struggle 'exercises a vast and in the highest degree important influence on the development of ideology'.[56] However, this does not mean that the movements of human thought have no specific laws of their own. In order to understand the thought of an epoch it is necessary to study the thought of the preceding epoch. True, the ideologists of one epoch may follow or revolt against the ideas of the previous epoch. But even in the latter case they never wage a struggle against the totality of former ideas, but only against those which best express the domination of the old order; many other ideas will be shared. Hence 'the ideologies of every particular age are always most closely connected – whether positively or negatively – with the ideologies of the preceding age'.[57]

It must be noticed that Plekhanov is speaking of ideologies in the plural, as belonging to different classes. He also uses ideology as synonymous with the 'state of minds' of any given age, so that one can hardly distinguish ideology from ideas in general. In sum, one finds in Plekhanov's writings a progressive use of the concept of ideology with a positive meaning. In spite of this, Plekhanov continued the struggle which Labriola had waged against the unilateral and crude understanding of the 'economic factor' and tries to show the active role of 'political' and 'ideological' factors. It is the economic structure, the sum total 'of the mutual relations people enter into in the process of their productive activities',[58] that determines which factor will be predominant. As Plekhanov puts it, 'the "economy" sometimes influences human behaviour through the medium of "politics", sometimes through the medium of philosophy, and sometimes through art or some other ideology . . . most often, it influences people through the joint operation of all these factors'.[59]

Plekhanov anticipated many of the ideas which later become famous in Lenin's writings and political practice. As early as 1883, Plekhanov wrote that 'without revolutionary theory there is no revolutionary movement in the true sense of the word'.[60] One year later, in *Our Differences*, he advanced central ideas about political working-class consciousness and the need for the organisation of a workers' party. Echoing Kautsky, he maintained that the social democrat can do more for the working class than the social revolutionaries, for 'he will bring *consciousness* into the working class, and without that it is impossible to begin a serious struggle against capital'.[61] A statement even closer to Lenin's later formulations appeared in 1889: 'By going among the workers, bringing them science, arousing the class consciousness of the proletarians, our revolutionaries from among the "intelligentsia" can become a powerful factor of social development.'[62] However, Plekhanov did not think that the role of the intelligentsia was irreplaceable; even if it does not understand its role, nothing will stop the working class from becoming aware of its interests and creating its own intelligentsia. Furthermore, in contrast to Kautsky, he did not seem to hesitate in subsuming science uder ideology.

Still, up until 1898 practically none of the authors of the first generation of Marxists, and certainly not Mehring, Kautsky, Labriola or Plekhanov, openly called Marxism an 'ideology'. They referred to it as a 'theory' or 'science'. The first thinker of this generation who posed the problem whether Marxism itself is an ideology was Edouard Bernstein. The question which he sought to answer is to what extent modern socialism should be treated as realistic or as ideology.[63] In order to answer this question Bernstein compared modern socialism with earlier socialist theories. In this respect he affirmed that 'no one would deny that socialism as a doctrine was originally pure ideology',[64] because it was based upon ideas such as Christianity, justice and equality which were invoked in order to produce and justify social changes. The point was, however, whether modern socialism had overcome ideology, whether proletarian ideas on the state, the economy and history were free from ideology. Bernstein's unequivocal answer was 'absolutely not'.[65] Marxism presupposes a 'moral impulse', the motivation of ideals which are ideological. Proletarian ideas are, of course, realistic in their direction because they refer to material factors which explain the evolution of human societies, but they are still thought reflexes, and therefore they are 'necessarily coloured by ideology'.[66]

All theories about the future development of society, however materialist they may be, contain a basis of ideology in so far as material interests have to be perceived as ideas: 'Merely by looking at the sentence "the proletariat organised as a class" it can be seen how far ideology is necessary in order for the workers to think themselves as a proletariat.'[67] In identifying ideology with ideas and ideals, Bernstein did no more than to repeat what Mehring and Kautsky had already said; but he drew a conclusion which they had not drawn – that Marxism, therefore, must necessarily be an ideology. It is symptomatic of the absence of any clear negative concept of ideology that despite the fact that Bernstein was already under attack for his 'revision' of Marx, none of his Marxist critics took him up on this issue. Plekhanov even wrote a special essay[68] criticising Bernstein's article in which he objected to Bernstein's conception of materialism and to his inadequate method; yet no mention was made of the impropriety of calling Marxism an ideology. This shows that the first generation of Marxists did not consider it to be of the essence of Marxism to defend a negative concept of ideology against revision. In my view an important reason for this is the fact that they were not acquainted with *The German Ideology*. It is ironic and revealing that Bernstein was probably one of the few Marxists who had direct access to the original manuscript of *The German Ideology*. Not only did he publish a part of it in 1904, but he also deleted many of its passages.[69] This suggests that perhaps his revision went further than the first generation of Marxists could perceive.

The positive concept of ideology comes of age: Lenin

Important as the absence of *The German Ideology* may have been for the development of a positive concept of ideology, it cannot itself explain the emergence of the positive conception. Any explanation of the evolution of a neutral concept of ideology needs to go beyond the sphere of mere intellectual elaborations. After all, one must not forget the fact that theoretical reflection is necessarily affected by political struggles and by the forms of economic production. In this sense the causes of a complex process of intellectual development cannot be purely negative (in the sense of an absence) or accidental, nor can they be sought solely within the inner logic of that theoretical evolution. True, the elements which I have tried to show so far as favouring a change in the meaning of ideology are important and cannot be reduced to economic or political processes. Yet they are articulated with and conditioned by these processes. The last decades of the nineteenth century witnessed crucial changes in the economic organisation of capitalism with the appearance of monopolies and imperialist expansion. A new political climate emerged which favoured the growth of powerful working-class movements and parties, particularly in Central Europe.

Perry Anderson has justly remarked that this is the time of a shift of the 'geographical axis of Marxist culture towards Eastern and Central Europe' which corresponds with the moment of 'popular rebellions against the *ancien régimes* of Eastern Europe'. According to him, this factor 'created the conditions for a new type of theory, based directly on mass struggles of the proletariat and integrated naturally into party organisations'.[70] This is crucial to our understanding of the evolution of the concept of ideology, and begins to explain the central role which Lenin had in completing this process. It is true that in Kautsky, Plekhanov and Bernstein the elements of a positive concept of ideology were already well delineated. But it is only with Lenin that such a concept gained wide intellectual currency. This is little wonder as Lenin was the most cogent and most powerful producer of a Marxist political theory of class struggle. And, of course, this is partly explained by the historical situation in which he was formed. Lenin faced a politically convulsed country and had to create the 'concepts and methods necessary for the conduct of a successful proletarian struggle for power in Russia'.[71]

The connection between the accentuation of political class struggle and a positive concept of ideology is not apparent at first glance. Yet it seems reasonable to expect that in a situation of polarisation, the 'class point of view' and the 'class interests' acquire overwhelming importance, whereas in a situation of relative calm, the rule and ideas of the dominant class remain relatively unchallenged. The accentuation of the struggle necessarily leads to intense confrontation on all fronts, especially in the field of ideas. The dominant ideas appear openly connected with the political interests of the ruling class and can thus be subjected to strong criticism. Now, in this confrontation the critique of the ruling ideas appears as an expression of the political interests of the dominated classes. In short, the political ideas of the classes in conflict acquire a new importance and need to be theoretically accounted for. This can be achieved by extending the meaning of ideology. If the political ideas of the ruling class are identified with an ideology and the critique of this ideology is realised from a different class position which entails a different set of political ideas, it is very tempting to say – by extension – that the critique is carried out from a different ideological point of view.[72] Thus the critique of the ruling-class ideology appears as ideology too, as the ideology of the dominated class. But in so far as this happens, the negative connotation is displaced and the new epistemologically neutral concept of ideology becomes positive, indicating the point of view of all classes.[73] Thus ideology now refers to class political ideas instead of referring to the masking of contradictions. Paradoxically, this displacement is prompted by the very accentuation of contradictions which revealed the connections between ideology and the interests of the ruling class, thereby making it possible to mirror this relationship by understanding the connection between the critique of the ruling-class ideology and the dominated class in terms of the concept of ideology.

Lenin expresses in a theoretical fashion this practical movement, and in doing so he is undoubtedly influenced by Kautsky and Plekhanov, the two theoreticians of the first generation of Marxists that he most respected. From the very beginning, Lenin's understanding of ideology was consistently neutral. In a text written in 1894, one of his first writings of theoretical importance, Lenin distinguished, at a general level, 'material social relations' from 'ideological social relations'. The former take shape 'without passing through man's consciousness' and generate recurrence and regularity in the social phenomena, thus making scientific analysis possible. The latter are those relations that 'before taking shape, pass through man's consciousness' and they 'merely constitute a superstructure on the former'.[74] Here Lenin clearly identifies the totality of forms of consciousness with ideology and speaks freely of 'the ideological leaders of the proletariat'.[75]

Yet where the practical needs of the political struggle show the clearest influence upon the concept of ideology is in *What is to be done*? It is in this text that the relationship between different class interests and various ideologies is firmly established. Lenin depicts a highly polarised political struggle which determines that 'the *only* choice is – either bourgeois or socialist ideology. There is no middle course (for mankind has not created a 'third' ideology, and, moreover, in a society torn by class antagonisms there can never be a non-class or an above-class ideology)'.[76] Lenin concentrated upon the distinction between the spontaneous consciousness of the working class and the real, 'social-democratic' class consciousness. The former is an 'embryonic form' of consciousness which arises from the spontaneous practice of the class as expressed in trade unionism. The latter is a political and theoretical form of consciousness developed by intellectuals outside the spontaneous movement of the class. In Lenin's view, 'class political consciousness can be brought to the workers *only from without*', for 'the history of all countries shows that the working class, exclusively by its own effort, is able to develop only trade-union consciousness'.[77] Developing an idea from Kautsky, who, in his turn, had taken it from the Lasallean conception of a fusion between science and the working class, Lenin asserted that the theory of socialism grew out of the philosophical and economic theories elaborated by intellectuals, it arose 'quite independently of the spontaneous growth of the working-class movement . . . as a mutual and inevitable outcome of the development of ideas among the revolutionary socialist intelligentsia',[78] and should therefore be imported into the class by the party.

What is interesting from our point of view is that this distinction between two forms of class consciousness does not coincide with the distinction between bourgeois and socialist ideology. Ideology is defined by its connection to the interests of a class. But from this it does not follow that all the ideas produced by a class further the interests of that class. In particular, the spontaneous consciousness of the proletariat does not necessarily serve the interests of the proletariat. On the contrary, 'the *spontaneous* development of the working-class movement leads to its becoming subordinated to the bourgeois ideology'.[79] The reason for this is that, according to Lenin, bourgeois ideology is older and more fully developed than socialist ideology and can thereby generate more easily its own popularisation. Thus Lenin depicts the connection between ideology and class interests in terms which are functional rather than genetic. A class can 'think' in terms of the ideology of a more powerful class, and to that extent it can reproduce an ideology alien to its own interests. Equally, the same ideological label can conceal opposite interests. For instance, Lenin says that 'there is the socialism which expresses the ideology of the class that is going to take the place of the bourgeoise; and there is the socialism that expresses the ideology of the classes that are going to be replaced by the bourgeoisie'.[80]

As developed in *What is to be done?* Lenin's conception encountered strong criticism and opposition from other Marxists. Plekhanov, for instance, argued that the conception of a socialist theory developed independently from the working-class movement was fatally idealist. Utopian socialism was developed separately from the proletarian class, but not Marxism. Nor was it true that the spontaneous class movement could only achieve a trade-union consciousness. The Paris Commune and British Chartism proved that spontaneity did not necessarily mean trade-union consciousness. Plekhanov accused Lenin of conceiving of the working class as a passive subject being moved towards socialism by a non-historical spirit, the socialist intelligentsia organised into a party.[81] Trotsky spoke of 'substitutism' which concealed Lenin's distrust of the proletariat as a revolutionary class: as one could not count upon the class's own activity it was necessary to substitute for it a group which could utilise it as a force – hence the dangers of paternalism, manipulation and bureaucracy. Indeed, there were likely to follow other forms of substitution, namely the party apparatus for the party, and finally, a dictator for the central committee.[82]

Rosa Luxemburg, in her turn, accused Lenin of Blanquism, of trying to impose a conspiratorial organisation upon the masses. She did not entirely deny the need for centralism, but rejected the military strategy of an insurrectional group as one unsuited to social democracy. She recognised that even when the objective conditions were ripe, the majority of the workers would not be prepared to take power. But it was in the struggle itself that they could overcome their backwardness. The proletariat, as Marx had thought, learned from its own experience and mistakes, thus gaining consciousness of its objectives in struggle.[83] Nevertheless, none of these criticisms questioned Lenin's conception of ideology as the expression of the interests of a class. The criticisms of 'substitutism' and 'Blanquism' were not really accurate, for Lenin was not in fact propounding a belief in the party as the new revolutionary subject; he always maintained the necessity of a dialetical relationship between party and masses which denied any conception of the class as a mere passive subject. However, Plekhanov's observations on the idealism implicit in the conception of a separate development of Marxism from the working class are more penetrating, for on this Lenin did not offer any qualifications to his statements.

This was a long-standing problem in Lenin's conception. Already in *What the Friends of the People are and how they fight the Social Democrats* a contrast could be noticed between a very deterministic view of consciousness in general, and the apparent lack of determination of Marxism itself. Whereas consciousness in general could be understood by analysing the essential economic relations, Marx's theory was hailed as a scientific breakthrough, mainly explained by Marx's genius. *What is to be done?* did nothing but confirm this conception of science as if it existed outside social determinations. There would have been less of a problem if

Lenin had merely been trying to say that Marxism was not the automatic result of class struggle and that it was not a collective spontaneous creation of the proletariat. But his formulae seem to go further than that in suggesting that Marxism arose 'quite independently of the spontaneous growth of the working-class movement'.

It is interesting to note that in Lenin's conception socialist consciousness is explained in terms of a fusion of three different concepts: ideology, class consciousness and science. Socialist theory is supposed to be all three at the same time. It is the ideology of the proletariat because it expresses its interests. But for the same reason it is the authentic class consciousness of the proletariat, as opposed to its spontaneous trade-union consciousness. Furthermore, as the claims of the socialist ideology are true and have been developed by a scientific intelligentsia, they are also science. As Lenin puts it, 'every ideology is historically conditional, but it is unconditionally true that to every scientific ideology (as distinct, for instance, from religious ideology), there corresponds an objective truth, absolute nature'.[84] Hence so far as the working class is concerned, science, ideology and class consciousness come together. The contents of the socialist ideology are supplied by science and express the 'genuine class consciousness' of the proletariat. This conception should be contrasted with Marx's, for whom, although historical materialism was a science developed by intellectuals, class consciousness was directly inherent in the actual practice of the proletariat, and ideology was a form of distorted consciousness which concealed contradictory real relations.

So, with Lenin the concept of ideology is finally neutralised. If bourgeois ideology or religious ideology are unscientific, it is not because they are 'ideology' but because they are specifically 'bourgeois' or 'religious'. The negative connotation has been displaced from the notion of ideology. Even when Lenin combated revisionism, he did not attack Bernstein for his conception of ideology, nor did he oppose revisionism just because it was ideology. Revisionism was criticised as part of a 'petty-bourgeois world outlook'. Ideology is here conceived as the 'domain' of a theoretical struggle which expresses different class interests. These contradictory class interests are manifested in different class ideologies which are in 'ideological struggle' against one another. As Lenin insisted, 'the ideological struggle waged by revolutionary Marxism against revisionism . . . is but the prelude to the great revolutionary battles of the proletariat, which is marching forward . . . despite all the waverings and weaknesses of the petty-bourgeoisie'.[85] With Lenin, therefore, the process of the change in the meaning of ideology became crystallised. It goes without saying that the immense power of Lenin's work and his practical political achievements contributed to the eventual dominance of this conception of ideology. The basis of Lenin's political achievements lay, as Lenin himself realised and as Anderson has pointed out, in the revolutionary energies of the Russian masses, whose spontaneous practice 'rendered possible the great enlargement of Marxist theory achieved by Lenin'.[86] Yet while in the main this expansion affected unexplored areas of Marxist *political* theory, in the specific case of ideology it totally transformed Marx's original conception. One wonders whether this would have happened to the same extent had Lenin read *The German Ideology*. Be that as it may, Lenin's conception played a crucial role in shaping the new contributions to the concept of ideology which were to emerge as common after his death.

Lukács's concept of ideology

Lukács's Marxism proved no exception to this legacy. From his first essays in the 1920s the Leninist conception was at the centre of his intellectual concerns. This is particularly noticeable in his conception of ideology which, unlike other fields in which Lukács's creativity and originality were strongly asserted, had a distinct Leninist flavour. In fact, it is my contention that as far as the concept of ideology is concerned Lukács did not introduce any fundamental changes to the Leninist conception. In effect, Lenin's distinction between a bourgeois trade-union ideology which is the spontaneous consciousness of the working class and a proletarian scientific ideology which is developed by intellectuals is transposed by Lukács into his famous distinction between the 'psychological class consciousness' and the 'imputed class consciousness' of the proletariat.[87] Lukács's self-critical Preface to the new edition of *History and Class Consciousness*, written in 1967, expressly recognises that in making that distinction he 'meant the same thing as

Lenin in *What is to be done?*'[88] Although this claim has been disputed, the connection seems plain enough. Stedman Jones has argued that the main difference between Lenin's couplet spontaneity-science and Lukács's couplet empirical consciousness-ascribed class consciousness is that, whereas the former allows for the autonomy of science, the latter collapses science into consciousness.[89] There is an element of truth in this assertion; but in my view it would be equally true to say that Lenin collapses class consciousness into science so that in the end, although from different perspectives, both authors fail to distinguish adequately science from class consciousness.

Ultimately, I tend to agree with McCarney's interpretation which, although it recognises some differences, accepts the basic similarity of both couplets.[90] However this is not the only evidence which shows Lukács's basic endorsement of Lenin's conception of ideology. A summary review of Lukács's essays immediately reveals that he uses the terms 'ideology' or 'ideological' to refer both to the bourgeoisie and to the proletariat, without implying a necessary negative connotation. He maintains, for instance, that Marxism is 'the ideological expression of the proletariat in its efforts to liberate itself',[91] and that historical materialism is 'the ideology of the embattled proletariat'.[92] Elsewhere Lukács explains that '*The fate of the revolution* . . . will depend *on the ideological maturity of the proletariat, i.e. on its class consciousness*', and that "ideology" for the proletariat is no banner to follow into battle, nor is it a cover for its true objectives: it is the objective and the weapon itself'.[93] Simultaneously he speaks of the 'bourgeois ideology' and contrasts it to proletarian ideology. Whereas the former was decisive when the bourgeoisie struggled against feudalism but has been subsequently undermined from within, the latter is 'the most potent weapon' and has led to bourgeois 'ideological capitulation to historical materialism'.[94] Still, 'the ideological defeat of capitalism' will not be easy to achieve 'in view of the great distance that the proletariat has to travel ideologically'.[95] Besides bourgeois and proletarian ideologies there exists also an 'ideology of the broad masses of the petty bourgeoisie'[96] which regards the state as an absolute institution. If the proletariat fails to give to the state the minimum authority it requires, these petty-bourgeois groups can be driven back into the arms of the bourgeoisie.

In short, there is overwhelming evidence that Lukács conceived of ideologies as expressions of different class interests, and in struggle with one another. Before a practical solution can be found for capitalist contradictions, the 'ideological crisis' must be solved.[97] It is therefore surprising that most interpretations of Lukács's concept of ideology, and particularly those which have gained wide intellectual currency, do not seem to appreciate this fact. In effect, with one notable exception,[98] it is widely accepted that Lukács defined ideology as false consciousness. Roisin McDonough, for instance, suggestively entitles her article 'Ideology as False Consciousness: Lukács'.[99] Diane Adlam and others in their presentation of the first issue of *Ideology and Consciousness* maintain that 'the central tenet of his [Lukács's] work is that ideology is false consciousness, a distorting veil that hangs over the eyes of men . . . an illusion'.[100] From a totally different theoretical perspective Seliger affirms that 'having used "ideology" most of the time in the pejorative sense established by the founders, Lukács was inconsistent in taking it occasionally in a positive sense, as Bernstein and particularly Lenin had been doing'.[101] At least Seliger recognises that there is in Lukács a positive use of the concept. Yet it seems strange to say that this is only 'occasional'. Seliger's assertion that this 'occasional' use of a positive concept is inconsistent with the negative sense which Lukács is supposed to uphold most of the time is based upon a misunderstanding. In effect Seliger mistakes the critical appraisal of bourgeois ideology for the negative character of the concept of ideology. Lukács is certainly critical of bourgeois ideology, yet not because it is ideology as such, but because of the inherent limitations of the bourgeoisie. There is no contradiction in criticising bourgeois ideology as false consciousness and holding a positive concept of ideology. Such a positive notion entails the neutralisation of the concept so that it can account for different class interests. The epistemological assessment of various ideologies is carried out by Lukács in terms of the limitations or potentialities inherent in any particular class position, but it no longer stems from the concept of ideology itself.

Thus the accusation of inconsistency derives from a misunderstanding about the extension which Lukács confers on the concept of false consciousness. I shall come back to this point in a moment. Implicit in Seliger's account is another mistake which suggests that the negative sense of ideology established by Marx and Engels is equivalent to the idea of false consciousness. I have already shown in Chapter 1 that Marx's notion of ideology is more complex than this, and I shall show in Chapter 3 that Seliger's arguments on this do not stand up to scrutiny. Neither Marx nor Engels, nor indeed Lukács himself, defines ideology as false consciousness. But whereas Marx and Engels maintain a negative concept of ideology, Lukács upholds Lenin's positive concept of ideology. Let us examine Lukács's passages on false consciousness. The most famous quotation claims that 'men perform their historical deeds themselves and that they do so consciously. But as Engels emphasises in a letter to Mehring, this consciousness is false'.[102] The strength of this argument lies in the fact that Engels's reference to false consciousness occurs in the context of an attempt to define ideology in general.[103] Elsewhere, Lukács maintains that 'in the class struggles of the past the most varied ideologies, religious, moral and other forms of "false consciousness" were decisive'.[104] Here he seems to equate ideology and false consciousness. Finally, when Lukács argues that capitalism would not be able to maintain its position 'if the proletariat were to oppose it consciously and resolutely', he adds 'only ideology stands in the way of such opposition',[105] apparently suggesting that ideology has a negative character in general.

Admittedly, it is easy to jump to the superficial conclusion that for Lukács ideology is false consciousness. Many interpreters have done this. But quite apart from the many statements already quoted in which Lukács speaks of the ideology of the proletariat in totally different terms, a careful analysis of these quotations – which seem to proclaim the opposite – in fact demonstrates that this is no more than a first impression. Once the context is fully grasped the apparent contradiction disappears. In these three quotations Lukács is attempting to contrast a particular kind of consciousness, the real class consciousness of the proletariat, to either bourgeois ideology, or more generally, past ideologies. The first quotation is not meant to be a general definition of ideology, in so far as false consciousness is only 'an aspect of the historical totality' and 'a stage in the historical process'. True, this false consciousness can affect the empirically given consciousness of the proletariat, but it cannot affect its 'ascribed consciousness', for by virtue of its privileged historical position the proletariat can understand the 'true driving forces' of history. This proletarian class consciousness is not, therefore, false consciousness, and yet it is said to be ideological. Conversely, Lukács is quite explicit in explaining the cause of the falsity of bourgeois class consciousness: bourgeois class conscoiousness is false not because it is ideological, but because the bourgeois class position is structurally limited. As he puts it, 'The barrier which converts the class consciousness of the bourgeoisie into "false" consciousness is objective: it is the class situation itself.'[106]

So the factor which decides whether an ideology is false consciousness or true consciousness is the structural position of the class whose interests that ideology serves. The same idea underlies the second quotation. Past ideologies are said to be a form of false consciousness, but they are contrasted with the class struggle of the proletariat, for which 'the revelation of the unvarnished truth became both a war-cry and the most potent weapon'.[107] Equally when Lukács says that 'only ideology stands in the way' of the proletariat consciously opposing capitalism, he refers not to ideology in general but to bourgeois ideology and, more concretely, to the effect produced by legality and the state which appear as 'man's natural environment'. Against this ideological effect Lukács opposes Marxism as the 'ideological expression of the proletariat'.[108] Hence it is quite clear that Lukács has a positive or neutral concept of ideology and that his treatment of false consciousness applies to particular class ideologies other than the proletarian ideology. This does not mean that the proletariat as a class is exempt from false consciousness. It is important to emphasise that for Lukács false consciousness can also be found in the proletarian empirical or psychological consciousness. But this should not be confused with the 'true' consciousness which is Marxism, the proletarian ideology. So, Lukács's analysis of false consciousness does not intend to provide the essential elements of the concept of ideology itself, but rather the characteristics of bourgeois ideology.

None the less, the continuity between Lenin and Lukács has been also challenged from a different perspective. Poulantzas and also Stedman Jones have carried out an extensive critique of Lukács's conception of ideology from a structuralist point of view. In essence, they contend that Lukács's theory fails on three counts. First, because it conceives ideology as the world-view of a class, the ruling ideology has no specific autonomy and is assumed to be 'pure', that is to say it simply reflects the conditions of existence of the dominant class. The relationship between the class subject and its ideology is represented in genetic terms and this obscures the fact that the ruling ideology reflects a political relation between classes. As Poulantzas puts it, such a conception cannot 'establish the existence within the dominant ideology of elements belonging to the ideologies of classes other than the politically dominant class'.[109] This is contrasted to Lenin's more complex account of the relationship between classes and ideologies.

Second, bourgeois ideological domination appears without an institutional apparatus to sustain it. In Stedman Jones's words:

> Lukács's whole account of bourgeois ideological domination is reduced to the invisible emanations of reification from commodities . . . What is strikingly and completely missing in Lukács's account is, of course, the whole institutional superstructure of bourgeois class power: parties, reformist trade unions, newspapers, schools, churches, families are scarcely mentioned.[110]

This is contrasted to Lenin's consideration of the superiority of bourgeois ideological forms and institutions.

Third, it is alleged that Lukács's conception cannot explain the ideological contamination of the spontaneous working-class consciousness. As each ideology functions in a vacuum 'it is impossible to see the effects of ideological domination by the dominant ideology on working-class ideology'.[111] This leads to spontaneism, as 'working class ideology is considered to possess the keys to Marxist science'.[112] This is, of course, contrasted to Lenin's distrust of the working class' spontaneous consciousness.

Thus both Poulantzas and Stedman Jones oppose Lukács's conception to Lenin's in a way that may lead one to believe that there is no continuity between them. It seems to me that the criticisms, as much as the contrast between Lukács and Lenin, are rather surprising in the light of the evidence provided by Lukács's texts. For in my view they do not support such claims. This may be related to the position argued by Arato and Breines that many studies reduce Lukács's thought to that of some of his intellectual progenitors. Poulantzas, for instance, identifies Lukács with Max

Weber's historicism; but, as McCarney points out, his critique does not make any specific references to Lukács's writings.[113] Be that as it may, it is necessary to address oneself to the substance of the arguments put forward. First of all, it is simply a mistake to believe that for Lukács ideologies are seen 'as number-plates carried on the backs of class-subjects' – as Poulantzas puts it – if this characterisation implies any genetic relationship between the class and its ideology. What the critics overlook is the fact that Lukács does make a distinction between the ideology of the class – its ascribed consciousness – and the psychological consciousness of the class. So the relationship between the class and its ideology is functional and not genetic. In fact, for Lukács the class psychological consciousness, spontaneously developed by the class, does not constitute its real ideology and can be entirely at variance with it. If this is so, then one can hardly accuse Lukács of spontaneism and of not considering ideological contamination. Of course, he acknowledges the bourgeois contamination of the proletarian empirical consciousness just as Lenin did, but he cannot recognise the ideological domination of the ruling ideology over the ideology of the proletariat, because that would entail a bourgeois domination over Marxism, the true consciousness.

Indeed, as McCarney has aptly shown, 'not only is Lukács able to acknowledge and theorise the phenomenon of ideological contamination, but it has in truth a central place in his view of the historical process'.[114] No one can reasonably dispute that for Lukács the struggle of the proletariat to resolve its internal 'ideological crisis' is at the centre of his analysis. This ideological crisis stems from the fact that 'the class consciousness of the proletariat does not develop uniformly throughout the whole proletariat', and that 'large sections of the proletariat remain intellectually under the tutelage of the bourgeoisie'.[115] 'Even in the very midst of the death throes of capitalism, broad sections of the proletarian masses still feel that the state, the laws and the economy of the bourgeoisie are the only possible environment for them to exist in.'[116] Lukács's analyses of opportunism and utopianism as the main problems of proletarian consciousness bear witness to the same central concern. However, it is true to say that Lukács's account of bourgeois ideological domination over the working class differs from Lenin's. But this does not necessarily mean that it is mistaken or in any sense inferior to Lenin's account.

Lenin explained the ideological subordination of the spontaneous working-class movement to bourgeois ideology 'for the simple reason that the bourgeois ideology is far older in origin than the socialist ideology; because it is more fully developed and because it possesses *immeasurably* more opportunities for being spread'.[117] This account should be contrasted to Lukács's, which emphasises the fact that because the proletariat is the product of capitalism it is subjected to the typical mode of existence of such a system, which is inhumanity and reification. The phenomenal forms of the economy present themselves on the surface as natural relations between things, thus hiding the real relations between human beings. Because these real relations are concealed and are not easily perceived, the mind comes to regard the phenomenal forms as the true representatives of human existence. As the capitalist system reproduces this system of appearances 'the structure of reification progressively sinks more deeply . . . into the consciousness of man'.[118] So while for Lenin the ideological subordination of the proletariat seems to originate in the fact that the bourgeoisie has more powerful means of disseminating and transmitting ideas which have been produced outside working-class experience, for Lukács, on the contrary, it is the very situation and practice of the proletariat within capitalist society that induces its ideological subordination. In other words, the proletariat does not need to be indoctrinated with ideas produced elsewhere, it itself spontaneously produces reified ideas.

Without denying that the bourgeoisie does possess more means for the transmission of ideas and that its ideology is older and more fully developed, Lukács's explanation goes deeper to the root cause of ideological domination and has the merit of rediscovering the importance of Marx's analysis in *Capital* for the understanding of ideological phenomena within capitalism. It is ironic that in this he should anticipate the efforts of structuralist writers who, on the whole, have nothing but contempt for his conception. The fact that Mepham, for instance, does not once mention Lukács in his article on the theory of ideology in *Capital* [119] is symptomatic of this refusal to consider Lukács's contribution. This does not mean that Lukács's early conception of ideology is free from criticism. Indeed, he should have paid more attention to ideological apparatuses. But it is certainly not the point to criticise Lukács for a definition of ideology as false consciousness or because he ignores the problem of ideological contamination. Nor is it that he substituted a genetic explanation of the relationship between class and ideology for Lenin's functional explanation. The basic criticism which can be made, it seems to me, is that Lukács consistently overrates the role of ideology and ideological struggle to the point that they seem to substitute for real political practice and real class struggle.

In effect this is a charge of idealism which Lukács himself was the first to plead guilty to in the above-mentioned preface. As he retrospectively commented, 'what I failed to realise, however, was that in the absence of a basis in real praxis, in labour as its original form and model, the over-extension of the concept of praxis would lead to its opposite: a relapse into idealistic contemplation'.[120] The consequences of this 'relapse' are well known. It is not practice that transforms things, but rather it is 'the practical consciousness' which possesses the ability to transform things. Hence Lukács is able to say that proletarian thought gradually transforms itself 'into a *practical theory* that overturns the real world'[121], and that '*the strength of every society is in the last resort a spiritual strength*' from which 'we can only be liberated by knowledge'.[122] Consciousness acquires not only an almost total autonomy, but also the ability to produce practical effects on its own. 'When the worker knows himself as a commodity his knowledge is practical', contends Lukács; '*that is to say, this knowledge brings about an objective structured change in the object of knowledge*'.[123] It is no wonder, therefore, that he can also say that the 'reform of consciousness is the revolutionary process itself'.[124] True, ideology has acquire in this account a central role in the revolutionary process. But this reaction against the reductionist tendencies of positivist Marxism has been taken too far, to the point where the role of social determinations on ideology has almost disappeared.

Lukács corrected this idealist conception in his subsequent writings, while at the same time maintaining his critical view of mechanistic and reductionist conceptions of ideology, typical of vulgar Marxism. He maintained that 'anyone who sees ideologies as the mechanical, passive product of the economic process at their base simply understands nothing of their essence'.[125] Yet he also pointed out that 'any apperception of the external world is nothing but the reflection of a reality existing independently of the consciousness, in the thoughts, conceptions, perceptions, etc., of men'.[126] Simultaneously, Lukács reaffirmed his positive concept of ideology in unmistakeable terms. He spoke, for instance, of 'the ideologies, including literature and art'[127] and of Marx's and Engels's 'materialist ideology'.[128] With Lenin and Lukács, therefore, the positive meaning of ideology is firmly established within Marxism. But at this stage it has not yet fully developed its creative potentialities for Marxist theory and practice in the West.

Ideology and hegemony

The change from a negative to a positive concept of ideology was fully accomplished by Lenin and confirmed by Lukács in the wake of the new wave of revolutionary activity which shook Eastern Europe during the first two decades of the twentieth century. However, the success achieved in the Russian Revolution was not to be repeated elsewhere. A new era of recession in the class struggle opened which was particularly noticeable in Western Europe. Again, this historical change is marked by a corresponding innovation in the concept of ideology. However, this time there occurred no radical alteration of the meaning of ideology, but rather an exploration in depth of its relevance both for the maintenance and the possible overthrow of the Western capitalist system. In many senses this exploration was initiated by Lukács himself. The enormous importance that he conceded to ideological struggle as the key to revolution is a clear sign of this new approach, which, to a certain extent, attempted to compensate for adverse objective conditions. Yet the most accomplished and perceptive, though not systematic, exploration of ideology under these new difficult conditions was carried out by Antonio Gramsci. With him, the positive concept of ideology yields its most creative fruits.

For a start, Gramsci gave more consideration to the concept of ideology itself than either Lenin and Lukács. Whereas the latter conceived of ideology in a positive way without ever attempting to define it as a concept, Gramsci dwells on its definition and, despite the fact that he also had not read *The German Ideology*, is quite aware of the existence of a negative concept which he consciously rejects. With Gramsci, the alternative between a positive and a negative concept becomes conscious, the object of a theoretical option. Gramsci observed:

> It seems to me that there is a potential element of error in assessing the value of ideologies, due to the fact (by no means casual) that the name ideology is given both to the necessary superstructure of a particular structure and to the arbitrary elucubrations of particular individuals. The bad sense of the word has become widespread, with the effect that the theoretical analysis of the concept of ideology has been modified and denatured.[129]

It is immediately apparent, however, that Gramsci's idea of the negative concept of ideology does not correspond with Marx's. What he rejects is the conception of ideology as an arbitrary individual speculation, which Marx would have rejected too; but he was not aware of the existence of an alternative negative concept. In this sense, Gramsci was also affected by the lack of knowledge of *The German Ideology*.

Gramsci did not realise that it is also possible to oppose to the conception of ideology as arbitrary appearance, ideology as a necessary *distorted* superstructure of a particular structure. None the less, it is interesting to note that the origin of the 'bad sense of the word', as Gramsci understands it, is in a particular interpretation of the 'good sense of the word' itself. In his reconstruction of the process that leads to the erroneous negative concept, he maintained, first, that 'ideology is identified as distinct from the structure, and it is asserted that it is not ideology that changes the structures but vice versa'. Then, in the second place, 'it is asserted that a given political solution is "ideological" – i.e. that it is not sufficient to change the structure, although it thinks that it can do so', and finally 'one then passes to the assertion that every ideology is "pure" appearance, useless, stupid, etc.'[130] It is quite clear, therefore, that Gramsci identified the negative concept of ideology with a form of reductionism and economism: ideology would be a mere epiphenomenon which reflects but cannot change the structure and thus it would be inferred that it is useless, a mere appearance.

This led Gramsci to propound a distinction between 'organic ideologies' and 'arbitrary ideologies'. The former are necessary to a given structure, the latter are individual speculations. Having made this distinction, Gramsci concentrated on the analysis of organic ideologies. In this way he disposed of the negative concept and expanded the positive conception. In this view ideology is a specific 'system of ideas'[131] or 'a conception of the world that is implicitly manifest in art, in law, in economic activity and in all manifestations of individual and collective life'.[132] But ideology is more than a conception of the world or a system of ideas; it also has to do with a capacity to inspire concrete attitudes and give certain orientations for action. This is why Gramsci used the simile of religion in order to explain this aspect, and proposed that what Croce called religion he called ideology. Religion can be taken 'not in the confessional sense but in the secular sense of a unity of faith between a conception of the world and a corresponding norm of conduct. But why call this unity of faith "religion" and not "ideology", or even frankly "politics"?'[133] Hence ideology is conceived as the unity between a world-view and its corresponding rules of conduct.

An organic ideology, therefore, must be capable of 'organising' human masses, must be able to translate itself into specific orientations for action. To this extent ideology is socially pervasive, the source of determined social action. Men and women cannot act without being conscious, without having certain formulated social orientations. Ideology is precisely 'the terrain on which men move, acquire consciousness of their position, struggle, etc.'[134] The influence of Marx's 1859 Preface on this conception is obvious: it is in ideology that men and women become conscious of their conflicts and fight them out; it is in ideology that social classes become aware of their position and historical role; it is in and by ideology, therefore, that a class can exercise hegemony over other classes. Gramsci's concept of ideology is creatively developed in connection with the notion of hegemony, referring to the ability of a class to secure the adhesion and consent of the broad masses. This aspect had already been anticipated by Lukács, who had emphasised the fact that bourgeois rule could not be sustained by force alone and that in order for the bourgeoisie to organise the whole of society in its own interests it had to develop a coherent *Weltanschauung* to which men and women freely submitted.[135] He had also understood that for revolution to be possible, the dominant system of beliefs had to be shaken and that, in this sense, ideological emancipation anticipated other developments. However, the notion of hegemony acquires a particular connotation in Gramsci's conception in which it is related to the specific situation of Western

Europe. As Anderson has put it, hegemony serves 'to designate the decisively greater strength and complexity of bourgeois class rule in Western Europe which had prevented any repetition of the October Revolution'.[136]

However, the problem which faces any hegemonic conception of the world 'is that of preserving the ideological unity of the entire social bloc which that ideology serves to cement and to unify'.[137] In other words, ideology for Gramsci has an integrating effect, which is based on its ability to win the free consent of the people. This hegemonic quality of a world-view is manifested in the 'solidity of popular beliefs' which 'has the same energy as a material force'. The importance of ideology for class domination is therefore highlighted by comparing it with a material force. This conception led Gramsci to propose a non-reductionist understanding of the relationship between ideologies and material forces which he expressed in the notion of *historical bloc*. This notion seeks to convey the idea that 'material forces are the content and ideologies are the form, though this distinction between form and content has purely didactic value, since the material forces would be inconceivable historically without form and the ideologies would be individual fancies without the material forces'.[138] On the other hand, Gramsci condemned as 'primitive infantilism' the idea that 'every fluctuation of politics and ideology can be presented and expounded as an immediate expression of the structure'.[139] So although ideology cannot be adequately separated from its material contents there is no mechanical correspondence between ideologies and the social structure.

These two statements may seem contradictory, for if the structure and superstructure form a historical bloc, how can it be that the latter is not the immediate expression of the former? The elements of an answer are given by Gramsci. Although the superstructures reflect the tendencies of development in the structure, it is difficult to identify at any given time, statically, the structure. In addition the *tendencies* of development in the structure may not be realised. In other terms, by speaking of 'tendencies' Gramsci indicated that no absolute necessity is carried in the structure. So the structural correspondence can be 'studied and analysed only after it has gone through its whole process of development, and not during the process itself, except hypothetically'.[140] In Gramsci's view this accounts for the existence of political mistakes and errors in calculation on the part of political leaders which historical development later corrects. This is why it is impossible to relate every single ideological and political struggle to some definite elements in the social structure.

Just as ideology is the terrain on which the ruling class achieved hegemony, it is also in ideology that the proletariat can become conscious of its role and try to extend its hegemony over other non-ruling classes. This is an essential political task which the proletariat has to carry out in order to be able to control the state. However, it would be a mistake to think that Gramsci proposes that the working class should gain total ideological domination before conquering political power, as Poulantzas suggests.[141] Gramsci is quite aware that

> the complete modification of the total consciousness of the working class before the conquest of the state, cannot be proposed; this would be utopian, for class consciousness as such cannot be completely modified until the mode of life of the class itself is modified, which entails that the proletariat has become the ruling class.[142]

At any rate, it is undeniable that Gramsci concedes an enormous importance to class consciousness and proletarian hegemony as a means to achieve state power. In this, again, he is preceded by Lukács.

There are, however, three main differences between the Lukácsian conception of ideology and Gramsci's approach. First, whereas in Lukács the analysis of ideology remains at an undifferentiated level of high intellectual complexity, Gramsci considers ideology at different levels. He distinguishes four degrees of ideology, namely philosophy, religion, common sense and folklore.[143] Philosophy is the most systematic and rigorous form of ideology, the best expression of the conception of the world of a class. In this sense, Piotte has pointed out that the philosophical level corresponds to Lukács's ascribed consciousness.[144] As Gramsci puts it, 'philosophy is intellectual order, which neither religion nor common sense can be'.[145] This is true of all philosophies. Yet in so far as they represent the conceptions of the world of different classes, there are some differences between them. Gramsci focuses in particular on their relationship to contradictions and finds a crucial difference between the philosophy of praxis and other philosophies. According to him, 'all hitherto existing philosophies . . . have been manifestations of the intimate contradictions by which society is lacerated. But each philosophical system taken by itself has not been the conscious expression of these contradictions.'[146] Historical materialism is also an expression of contradictions but it has liberated itself from all unilateral elements: 'it is consciousness full of contradictions, in which the philosopher himself, understood both individually and as an entire social group, not only grasps the contradictions, but posits himself as an element of the contradiction and elevates this element to a principle of knowledge and therefore of action'.[147]

Whereas Lukács's analysis remained at the philosophical level of ideology by emphasising the 'ascribed consciousness' to the exclusion of the 'psychological' forms of class consciousness, Gramsci also considers other degrees of ideology as important, even for a Marxist world-view. In so far as religion is a source of practical orientations for action, in addition to it being a world-view, it is certainly an ideology, though it lacks the coherence and intellectual order of philosophy. In order for any philosophy to be truly 'original', in order for it to be creative, it has to be 'socialised', it has to permeate the culture of the people. In Gramsci's view, religion, particularly Catholicism, was especially successful in bridging the divide between a philosophical system and the belief of the masses. From here, Gramsci extracts the religious degree of ideology as a very important fact. As he puts it:

> in the masses *as such*, philosophy can only be experienced as a faith . . . in particular in the social group. The man of the people thinks that so many like-thinking people can't be wrong . . . while he himself, admittedly, is not able to uphold and develop his arguments as well as the opponent, in his group there is someone who could do this . . . he has no concrete memory of the reasons and could not repeat them, but he knows that reasons exist.[148]

Similarly, common sense, although it is a more incoherent and inarticulate conception than religion, 'the folklore of philosophy',[149] as Gramsci calls it, is the most widespread form of ideology among the subordinated classes. Common sense involves a good dose of 'good sense', and to this extent 'it is not possible to separate what is known as "scientific" philosophy from the common and popular philosophy which is only a fragmentary collection of ideas and opinions'.[150] Even more, according to Gramsci, common sense deserves 'to be made more unitary and coherent'. True, the philosophy of praxis must criticise common sense, yet in a manner different from Lenin's and Lukács's critique of spontaneity, for the philosophy of practice (Marxism) must base itself initially on common sense 'in order to demonstrate that "everyone" is a philosopher and that it is not a question of introducing from scratch a scientific form of thought into everyone's individual life, but of renovating and making "critical" an already existing activity'.[151] Finally, the folklore is the lowest degree of ideology, a collection of disparate elements from various world-views without much coherence.

Second, although Lukács accords just as much importance to class consciousness as Gramsci does, he does not fully explain how it is that it comes to be formed and who are the agents in its development. Gramsci, on the contrary, strongly underlines the role of intellectuals in the formation of class consciousness. According to him, every fundamental social class 'creates with itself, organically, one or more strata of intellectuals which give it homogeneity and an awareness of its own function not only in the economic but also in the social and political field'.[152] These are the 'organic intellectuals', who must be distinguished from the 'traditional intellectuals', who are related to classes which have no essential role in a particular society. So although it is perfectly true to say that for Gramsci classes become conscious of their role and extend their hegemony on the terrain of ideology, it is also true that they can do so only by the mediation of organic intellectuals. Consciousness is gained in ideology, but through the agency of intellectuals. As Gramsci claims, 'a human mass does not "distinguish" itself, does not become independent in its own right without, in the widest sense, organising itself; and there is no organisation without intellectuals'.[153]

This is true of the ruling class and of the proletariat. In order for a class to secure its hegemony, it needs the creation of intellectuals who will elaborate, modify and disseminate its class conception of the world. In this sense, ideology is necessarily produced by and depends upon a long, difficult and contradictory process of creation of intellectuals. This process, in which there are advances and retreats, dispersals and regroupings, is described by Gramsci as a dialectic between the intellectuals and the masses. Hence the extension of hegemony is simultaneously a continuous process of construction and reconstruction of a conception of the world and a continuous process of formation and reconstitution of intellectuals. There is no place in Gramsci's theory for a conception of a separate group of intellectuals producing a fully developed ideology which is then taken to the masses from without. The dialectic between the intellectuals and the masses entails that they do not impose an external theory, but make critical and renovate an already existing activity. This is why Gramsci can say that 'mass adhesion or non-adhesion to an ideology is the real critical test of the rationality and historicity of modes of thinking'.[154]

Third, whereas Lukács pays scant attention to the material institutions through which ideologies are produced and disseminated, Gramsci gives especial attention to the institutional framework which serves as the place of production and channel of diffusion of ideologies. In particular he mentions the educational system, religious organisations, publishers and communication media in general. These institutions, which may well be called 'ideological apparatuses'[155], are the material supports of ideology. The conjunction of various ideologies including the ruling ideology plus the ideological apparatuses forms what Gramsci calls *civil society*, one of the two essential parts of the superstructure.[156] The other part, *political society*, includes the state apparatuses which monopolise the use of coercion and can therefore enforce their rulings.[157] As Piotte has pointed out, 'civil society, according to Gramsci, is the moment whereby the economic necessity is transformed into a political programme which is an "ought-to-be", it is the moment whereby necessity becomes consciousness of necessity and therefore freedom'.[158] This passage from economic necessity to the ethico-political moment, from the structure to the superstructure, from objective to subjective, from necessity to freedom, is what Gramsci calls *catharsis*.[159] The ethico-political moment is the moment in which the proletariat becomes conscious of its role in ideology.

It can now be appreciated why it is that, in my view, Gramsci represents the most creative development of the positive concept of ideology. For a start it is apparent that Gramsci breaks fresh ground by analysing in a highly suggestive manner the role of intellectuals and ideological apparatuses in relation to ideology. These aspects had not been given much consideration by Lenin or Lukács. But this is only a minor point. The main problem with Lenin's and Lukács's conceptions of ideology was that they could not resolve dialectically the opposition between spontaneous consciousness and socialist ideology, between psychological consciousness and ascribed consciousness, between philosophy and common sense. So these pairs become dichotomies which separated the perfect and fully lucid world of science from the distorted and incoherent world of spontaneous consciousness. Marxism was developed as a science by the intelligentsia outside the working class and imported into it as a substitute for a false psychological consciousness able only to express bourgeois ideology.

Gramsci was fully aware of these oppositions, and actually made them the object of his reflections. But his analysis of the relationships between the two poles was far more subtle and less unilateral in that he theorised a double current of determinations bridging the divides between them. True, the philosophy of practice is developed by intellectuals, as are all conceptions of the world, but three qualifications should be made: first, the organic intellectual is created as such by the class and thus there cannot be an absolute distinction between intellectuals and non-intellectuals; second, there is no question of introducing from scratch a science, but of renovating and making critical an already existing activity – in other words, the philosophy of praxis does not substitute for a deficient consciousness but recognises and expresses a collective will, a historical orientation which is already present in the class; and third, the philosophy of praxis, the proletarian ideology, can be lived as a faith and as 'good sense' which is informed by some fragmentary philosophical elements. So the various degrees of ideology allow one to conceive forms of proletarian consciousness which are neither the clearest Marxist theoretical consciousness nor bourgeois ideology pure and simple. Hence although Gramsci accepted the existence of ideological contamination, he did not reduce proletarian non-philosophical forms of consciousness to bourgeois falsities. Whereas for Lenin and Lukács proletarian ideology had to express the true interests of the working class, and anything short of that was bourgeois ideology, for Gramsci the proletarian ideology can express those interests imperfectly. This is primarily because for Gramsci ideology is not just a philosophical world-view, but it must necessarily entail orientations for action and must be 'socialised' in the masses. To this extent ideology has to be continually refashioned in order to become adequate for new historical situations.

3

The Marxist Concept of Ideology: A Continuing Controversy

Some consequences of the change in the character of ideology

The process of change in the meaning of ideology which I have described in the last chapter entails at least three consequences. First, the concept of ideology is neutralised and loses its critical connotation. Second, the relationship between ideology and class is altered. Third, the relationship between ideology and contradiction is changed. In effect, whereas Marx's negative concept is critical and restricted in scope, capable of discriminating between adequate and inadequate ideas, the positive conception, by extending the concept so that it covers the political ideas, and more generally the world-view of each class in society, cannot by itself assess the adequacy of the ideas contained in any of them. By becoming comprehensive, the concept of ideology can no longer discriminate between various forms of knowledge. True, the use of a positive concept of ideology does not prevent Marxist thinkers from differentiating between 'bourgeois ideology' and 'proletarian ideology'. But the difference has nothing to do with the notion of ideology itself, for it is evaluated by using other criteria, such as the character of class interests or the structural position of the class within the mode of production. Hence, if bourgeois ideology is deemed distorted, its falsity is imputed to its bourgeois origin and not to its being an ideology.

There is nothing inherently mistaken in differentiating ideologies by ascertaining the specific character of the class interests which lie behind them. The problem is that the distinction can be easily transposed into an extrinsic criterion of truth which mistakenly discriminates between false and true ideologies on the basis of ascribing them to different classes, without considering their intellectual content. The negative concept of ideology, on the contrary, is in itself an intrinsic discriminating criterion which passes judgement upon ideas, whatever their class origin. For Marx the 'ideological' is the attribute of any thought that conceals contradictions. In so far as the concealment of contradictions cannot but help perpetuate the actual system of domination, ideology necessarily serves ruling-class interests. For the positive version, on the contrary, the 'ideological' is the quality of any thought that serves class interests, whatever they may be. So the relationship between ideology and class is altered. Whereas for Marx the idea of a 'proletarian ideology' is totally foreign, for the new generation of Marxists each class produces its own ideology, or at least an ideology that serves its interests can be ascribed to it.

The positive conception also changes the relationship between ideology and contradiction. Dominant and dominated ideologies confront one another in the field of ideology. This means that ideology is conceived as the terrain of a struggle,[1] or 'the medium through which the class struggle is conducted in theory'.[2] Whereas for Marx ideology originates *on* the terrain of contradictions, for the positive version ideology *is* the terrain of contradictions in theory. This is also expressed by saying that ideology is a totality, an objective level of society divided by class struggle. For Marx, ideology is not the totality of class-determined ideas, but a modality of certain ideas which explain away contradictions. While the positive conception understands ideology as a particular space within which class struggle occurs, Marx understands ideology as a particular effect in the field of ideas of the existence of contradictions. So for Marx the 'space' of the struggle is constituted by the general field of ideas, not exclusively by ideology. The definition of ideology in terms of a 'space' or 'terrain' exemplifies what I mean by neutralisation. Ideology becomes the battlefield but it is no longer an instrument in the battle. It therefore loses the critical and combative character it used to share with many other Marxist concepts such as alienation, contradiction, inversion, domination, repression, exploitation, oppression. All of them refer to undesirable situations at various levels of society so that when they are applied they cannot but imply, by their very content, a critique of a distorted state of affairs.

It is most important to recognise that within the Marxist tradition the negative and the positive concepts of ideology are both theoretically incompatible and historically successive. A failure to recognise them as theoretically incompatible may lead to attempts at fusing the two versions in one. But even if one accepts their incompatibility, a failure to recognise the occurrence of a real historical change from one to the other may lead to attempts at dismissing one of them as a mistake or a misinterpretation. These are the two most important and common errors in the discussion of the Marxist concept of ideology. In effect, the attempt at reconciling both versions has been tried time and again within Marxism. The reason for its resurgence, despite its lack of success, is not merely theoretical; in reality there is the more or less disguised urge to reconcile Marx with his intellectual heirs, particularly Lenin. It is as if the recognition of a change of perspective has been detrimental to Marxism and is seen as theoretically unacceptable. Admittedly, the lack of a single approach generates other problems. Not the least are the confusions about the meaning and scope of the concept which bedevil Marxism up to this very day. Yet the problem is made worse by trying artificially to reconcile both versions. An example of the problems involved is provided by Althusser's conception of ideology, which will be dealt with further below.

But there is also the error which consists in denying the historical change in the meaning of the concept. Very often the differences between the negative and the positive concepts of ideology are recognised only in order to dismiss one of them as invalid. Ideology is considered to have always possessed either a positive or a negative character – no change has occurred, and to suppose so is the result of misinterpretation. Most of the time this error has been committed by asserting that the negative version is a mistake, either because it is an interpretation which lacks a firm basis in Marx's writings or because Marx himself is seen to have abandoned it in his mature writings. While McCarney adopts the first line of argument, most structuralist critics adopt the latter. I shall discuss them further below. Against these positions it is necessary to show that Marx did hold to a critical concept and that, if there is any mistake, this is to try to twist his thought into its opposite. It is also necessary to show the specificity of Marx's contribution and its relevance for theoretical analysis. However, it is important to recognise that the fact that Marx held a negative concept of ideology does not of itself invalidate other positive approaches which operate with a different logic. I am against trying to read in Marx a positive conception of ideology, but I am in favour of recognising the contributions of other Marxist theoreticians who approach the problem from a different angle. For in this matter there should not be any question of erecting Marx's version as the paradigm against which later contributions are, as a matter of principle, disfavourably contrasted. The creativity of Gramsci's contribution, for instance, is certainly not diminished just because it changes Marx's original version.

Althusser's ambiguity

Althusser has presented the most influential exposition on ideology in the last two decades. Yet it is surprisingly ambiguous. The influence of Lenin's theory is apparent, but this does not prevent Althusser from keeping some elements of a negative conception which he tries to articulate with the Leninist approach to ideology. Since I have expounded and criticised at length Althusser's theory of ideology elsewhere,[3] I shall concentrate here on some of the problematic aspects of his attempt to reconcile both versions. Althusser distinguishes between the theory of ideology in general and the theory of particular ideologies. The object of the theory of ideology in general is 'an omni-historical reality, in the sense in which that structure and functioning are immutable, present in the same form throughout what we can call history'.[4] In this theory the function of ideology is to secure cohesion among human beings, and between them and their conditions of existence, thus allowing the reproduction and survival of society. Ideology in this perspective is a 'cement' that holds society together. The theory of particular ideologies focuses on historical social formations where the existence of specific class divisions 'overdetermines' the general function of ideology, so that the function here is more specifically to secure the domination of the ruling class by making the 'exploited' accept their conditions.

This distinction has been justly criticised from many points of view,[5] yet whatever its problems it entails a consistently negative concept of ideology. In effect, if ideology is a 'cement' that secures the cohesion of society, it is because 'the opacity of social structure makes necessarily *mythical* the representation of the world necessary for social cohesion'.[6] On the other hand, if ideology secures the domination of the ruling class, it is because it is 'a representation of the imaginary relationship of individuals to their real conditions of existence', and because it 'interpellates' individuals and constitutes them as 'subjects' who accept their subordinated role within the system of production relations.[7] It may well be that Althusser's 'imaginary transposition' is different from Marx's 'inversion', but at any rate both concepts entail a distortion, a misrepresentation. That Althusser holds this negative concept is also confirmed by his contention that science is radically different from, and indeed opposed to, ideology. Whereas ideology is inadequate and abstract knowledge, science is concrete and adequate knowledge. They are connected by the fact that 'scientific practice starts with the abstract and produces a (concrete) knowledge';[8] that is to say, science works on ideological raw materials and transforms them into adequate knowledge. But the final result is radically different from the raw material: between ideology and science there is an 'epistemological break'.

However, Althusser also affirms that ideology can express the protest of the exploited classes and that, therefore, there are dominated ideologies. As he puts it, 'within ideology in general the existence of *different ideological tendencies* is observed, which express "representations" of the different social classes'.[9] This version seems to entail a positive concept of ideology in so far as it accepts the existence of different class ideologies. How can this distinction of ideological tendencies be reconciled with the above-mentioned negative concept? Althusser's solution does not remain the same throughout his development. In his early writings he explicitly seeks to reconcile both versions by arguing that the dominated ideologies are subordinated to, and express themselves in terms of, the ruling ideology. The spontaneous ideology of the working class remains trapped in the structure of the ruling ideology and cannot, by itself, get rid of it. By resorting to Lenin's account, Althusser contends that 'in order for the "spontaneous" working-class ideology to transform itself so that it can become liberated from bourgeois ideology, it is necessary that *it receives from without the help of science*, and that it transforms itself under the influence of a new element, radically different from ideology: precisely science'.[10]

Hence all ideologies are somehow distorted in so far as they are subordinated to the ruling ideology, but at the same time they represent different classes. However, this does not solve the basic problem. If the general function of ideology is to secure everyone's adhesion to the system and if the particular 'overdetermined' function of ideology is to secure the domination of the ruling class, how can this very ideology be the vehicle of protest? If ideology is said to 'interpellate' individuals and to 'constitute' them as 'subjects' obedient to the system, how can they, through an ideological tendency, become critical of the system? Although this seems very difficult to conceive, at least Althusser has tried, at this stage, to remain faithful to the negative character of ideology. Whereas Lenin equates the 'imported science' with ideology and freely speaks of a 'scientific ideology' or 'socialist ideology', Althusser denies the ideological character of science. Yet the accommodation of the negative character of ideology with the existence of various ideological tendencies is achieved at the cost of contradicting the original definition and function of ideology.

In a later stage Althusser tries to answer the accusations of functionalism which greeted his article on the ideological state apparatuses. But in the course of his defence he seems definitely to abandon the idea of a negative concept of ideology while keeping the general mechanism of 'interpellation'. In effect, opposed to bourgeois ideology there exists a proletarian ideology upon which the communist party constitutes itself. This ideology 'interpellates individuals as subjects, but exactly as militant-subjects'.[11] Ideology therefore no longer constitutes individuals as subjects obedient to the system. That may be the specific role of bourgeois ideology. But the proletarian ideology constitutes individuals as subjects against the system. Contrary to his early writings, Althusser now argues that the proletarian ideology is not the purely spontaneous ideology of the working class, but it is informed by objective knowledge provided by Marxism. It is therefore a very particular ideology: 'it functions at the level of the masses as all ideology (by interpellating individuals as subjects) but it is soaked in historical experiences and enlightened by principles of scientific analysis'.[12] The general opposition between science and ideology has therefore disappeared. But with it the originality of Althusser's contribution has gone, too.

However, this new development is compatible with another

tenet of Althusser's theory which he developed from the very beginning, and which cannot be easily reconciled with the opposition between science and ideology. Althusser argued that ideology is one of the three objective levels of society which includes 'the forms of social consciousness'. In his own words, 'all social formation is an "organic totality" which encompasses three essential 'levels": the economy, politics and *ideology or forms of social consciousness*'.[13] Two consequences can be drawn from this conception. First, ideology as an objective level is inclusive of all ideas. Second, ideology is independent from the subjectivity of individuals who are subjected to it. I am going to deal with the second aspect further below. As far as the first aspect is concerned, the inclusiveness of ideology make it more difficult to conceive the whole of it in negative terms. The problem can be expressed thus: if ideology is an 'imaginary transposition' and at the same time includes all ideas, does this mean that no idea can be a true representation of reality? Althusser's solution is not clear, but he seems inclined to exclude science from this objective level called ideology.[14] The problem of this solution is twofold. First, it is difficult to deny that science is a form of social consciousness. Second, even if that were possible, where, then, is one to locate science within the 'organic totality'? Of course, by scrapping the opposition between science and ideology the problem disappears – and this is what Althusser accomplishes in the end, but only at the cost of destroying what had been the cornerstone of his theoretical construction.

The structuralist objections against false consciousness

Although there are in Althusser some strong elements of a negative concept of ideology, from the start he opposes Marx's formulations in *The German Ideology*. In Althusser's view this text conceives of ideology 'as a pure illusion, a pure dream, i.e. as nothingness. All its reality is external to it.'[15] He proposes, on the contrary, that ideology has a material existence in so far as it exists in material apparatuses and practices. Simultaneously, as I have already shown, ideology for Althusser is independent of the subjectivity of individuals. These two tenets have provided Althusser's followers with arguments against a conception of ideology which they consider to be the epitome of a mistaken historicist approach, namely the idea of ideology as false consciousness. In effect, the conception of false consciousness seems to convey the notion that ideology has an 'ideal' or spiritual existence and that it is very much dependent on the subjectivity of individuals. It is no wonder, therefore, that they make of this concept – which is mistakenly attributed to Lukács, not to speak of the young Marx – the centre of their attacks.

Nevertheless, one has to be aware of the fact that not all the followers of Althusser criticise the very notion of a negative concept of ideology. As I have shown, Althusser himself oscillates between a negative and a positive conception. This ambiguity is at the bottom of a division of the Althusserian field into two groups which underline different versions. Those who emphasise ideology as an objective level of society and the existence of a revolutionary ideology tend either to ignore, or even to criticise, the 'misrecognition aspect' as a necessary component part of ideology. Here one finds authors like Laclau, Hirst and Mouffe.[16] The other group emphasises the idea of an 'imaginary transposition' and its opposition to science, and therefore maintains a negative concept of ideology. Here one finds Poulantzas, Godelier and Mepham.[17] Both groups criticise the equation of 'ideology' with 'false consciousness', but the former goes further to eliminate any necessary negative aspect, whereas the latter keeps the critical connotation as essential to the concept. They can express this difference by using Althusser's own language at different stages. For those who continue to maintain a negative version, ideology 'interpellates' individuals as subjects in a fundamental misrecognition which is bound to reproduce the system. For those who abandon a necessary negative connotation of the concept, ideology 'interpellates' individuals as subjects, but this can be either for the maintenance of the system or for its transformation.

The objections against 'false consciousness' cover three aspects, two of which are shared by all Althusserians while the third is put forward only by those who want to eliminate all negative connotations from the concept. The first objection has to do with the conception of ideology as an objective level of social reality, which makes it independent from individual subjectivity. The best formulation here is provided by Althusser himself in rather strong terms. He argues that ideology is a system of representations, 'but in the majority of cases these representations have nothing to do with "consciousness": they are usually images and occasionally concepts, but it is above all as *structures* that they impose on the vast majority of men, not via their "consciousness"'.[18] It is not the subject that produces ideas, but it is rather ideology that produces ('interpellates') the subject. As Coward and Ellis put it, ideology is 'a practice of representation, a practice to produce a specific articulation, that is, producing certain meanings and necessitating certain subjects as their supports',[19] or, as Mouffe summarises it, ideology is 'a practice producing subjects'.[20]

The second objection has to do with the materiality of ideology. Althusser contends that 'the "ideas" or "representations", etc., which seem to make up ideology do not have an ideal (*idéale* or *idéelle*) or spiritual existence, but a material existence'. By this he means that 'an ideology always exists in an apparatus, and its practice, or practices. This existence is material.'[21] Of course, this materiality is not the same as that of a paving-stone; it refers rather to a modality of which languages and rituals are good examples. Nevertheless, ultimately they too are rooted in physical matter.

The third objection goes beyond the other two in that it rejects the very idea of falseness. Ideology, for this group of authors, is not a distorted representation of reality: first, because ideology represents men's and women's lived relations to their conditions of existence and not those conditions directly; second, and more fundamentally, because, as Hirst puts it, 'how can something which has effects be false? It may derive from forms of the imaginary but it is not false. It would be like saying a black pudding is false, or a steam roller is false.'[22] Falseness in this perspective is synonymous with illusion and can also mean the intention to deceive on the part of individual subjects. As ideology is an objective level of the social totality, it obviously cannot be illusory nor can it be related to any subjective intention to deceive.

It is not my purpose to defend a concept of ideology defined as false consciousness, nor do I disagree with every single aspect of these criticisms. However, the critical examination of these three objections is instructive for any negative concept of ideology and this is why I propose to deal with them in order.

The problem of the subject

Ideology conceived exclusively as an objective instance separated from the subject introduces a dualism between subject and object whereby the subject appears as passive and constituted by the object. This is what is involved in Godelier's description of ideology whereby 'it is not man who is mistaken about reality, it is reality which misleads him'.[23] In this perspective subjects are nothing but supports, they are 'produced' for certain representations, they are the place of crystallisation of certain objective practices. Whereas for Marx practice had been the mediation which allowed us to think the unity of subject and object, in this position practice acquires objectivitiy which separates it from the subject. For Marx the subject was produced by/in its own material practice. In *Capital* he affirmed that man, by 'acting on the external world and changing it, he at the same time changes his own nature'.[24] This is very different from holding that the subject is produced for/in ideological representations. In this account ideology appears as determinant but its own determination is obscured. The determination of consciousness by material practice has been transposed into the determination of the subject by ideology. This is in fact a variation on the structuralist theme of Marxism as an 'anti-humanism' and as a 'non-historicism'.

Althusser sets out to prove that humanism is an ideological concept which Marx replaced in his mature work by scientific concepts like 'social formation', 'productive forces', 'relations of production', and so on. To Marx's dictum in *The Eighteenth Brumaire of Louis Bonaparte* that human beings make their own history but not as they please, he opposes Marx's argument against Adolph Wagner that the former's analytic method does not start from man but from the economically given social period.[25] According to Althusser, the problematic of man as the subject is replaced by new concepts. However, as Mepham has shown,[26] Althusser provides several different 'anti-humanist' formulae which do not coincide with one another. A first formula reads: 'It is the masses which make history, the class struggle is the motor of history.'[27] A second formula has in turn two versions: (i) 'The subjects of history are given human societies';[28] and (ii) 'The true subjects of the practices of social production are the relations of production. Men are never anything more than the bearers/supports/effects of these relations.'[29]

Neither Althusser nor Mepham has come up with a definite answer as to which one of these formulae is to be taken as the truly 'anti-humanist' formula. The new scientific formula turns out to be a contradictory group of formulae which neither Althusser nor Mepham can adequately sort out. For it seems obvious that masses, class struggle, societies and relations of production are not equivalent terms. Still, Mepham surprisingly endorses Althusser's claim of having replaced an 'ideological formula' by a 'scientific' one. He recognises that the 'humanist formula' was used 'as an important political weapon by Marx, Engels and Lenin. It was used to combat, for example, certain forms of crude mechanical determinism.' But he immediately adds that 'it is not philosophically, scientifically or politically adequate and it is important to find a better weapon if we can'.[30] One wonders how a formula which is an 'important political weapon' can be reconciled with the fact of not being scientifically adequate. Even more, Althusser accuses the philosophers who use this formula of 'mixing everything up' and of disarming revolutionary militants and theoreticians. How then can it possibly be an important political weapon? It might be argued that a non-scientific formula may have the efficacy of all ideology, but if this is so it would mean that an ideology such as mechanical determinism can be combated by means of another, equally distorted, ideology. This is a contradiction even for the Althusserian conception of ideology and its relation to science.

I think one can agree with Althusser that Marx abandoned the Feuerbachian idea of man as a general essence after the 'Theses on Feuerbach'. But he did not abandon it because it was impossible to conceive of the essence of man as the origin, cause and goal of history, as Althusser contends.[31] Actually the Feuerbachian man was not the origin, cause or goal of any history. Marx abandoned the Feuerbachian idea of human essence precisely because it abstracted from the historical process.[32] As Rancière has cleverly put it, Marx did not criticise Feuerbach because his conception of history had a subject, but rather because his subject did not have a history.[33] To Feuerbach's abstract 'man', Marx opposed concrete empirical men as divided in classes and reproducing their existence. The question was not whether (or not) it was possible to think of a subject, but rather whether man was an abstract essence or concrete historical individuals subsumed under specific social relations.

True, for Marx isolated individuals are not the principal actors in history. In the 1857 Introduction he affirmed that the individual and isolated hunter and fisherman, with whom Smith and Ricardo begin, belongs among the unimaginative conceits of the eighteenth-century Robinsonades.[34] This is, in its turn, reflected in Marx's very concept of society: 'Society does not consist of individuals, but expresses the sum of interrelations, the relations within which these individuals stand.'[35] Yet this does not mean that he has done away with the problematic of the subject. On the contrary the idea of the subject keeps reappearing in Marx's writings, but always within the context of social relations. His objection to the eighteenth-century Robinsonades had to do with the conception of isolated individuals whose social relationships were overlooked. This is why, when he speaks of *men* making history, he means neither the essence of man, nor an aggregation of isolated individuals. He obviously means men as divided into classes. This is the context in *The Eighteenth Brumaire of Louis Bonaparte* – one of the sources of the so-called 'humanist formula' – which is fundamentally a class analysis. This is also the case in the 1859 Preface where *men* are said to enter into definite relations that are indispensable and independent of their will. Similarly, in *The German Ideology*, Marx and Engels spoke of classes achieving an independent existence 'over and against' individuals. This is why, when Althusser says that we can only speak properly of a class humanism and not of personal freedom, he misses Marx's point that liberation means the abolition of all classes, including the proletariat. True, before that, men are inconceivable without these historical frames, but they are the agents who practically produce them, even though they do not control them. This idea is to be found not just in *The German Ideology* – a suspect text for Althusser – but also in the *Grundrisse*:

> the conditions and objectivations of the process are themselves equally moments of it, and its only subjects are the individuals, but individuals in mutual relationships, which they equally reproduce and produce anew. The constant process of their own movement, in which they renew themselves even as they renew the world of wealth they create.[36]

The materiality of ideology

The second objection is concerned with the contention that ideology is material and not spiritual. It seems to me that in dealing with ideology one cannot just talk of its materiality *tout court* or deny its relation to consciousness without falling into some confusions. It is precisely because ideology has to do with consciousness that one has to qualify the character of its materiality in order to avoid a crude reductionism. Paul Hirst has argued that in denying the ideal or spiritual character of ideology, Althusser has tried to displace the opposition ideas–matter, a residue of vulgar materialism[37] with which Marx and Engels were forced to engage, in *The German Ideology*, and which later they abandoned. According to Hirst, 'for Althusser, ideas are real and not "ideal" because they are always inscribed in social practices and are expressed in objective social forms (languages, rituals, etc.). As such they have definite effects. Althusser asserts the materiality of ideology.'[38]

I shall try to show first that Marx's and Engels's formulations about consciousness in *The German Ideology* are exactly the opposite to vulgar materialism, and also that they convey a far more complex picture than Hirst would have us believe. Second, I shall attempt to prove that although Hirst's formulations seek to surpass vulgar materialism, they are not totally successful in doing so, nor do they avoid a kind of objectivism which reduces the forms of consciousness to a merely external mode of existence.

As to the first point, one has to say that indeed a sharp distinction between purely ideal forms and purely material aspects of society is not acceptable within Marxism. What Marx calls 'forms of social consciousness' or just consciousness are certainly inscribed in social practices and can only be individually incorporated through their materiality. Yet it seems very strange to argue that Marx was not aware of this in *The German Ideology*, which is precisely the place where one of his most forceful formulations on this is to be found. It is worth while quoting it at length:

> Only now, after having considered four moments, four aspects of the primary historical relationships, do we find that man also possesses 'consciousness', but, even so, not inherent, not 'pure' consciousness. From the start the 'spirit' is afflicted with the curse of being 'burdened' with matter, which here makes its appearance in the form of agitated layers of air, sounds, in short, of language. Language is as old as consciousness, language *is* practical consciousness that exists also for other men,

> and for that reason alone it really exists for me personally as well; language, like consciousness, only arises from the need, the necessity, of intercourse with other men. Where there exists a relationship, it exists for me . . . Consciousness is therefore, from the very beginning a social product, and remains so as long as men exist at all.[39]

One cannot possibly argue that this passage smacks of vulgar materialism. On the contrary, it affirms the connection of consciousness with materiality in a multidimensional manner which excludes any reductionism and oversimplification. For a start, Marx denies the idea of a 'pure consciousness' totally separated from materiality. However, he refers to a materiality which is different from and more complex than that which one can attribute to natural or physical objects. True, consciousness must necessarily have an aspect of this, too, an external entity which allows it to be communicated and apprehended. At the very least, there will be sounds, 'agitated layers of air', language. As Marx puts it, language is practical consciousness, the objectivation of consciousness in material form. But consciousness is not only that and it cannot be reduced to that material element. Consciousness is also, but not only, an external, material reality. There are also two other essential dimensions of consciousness. First, Marx insists that from the very beginning it is a social product; consciousness originates and exists in networks of relations, it arises from the necessity of intercourse. Second, Marx adds that where there exists a relationship, it exists for the individual; in other words consciousness exists also within us, it is also internal to human beings. The existence of consciousness is not therefore merely physical as language and books, nor is it merely social as an instance of society external to the subject, but also, from the beginning, it is internal to and involves the subjects. These three dimensions of consciousness must be taken into account if one is to avoid reductionism.[40]

It is not possible, and it does not make sense, to oppose any of these dimensions to the others. Consciousness is simultaneously social, internal to the subjects and requires physical modifications in order to exist. Consciousness is not imposed on subjects from without because it is social; rather, it is also internal to the subjects because it is social. The separation between internal and external does not help as far as consciousness is concerned because consciousness is both at the same time: it can be internal only because it is social and it is social only in so far as it is internal. Here lies the problem of any theory which considers consciousness only as an external instance which somehow constitutes the subject. This brings us to the second point. Hirst claims that Althusser surpasses vulgar materialism because he does not reduce materiality to the natural or physical, because it also gives reality and material entity to all aspects of society including ideas. Fair enough, Althusser and Hirst certainly avoid the reductionism of understanding ideas as mere epiphenomena of economic processes. But in so doing they fall into another kind of reductionism which was also castigated by Marx as typical of the old materialism.

In effect, Hirst's conception of vulgar materialism is rather narrow and confined to the conception of ideas as epiphenomena. In the 'Theses on Feuerbach' and in *The German Ideology* Marx also proposed other elements for a critique of vulgar materialism. For instance, he criticised the materialist doctrine that men and women are the product of circumstances and accuses Feuerbach of abstracting from the historical process. But his main objection exactly illustrates my point: 'The chief defect of all hitherto existing materialism (that of Feuerbach included) is that the thing, reality, sensuousness, is conceived only in the form of the *object or of contemplation*, but not as *sensuous human activity*, *practice*, not subjectively.'[41] In their attempt to give consciousness an unquestionable reality, Althusser, and Hirst after him, have fallen into the trap of considering such a reality only in the form of the object, as an external materiality, not subjectively. They have avoided one kind of reductionism at the cost of falling into another, namely the reductionism of considering consciousness and ideology to be objects confronting subjects from without. It is as if the reality of social consciousness could be guaranteed only by its objectivation. I do not deny this dimension of consciousness. I only say that one cannot reduce consciousness to it or, as Marx would put it, one cannot conceive of it only in the form of the object. There is no reason why objectivity, effectivity and reality should be exclusively confined to external materiality. As Marx reminded us, human activity itself is objective activity; that is to say, what we consider subjective is also objective and real.

The problems of false consciousness and distorted communication

The third objection has to do with the very notion of falsity as applied to social phenomena. The nub of the argument is, as Hirst has put it, that something which has effects, like ideology, cannot be false. But this argument presupposes a peculiar concept of falsity; in fact, it seems to equate falsity with non-existence or non-reality. This is shown by the fact that Hirst uses falsity as a synonym of 'illusion', thus transposing an epistemological reality into an ontological absence. There is no reason why one should oppose falsity to existence. A false statement is quite real, it exists and has effects and yet it entails a distortion. Even Althusser understands this by admitting that although ideology does not correspond to reality it does make allusion to reality.[42] There is nothing wrong in preferring a positive concept of ideology to a negative one. But it is a mistake to try and demonstrate the impossibility of a critical concept in this way.

However, it is very important to emphasise that one cannot simply equate the negative concept of ideology with false consciousness, nor can one easily attribute this notion to Marx. For a start Marx himself does not use this expression. Its real source is Engels's letter to Mehring where it is affirmed that 'ideology is a process which is indeed accomplished consciously by the so-called thinker, but it is the wrong kind of consciousness'.[43] There would be nothing wrong with this statement if it were not interpreted as a formal and full definition of ideology. In other words, the problem with this statement is not that it is fundamentally mistaken but only that it is incomplete. It is possible to show that 'false consciousness' is a problematic expression when it is equated with ideology without any further addition.

There are in my view three main difficulties with this notion. First, it is an ambiguous expression in so far as it *may* convey the idea that ideology is an invention of the individual consciousness, a delusion, a mirage without any base in reality. Indeed Engels's explanatory phrase which follows the above-mentioned statement lends itself to this interpretation, for it says that the thinker 'imagines false or illusory motive forces'. To this extent Althusser's warning against a reduction of ideology to individual consciousness is partly justified. But the problem is ambiguity and not that the concept of false consciousness, of itself, means the intention of deception by individual subjects. Second, ideology appears as a mere intellectual or epistemological problem which can be put right by criticism. The notion of false consciousness does not make any explicit reference to the elements in social reality itself which contribute to its emergence.

Third, and most important, the expression 'false consciousness' by itself does not specify the falsity which ideology entails. Hence, under its cover all kinds of errors and mistakes appear as ideological; in fact, ideology becomes synonymous with error and loses its identity as a distinct concept. Admittedly the vagaries of a mentally deranged person, a logical error in mathematics or a mistake in measuring the temperature of a room are all distortions, but I can see no reason why they should be treated as ideological distortions. The problem with false consciousness is that, apart from being an ambiguous expression which elides a reference to its social basis, it is not specific. There is no doubt that for a negative concept of ideology to exist ideology must be a distortion, but the problem is to specify in what respect and to be able to show the particular character of the distortion. Otherwise ideology substitutes for error and there is nothing especially new about it. The concept of false consciousness, on its own, is ambiguous: it does not clarify its dependence on real social problems and fails to determine the character of its falsity; therefore, it is not an adequate definition of ideology.

It is perhaps opportune to mention in this context some aspects of Habermas's contributions which have a bearing upon the concept of ideology. Not that one could associate Habermas with a concept of false consciousness. In fact, he propounds the idea that 'today the problem of language has replaced the traditional problem of consciousness; the transcendental critique of language supersedes that of consciousness'.[44] Nevertheless, this very interest in the theory of language and communication (in so far as it affects the concept of ideology and once it is sufficiently developed) constitutes a shift from Habermas's first approach to ideology which leads, through a different way, to some of the problems which I have attributed to the notion of false consciousness. In his early approach Habermas contends that in advanced capitalism class antagonisms have become latent and that therefore ideology is no longer based on the market and the principle of equal exchange, but has become a form of technocratic consciousness which has the effect of depoliticising the masses. Technocratic consciousness blurs the difference between communicative interaction and purposive-rational action by justifying decisions as if they were 'technical' and not 'political'. Although Habermas disagrees with Marcuse's view that science and technology are inherently ideological, he accepts that they are not entirely innocent either, and despite their necessary progressive character they have also become the source of the new ideological consciousness.[45]

I have critically examined this theory elsewhere in the context of a discussion of the relationship between science and ideology.[46] Although it points to a trend which other Marxist authors like Althusser recognise,[47] it consistently underestimates the importance of class struggle and of bourgeois liberal ideology in advanced capitalist societies. Yet in spite of these problems Habermas's position is still able to link ideology with class-based domination. As he puts it:

> today's dominant, rather glassy background ideology, which makes a fetish of science, is more irresistible and farther-reaching than ideologies of the old type. For with the veiling of practical problems it not only justifies a *particular class's* interest in domination and represses *another class's* partial need for emancipation, but affects the human race's emancipatory interest as such.[48]

It is interesting to note, at this early stage, that Habermas combines the universal emancipatory interest of the human race with the particular emancipatory interest of the dominated class. Yet he does not clarify their relationship. For the Marxist tradition both interests are inextricably linked in so far as 'the condition for the emancipation of the working class is the abolition of all classes';[49] that is to say, the abolition of itself and its opposite. Moreover,

> since the conditions of life of the proletariat sum up all the conditions of life of society today in their most inhuman form; since man has lost himself in the proletariat . . . (this) cannot abolish the conditions of its own life without abolishing *all* the inhuman conditions of life of society today which are summed up in its own situation.[50]

Still, Habermas considers both aspects at this stage even if their relationship is not clear.

Habermas's subsequent development of a theory of communicative competence shifts the emphasis from the concrete veiling of the ruling-class interests to the universal communicative situation in which no genuine consensus can emerge. In this new context ideology is understood as 'systematically distorted communication', as a system of norms and views which are validated in a communicative framework and which impede discursively achieved and constraint-free consensus. Habermas wants to analyse communication from the point of view of a 'universal pragmatics', attempting to find general norms which apply to all speech situations, as against an 'empirical pragmatics' which investigates the contextual and extra-linguistic conditions of communication. As he states it, 'I have proposed the name *universal pragmatics* for the research program aimed at reconstructing the universal validity basis of speech.'[51] Briefly, he suggests that in every exchange of speech acts there implicitly exists the idea of a genuine consensus which makes reference to an 'ideal speech situation'. According to Habermas, 'consensus can arise only through appropriately interpreted, *generalisable* interests, by which I mean needs *that can be communicatively shared*'.[52] This rarely occurs in practice, but it is expected, or assumed, in all speech. As he puts it, 'in taking up a practical discourse, we unavoidably suppose an ideal speech situation that, on the strength of its formal properties, allows consensus only through *generalisable* interests'.[53]

A consensus achieved in this ideal situation – a 'rational consensus', Habermas calls it – is therefore a norm against which all validity claims have to be measured, and it becomes the only possible criterion from which to judge concrete situations of systematically distorted communication. Ideology in advanced societies does not merely legitimate norm systems, but does so

> through the anchoring of the belief in legitimacy in systematic barriers to will-forming communication. The claim that our norms can be grounded is redeemed through legitimating global views of man and nature. The validity of these global views is in turn secured in a communication structure which excludes discursive will-formation . . . The barriers to communication which make a fiction precisely of the reciprocal imputation of accountability, support at the same time the belief in legitimacy which sustains the fiction and prevents its being found out. That

> is the paradoxical achievement of ideologies, whose individual prototype is the neurotic disturbance.[54]

According to Habermas, 'the specific achievement of such ideologies consists in the inconspicuous manner in which communication is systematically limited'.[55] This is why the unmasking of ideology can only be achieved by comparing historical and concrete norm systems with the ideal situation of a rational consensus; that is to say, with an ideal norm system which is supposed to have been achieved discursively and without any constraint. I shall come back to this point in Chapter 6.

It is worth noting, furthermore, that Habermas's model of distorted communication is neurosis and other 'pathological speech disturbances to be observed, for example, among psychotics'.[56] To this extent the critique of ideology becomes a form of psychoanalysis.[57] Just as the neurotic patient is not conscious of his/her inner repression and has to be led by the psychoanalyst to recognise it through a process of language analysis, so human beings in society at the level of collective action may participate in situations of pseudo-communication in which the false assumption of consensus makes it impossible for them to recognise any communication disturbances. They therefore have to be led by critical theory to recognise them through a process of reflection. As Held points out, 'it is Habermas's contention that by conceiving of social institutions as the result of repressed needs and, therefore, as the source of distorted and limited communication, Freud was able to give a better account of ideology than Marx'.[58]

Habermas's account of ideology has been criticised from various angles.[59] Nevertheless, most criticisms coincide on the main points. For instance, the use of psychoanalysis as a model for ideology-critique has been attacked because it transfers the individual interaction between patient and analyst to social interaction between groups and classes. The analogy is clearly deficient. Furthermore, psychoanalysis entails conscious co-operation on the part of the patient, whereas classes stand in a relationship of conflict and domination which makes the analogy even more implausible. Additionally, it seems to me that to conceive of neurosis as the prototype of ideology empties both phenomena of their specific contents by focusing on the abstract and formal aspect that they share – the fact of their being cases of distorted communication. What I said of false consciousness also applies to distorted communication. It is a definition which is not specific, and therefore ideology loses its identity as a distinct concept. There is no doubt that a critical concept of ideology entails a distortion, but not all distortions are necessarily ideological. The point is to delimit the specific character that ideological distortions possess. As Held has rightly pointed out,

> by seeing both ideology and neurosis through a communication paradigm, Habermas risks deflecting attention from the specificity of each; that is, from the link of neurosis with the dynamic of desire and the necessity of repression in the achievement of self-identity, on the one hand, and on the other, the connection of ideology with the clash of material interests.[60]

Furthermore, just like false consciousness, the notion of distorted communication does not make any explicit reference to the social basis of ideology. Habermas's first approach to ideology was at least able to relate technocratic consciousness to class-based domination, to material interests. For the theory of ideology as distorted communication, on the contrary, material interests and domination do not seem to play a role, or, as Giddens has pointed out, the very idea of domination is made equivalent to distorted communication.[61] This means that the real problem of capitalist society is considered to be superstructural. Domination is no longer based on class differences or material inequality; domination is now an ideological problem which can be located at the level of those consensual structures where communication is systematically distorted. Hence it does not make sense to continue to speak of the particular emancipatory interest of the oppressed class. Now emancipation can only be predicated on the human race as a whole. The universal interest of human kind replaces the particular interests of dominated classes. The abstract consideration of distorted communication replaces the concrete analysis of capitalist contradictions.

In these circumstances it is hardly surprising that Habermas should fail to identify the revolutionary subject which will carry out the struggle for emancipation. In fact, the very notions of emancipation and struggle acquire a new meaning which refers them more to intellectual processes of reflection and discursive argumentation than to concrete political activity orientated to overcome material domination. As class-based domination is no longer the support of ideology, emancipation is no longer the business of any class in particular. The logic of Habermas's theory suggests this now lies with some groups of intellectuals because they alone can engage in a process of critical reflection that illuminates the existence of systematically distorted communication. In fact, the equation of domination with ideology is profoundly misleading and merits criticisms similar to those Marx levelled against the young Hegelians, especially in his belief that they considered false conceptions and mistaken ideas 'as the real chains of men' and that they therefore 'fight only against these illusions of consciousness'. They need to be reminded, however, 'that they are in no way combating the real existing world when they are merely combating the phrases of this world'.[62] Similarly, for Habermas distorted communication appears as domination, and therefore the fight must be directed against a consensus established under coercion. He tends to forget, however, that in combating systematically distorted communication he is not necessarily combating real material domination.

Two mistaken interpretations of Marx

The fact that Marx never used the notion of 'false consciousness', and above all the fact that he specified the ideological distortion in terms of the concealment of contradictions in the interest of the ruling class, make it impossible to sustain the proposal that his concept of ideology can be simply equated with false consciousness. Nevertheless, Marx still held a negative concept of ideology and this fact continues to be at the centre of the debate about the Marxist concept of ideology, and indeed about the very interpretation of Marx's contribution. Two current interpretations of Marx's concept of ideology hinge upon this theme, though they arrive at totally opposite results. Seliger seeks to prove that Marx conceived of ideology as false consciousness and that, therefore, Marx's conception is inherently dogmatic. McCarney seeks to show, on the contrary, that Marx not only does not hold ideology to be false consciousness but also that he does not even endorse a negative concept of ideology, and that, consequently, Marx's concept is epistemologically neutral. I intend to show that both these accounts are mistaken because they find no support in Marx's writings.

Seliger is aware that Marx does not use the expression 'false consciousness', but for Seliger this makes no difference because Marx uses equivalent terms like 'incorrect', 'untrue', 'illusion', etc. Furthermore, Seliger acknowledges that there is no systematic treatment or clear-cut definition of ideology in Marx. None the less, he affirms that for Marx and Engels ideology is 'thought that [is] distorted, because all socially relevant thought [is] dependent on economic and social conditions',[63] or to put it in different words, 'the dependence of ideas on the relation between economic and social conditions affects adversely the truth-value of ideas'.[64] Seliger does not seem to realise that he is unwittingly mistaking Mannheim's conception of ideology and relationism[65] for Marx's conception. Marx never believed that all ideas were distorted because they were socially determined, nor did he ever affirm such a thing. Of course, if one could prove that Marx naively fell into such an obvious contradiction the inevitable consequence would be that Marx's thought is dogmatic because, on the one hand, it would affirm the universal precariousness of knowledge, and on the other, it would exclude itself from the general rule without any justification. This is what Seliger sets out to show. But the evidence he tries to produce does not stand up to scrutiny.

Seliger himself is aware that on numerous occasions Marx rejects the equation between ideas in general and ideological distortions, and that he does not only exclude his own thought from ideology but also praises the scientific achievements of classical political economy. Yet instead of taking these statements as clear indication that Marx does not really think that all ideas are irretrievably distorted, he states that 'the occasional praise they [Marx and Engels] bestowed on the classical economists is by no means unimportant, but is actually supplementary evidence of their deviation from the dogmatic standpoint'.[66] Thus Seliger accepts that there are statements in Marx's writings which do not fit with the identification of ideology with all ideas, but as they are not systematically and consistently presented the dogmatic version prevails. The idea is not only that in Marx there are ambiguities – a fact which I recognise – and not only that these are statements which cannot easily be reconciled, but also that ultimately, and this

Seliger consistently affirms, Marx's most genuine concept of ideology is dogmatic. It supposes 'that the entire intellectual superstructure prevalent prior to the demise of capitalism is ideological in the sense of being intrinsically false'.[67]

How does Seliger prove that this is so, and that for Marx the dependence of ideas on social being results in distortion? He selects some quotations from *The German Ideology*, especially the one which claims: 'If in all ideology men and their circumstances appear upside-down as in a *camera obscura*, this phenomenon arises just as much from their historical life-process as the inversion of objects on the retina does from their physical life-process.'[68] As is patently obvious, this quotation in its English version does not support Seliger's contention; it only refers to the social determination of ideology without implying that all ideas are distorted. But Seliger proposes a different translation which begins 'If in the whole ideology', and then as if this were not sufficient to convey his own interpretation, he adds, in between brackets, a sentence of his own – '[the entirety of ideas]'[69] – so that nobody can doubt that Marx is equating ideology with all ideas.

It seems to me obvious that Seliger is forcing the text to say something which is by no means self-evident in the context. Even if one accepted his translation 'If in the whole ideology', this phrase does not of itself means that Marx is thinking of all ideas. On the contrary, it is possible to argue, like McCarney, that the use of the definite article with an adjective in the original '*in der ganzen Ideologie*' 'might rather be taken to suggest that it is some particular ideology that is in question'.[70] I do not necessarily agree with this interpretation either, but at least it shows that Seliger's confident interpretation is based on a less than solid foundation. The forthright equation of the phrase 'in the whole ideology' with 'the entirety of ideas' only reveals that Seliger starts his analysis with the preconception that this is what Marx really means. In other words, he dogmatically – and without justification – assumes what he has to prove.

I recognise that Marx's and Engels's sequence of exposition leading to this quotation is not felicitous. Without warning or clarification they pass from a general principle of determination – 'consciousness can never be anything else than conscious existence' – to the particular determination of ideology: 'If in all ideology', and so on. This may be confusing. But it by no means entails the necessary equation between ideology and consciousness. It would have been desirable if Marx and Engels had demarcated more explicitly the analysis of ideology from the analysis of the social determination of consciousness. But at least they never used consciousness and ideology as interchangeable terms, and this can be clearly seen in *The German Ideology*. Besides, one has to be aware of the fact that the distinction between ideology and consciousness is not absolute and that although they cannot be identified with one another, ideology is certainly a part of social consciousness and is socially determined as much as other ideas. This in itself makes it more difficult for the interpreter to understand the nature of their difference.

The difficulty of comprehending ideology as a distinct part of social consciousness underlies Seliger's second argument, which suggests that Marx claims that from the moment the division between material and mental labour appears 'consciousness *can* really flatter itself that it is something other than consciousness of existing practice',[71] and that therefore he is 'logically committed to the assumption that until the advent of communism the clash between consciousness and reality is unexceptional and inevitable'.[72] In fact, Marx was proposing nothing of this sort. He was only saying that consciousness *can*, and not that it necessarily and in all circumstances does, flatter itself that it is totally autonomous. That this is so is shown by the fact that he specified the particular forms of consciousness he was thinking of, namely 'pure' theory, theology, philosophy, ethics, etc. It is even possible to argue that Marx was not so much concerned with indicting the whole of philosophy, ethics, etc., but rather the attempts to create 'pure' theory, philosophy, etc. Again, Seliger mistakes a particular form of idealistic consciousness as expressed in, say, theology for the entirety of ideas of a society.

Seliger goes on to maintain that it is possible to demonstrate Marx's identification of ideas with distortions in the rest of Marx's writings. But the proofs he adduces are no better than the ones we have seen. For instance, referring to the *Manifesto*, Seliger contends that 'together with classes, all ideologies and ideological consciousness will disappear. This can only mean that all hitherto known forms of consciousness have been "false".'[73] This is a *non sequitur*, and it can only be affirmed if one has previously demonstrated that ideology is equivalent to all forms of consciousness.

But this is what he is supposed to be demonstrating here. Again, Seliger assumes *a priori* what he has to prove. He also quotes that section in *Capital* in which Marx states that the conceptions of the agents of economic relations are different from, 'and indeed quite the reverse of, their inner but concealed essential pattern and the conception corresponding to it'.[74] As it is quite obvious that Marx is distinguishing two different forms of consciousness, one ideological and the other non-ideological, Seliger must shift the ground of his argument. The problem is now that 'the conception corresponding to the essential pattern' is 'available in Marx's "real positive science"';[75] that is to say, Marx is dogmatically excluding himself from the universal distortion. This is similar to what he proposed in the 1859 Preface, where he opposed ideological forms to science.

Curiously enough, instead of taking these statements as proofs that Marx did distinguish between ideology and science, Seliger uses them to prove Marx's dogmatism. It is worth noting that in neither of these two places is Marx specifically and directly speaking of his own science and that, furthermore, he recognises elsewhere that some understanding of the 'essential pattern' was achieved by bourgeois classical political economy. But even if he was referring to his own science as different from ideology, why should he be 'dogmatic'? Does he not give reasons for the position he takes, whatever we may think of them? Why should a claim to validity be dogmatic? Does not Seliger's book posit a similar claim?[76] Ultimately, Seliger's accusation of dogmatism is nothing but an unsubstantiated and dogmatic attempt to discredit the overwhelming evidence that Marx distinguishes between ideology and other forms of consciousness.[77] Seliger does not only fail to produce positive evidence to support his interpretation of Marx's concept of ideology but also fails to dismantle the evidence against his case.

The arguments for neutrality

McCarney's interpretation starts from the premise that for Marx 'ideology is not an epistemological category' and that consequently 'it has no necessary connection with what is cognitively suspect or deficient in any of the ways these qualities may show themselves'.

All claims about a critical concept of ideology 'have no basis in Marx's thought' and are 'dealing in a fantasy'.[78] McCarney's reading of Marx is strongly influenced by the 1859 Preface, on which he bases his interpretation of ideology as beliefs which serve class interests. In order for this concept to embrace the standpoint of all classes, an 'epistemic neutrality' is required. He is well aware that the major problem for his thesis is constituted by *The German Ideology*, and thus he proposes to show that it has been systematically misread.

McCarney's first argument concerns the general status of *The German Ideology*, which he thinks is not a 'theoretical' work. According to this view, the text does not set out to develop a theoretical account of ideology, it fails to provide a definition of the concept, and rather than being concerned with ideology as such it is merely concerned with a particular variety, 'the German ideology'. Consequently, 'ideology tends to appear in a poor light simply because Marx is almost exclusively concerned with ideological beliefs which he rejects'.[79] It is true that Marx does not provide a 'dictionary-type' definition of ideology, but one cannot deny that he does provide numerous theoretical elements which contribute to a definition. In this sense one must be careful not to underestimate the theoretical value of the text simply because it is a polemical work. One cannot separate theory from a particular analysis as if they were entirely disconnected spheres.

How can the analysis of the German ideology be carried out without using theoretical instruments which include a notion of what ideology is? McCarney's point is to deny that *The German Ideology* is specifically concerned with clarifying that notion in general as a previous step to a particular analysis. This is true, but in no way prevents one from working out the more general features of the concept. This is also the case of other key concepts such as *class* or *contradiction* which are widely used by Marx but never specifically defined. They, too, have to be theoretically worked out from their specific utilisation. Besides, that Marx and Engels did not only consider the specific case of the German ideology but were also speaking of ideology in general is shown by one of the few headings provided by the original text itself: 'Ideology in general, German Ideology in particular'.[80]

Hence the fact that one does not find a formal definition of ideology in *The German Ideology* does not, by itself, help McCarney's thesis. He still has to prove that his interpretation can be worked out from the text and that the 'poor light' in which ideology appears is not a general feature of the concept. This is not easy because the overwhelming evidence provided by the text suggests a different interpretation. Unable to find any substantial positive support for his version, McCarney resorts to the negative and painfully difficult attempt at dismantling the evidence against his case, in the hope of winning by default, as if casting doubts on the opposite interpretation would make his the necessary one. The procedure is fundamentally flawed, for even if he succeeded in casting some doubts on the contrary evidence he would still be unable to work out his own version from the text on account of its particularity. So we would arrive at the paradoxical conclusion that the only text of Marx's which deals with ideology at some length – whatever problems we may find in it – is of little or no value for working out a general concept of ideology.

However, I do not think that McCarney is very successful in countering the evidence which *The German Ideology* provides against his case. Take, for instance, his treatment of expressions such as 'ideological deception', 'ideological distortion' and 'the illusions of the ideologists' which abound in the text. According to McCarney, they do not lend support to the epistemological thesis but constitute rather a problem for it to solve. For if the negative concept of ideology is correct, then these expressions have a pleonastic character. And it is unthinkable that Marx would have fallen for unnecessary and redundant expressions on such a scale. So the extensive use of 'ideological distortion' means that there are ideologies which are not distorted.[81] This argument is not convincing because in order for a pleonasm to exist, the allegedly repeated terms must have equivalent meaning so that one of them is unnecessary. Now 'ideological' and 'distortion' are not equivalent for Marx. Although all ideology is distorted, not all distortions are ideological. As I showed in Chapter 1, Marx restricts the concept of ideology to a specific kind of distortion which conceals contradictions, and does not identify ideology with error in general.

Another argument seeks to dispose of the stubborn passage 'If in all ideology men and their circumstances appear upside-down as in *camera obscura* . . .', which clearly indicates a negative concept of ideology. McCarney, like Seliger, translates '*Wenn in der ganzen Ideologie*' into 'If in the whole ideology', but, contrary to

Seliger, he thinks this restricts the citation only to the German ideology. As the 'if' still bothers him, he assumes that the German '*Wenn*' is here 'concessionary' and not 'suppositional' in character, which authorises him to scrap it altogether from the translation. Yet as these procedures have altered the evenness of the text by making it switch abruptly from a general context to the particular, a further defence is needed which proposes that 'smoothness of texture is not a notable feature of Marx's work'.[82] Finally, even if one leaves the translation as it is, he claims that the statement is counterfactual, meaning: 'Even if, as is not the case, all ideology has an idealist character, still that fact too could be explained on the materialist hypothesis.' In conclusion he can now claim with some relief 'that the threat to our thesis from the *camera obscura* passage has vanished'.[83]

With these extraordinary expedients McCarney accommodates the text to his own position. Without going into the technical details of the translation it does seem that the whole procedure smacks of scholasticism. A chain of small changes, the necessity of which is not proven, succeeds in twisting the general sense of the whole text. I do not claim that the precise sense of this text is obvious or clear, but even with problems of interpretation the general sense of the text massively supports the idea of a negative concept of ideology. This is the only sensible answer to McCarney's perplexed question as to why, if his interpretation is right, 'the nature of the pattern has been so widely misconceived'.[84] In other words, the answer is simply that the pattern has not been misconceived at all. This is also the only right answer to a question which, according to McCarney, 'may be a source of residual unease about the argument'; that is, the question of 'Marx's apparent reluctance to speak of ideology in connection with the proletariat and, in consequence of the ideological significance of his own work.'[85] This so-called 'apparent reluctance' is a gross understatement, for Marx never called his own thought or the political thought of the proletariat ideological. The reason for this is again very simple: the negative character of ideology.

But, of course, these questions are not so easy for McCarney to answer and therefore he is obliged to continue his painstaking elaborations in order to find solutions that fit his own version. Again, these solutions are not at all convincing. For example, in looking for the causes of the widespread acceptance of a negative concept of ideology, he points to Engels as a mediating factor. In particular he blames Engels for using the expression 'false consciousness' in a letter to Mehring.[86] Yet as he cannot give the impression that Engels understands ideology in a critical sense – that would be damaging to McCarney's thesis – he is compelled to minimise the error and treat it as an isolated aberration. On the whole, it appears to McCarney that Engels was right. So the conclusion is that the expression 'false consciousness' was lifted out of the original context and without regard for 'the particular shade of meaning that Engels wished to attach to it'. Thus it is demonstrated 'how slight was the impulse originally given to the hare of "false consciousness" which has been running so vigorously ever since'.[87]

McCarney does not seem to realise that by trying so desperately to save Engels from the indictment of propounding a negative concept of ideology, he undermines the answer to his original question. If the arguments for finding in Engels a negative concept are so baseless and the original impulse to the hare of false consciousness is so slight, how can one justify their widespread impact? The original question is left without an answer, unless one is prepared to accept with McCarney that the real cause is a gigantic travesty. I am not personally in favour of understanding ideology as false consciousness, but the least one can say about Engels's role is that having been the co-author of *The German Ideology* it is not at all surprising that he kept referring to ideology in a negative sense. This is the reason why neither Marx nor Engels ever talked about a proletarian ideology in a positive sense. McCarney attributes this to an 'obsessional concern with unmasking the ruling ideas' which 'tend to appropriate the entire field of discourse'.[88] But this is a very flimsy and arbitrary argument. With such a reasoning one could make Marx think anything and blame his 'obsession' for not mentioning it. The suggestion that Marx did not mention proletarian ideology because the proletariat was also the destroyer of ideology in general is equally weak and proves nothing but the contrary. In order for the proletariat to be able to destroy ideology in general, its own thought must be free from ideology.

McCarney approvingly contrasts the practice of Lenin and Lukács with Marx's 'failure to say much about the ideology of the proletariat'.[89] But he fails to understand the real nature of their historical difference. It is true that the generation of Marxists which includes Lenin, Lukács, Gramsci and others strongly relied on an interpretation of the 1859 Preface for their elaborations on ideology and that they accepted the existence of a proletarian ideology. But McCarney does not take into account the fact that they did not have access to *The German Ideology* and, more important, the fact that they faced a totally different political reality. So the fact that their emphasis was different from Marx's is quite understandable. McCarney's problem is that he cannot easily reconcile Lenin, Lukács and Gramsci with Marx. Yet instead of accepting the difference and showing its source, he embarks on the hopeless task of trying to adapt *The German Ideology* to a version which not only was developed more than half a century later but was also developed without a knowledge of that very text. This laborious enterprise cannot succeed despite McCarney's skilful endeavours.

Ideology as interpellation

Among the positive conceptions of ideology Laclau's contribution represents an innovation with respect to the traditional Leninist and Lukácsian conceptions which emphasise the existence of 'paradigmatic' class ideologies. Laclau contends that the elements of concrete ideologies such as liberalism, nationalism, fascism, etc., have no necessary class belonging and that their class connotation can vary as 'the result of the articulation of those elements in a concrete ideological discourse'.[90] In other words, these are not 'pure' ideologies produced by classes as complete totalities; there exist ideological elements which are neutral if taken in isolation, and which can be articulated to concrete class discourses. The conjunction of these ideological elements constitutes the ideological level of a social formation. In order to understand how these elements work, Laclau resorts to Althusser's idea that ideology interpellates individuals as subjects; individuals are 'recruited' or 'constituted' as subjects subordinated to the ruling class or as militant subjects who fight against the ruling class. Hence the ideological level of a society is made of different types of interpellations. An ideological discourse articulates several interpellations in a relative unity.

Laclau identifies a special kind of interpellations which he calls 'popular-democratic' interpellations; that is to say, ideological elements which interpellate individuals as 'the people', as the underdog opposed to the powers that be. He distinguishes these interpellations from class interpellations which constitute individuals as a class and which seek to integrate popular-democratic interpellations into the class ideological discourse. As he puts it,

> *the popular-democratic interpellation not only has no precise class content, but is the domain of ideological class struggle par excellence*. Every class struggles at the ideological level *simultaneously* as class and as the people, or rather, tries to give coherence to its ideological discourse by presenting its class objectives as the consummation of popular objectives.[91]

Fascism successfully articulated the popular-democratic interpellations to the discourse of the monopoly fraction of the bourgeoisie, successfully identifying nationalist and anti-plutocratic popular traditions with racism. This was possible because the working class under the influence of the Third International failed to integrate into a socialist discourse those popular traditions, and developed a political strategy based on narrow-minded economism and class reductionism.

Within the framework of a positive conception of ideology, Laclau's attempt to deal with ideologies in a non-reductionist fashion by looking into their 'articulating' principle is certainly appealing. The idea that classes 'articulate' to their ideological discourses elements which are not necessarily their own creation is valuable. Furthermore, Laclau's critique of the theory of 'paradigmatic' ideologies is quite necessary. In the Leninist and Lukácsian traditions, Marxism is supposed to be the ideology of the working class, and all the spontaneous traditions and 'empirical' forms of consciousness of the class are suspect. By objecting to the abstract reduction of working-class ideology to Marxism-Leninism, Laclau puts himself in the Gramscian tradition which appraises in a much more satisfactory way the various levels of ideology and which grants far more relevance to the reworking and reinterpretation of theory in the context of spontaneous popular traditions.

None the less, Laclau propounds these points by basing himself on two arguments with which in their present form I tend to disagree. One is the distinction between two separate kinds of contradictions, namely the people–power bloc contradiction and the class contradiction. I shall discuss this point in Chapter 4. The other is the principle that 'the class character of an ideology is given by its *form* and not by its *content*'.[92] I shall critically examine this proposition in Chapter 5. Neither of these arguments is in my view strictly necessary to support a non-reductionist conception of ideologies, as Gramsci's position illustrates only too well. For the time being, however, and without pre-empting the discussion of these two propositions, I want to argue that Laclau's analysis of ideologies, and particularly of fascism, still presupposes – although it does not recognise it – the operation of a negative concept of ideology. In this sense Laclau's explicit rejection of ideology as a kind of distortion contradicts some of the presuppositions of his own analysis.

When inquiring into the ultimate causes of fascism he concludes that they are connected with a dual crisis: a crisis of the power bloc and a crisis of the working class. Both are ideological crises in Laclau's terms because the ruling class is unable to neutralise popular-democratic interpellations and the working class is unable to articulate them in a socialist discourse. If we focus on the latter, we shall see that the reason given by Laclau for this inability of the working class is a kind of *reductionism* in its practice which, in its turn, produces *economism*. But then one may ask: what does reductionism and economism boil down to? In trying to answer this question Laclau cannot but explain that they are errors and distortions in the understanding of contradictions. In effect, according to him, class reductionism transformed 'the class barrier into an absolute criterion of separation between the working class and the rest of society',[93] thus disregarding the autonomy of popular-democratic struggles. Economism, in its turn, entailed two further distortions, namely the assumption that the middle sectors and the peasantry would become increasingly proletarianised and the idea that 'the purely economic contradictions inherent in capitalist accumulation would provoke, by the simple unfolding of its internal mechanism, the crisis of the system'.[94]

One can agree or disagree with the content of Laclau's assessment, but nothing can be more evident than the fact that in order to explain the ultimate causes of the emergence of fascism he is unconsciously utilising the elements of Marx's concept of ideology, and in particular the forms which concern the misunderstanding and displacement of contradictions. In this sense it would be true to say that at the origin of fascist ideologies in Laclau's terms lie ideological distortions in Marx's terms. From a more general perspective one can say that inasmuch as those working-class practices and conceptions which are criticised by Laclau misrepresented and therefore concealed the real character and evolution of contradictions, thereby hindering the working-class movement, then they were ideological in Marx's sense of the term; and what Laclau accomplished without acknowledging it is a critique of ideology. One can agree or disagree with Laclau's critique, but the nub of his critique is not dependent on whether one class or the other provides the articulating principle of the discourse. Rather, it is dependent on whether or not the discourse of the working class at a certain historical moment provides a correct understanding of contradictions.

4

Inversion and Contradiction

From the Hegelian inversion to the Marxist inversion

As I have already shown, Marx's treatment of ideology repeatedly refers to 'inversions' and 'contradictions'. It is necessary to clarify these concepts and explore their relationships so that the significance and scope of the notion of ideology are better appreciated. I shall deal first with the concept of *inversion*. It is of course not at all surprising that this notion, as many others that Marx uses, should be taken from Hegel. It appears in *The Phenomenology of Mind* in the context of the distinction – which Marx also borrows – between the sphere of appearances and the inner world. Hegel wanted to assert that the inner reality of things is concealed by, and indeed is the reverse of, their phenomenal forms. As he wrote, 'by the law of this inverted world, then, the self-same in the first world is the unlike of itself, and the unlike in the first is equally unlike to itself . . . what by the law of the first is sweet, is, in this inner, inverted reality, sour; what is there black is here white'.[1]

This inversion affects the natural world as much as the spiritual world. It is not just that what appears sweet is in fact sour, or that oxygen becomes hydrogen, but also that the punishment of a crime is really self-punishment and that what is despised in one world is honourable in the other. In short,

> looked at on the surface, this inverted world is the antithesis of the first in the sense that it has the latter outside itself, and repels that world from itself as an inverted reality; that the one is the sphere of appearance, while the other is the inherent being; that the one is the world as it is for an other, the other again the world as it is for itself.[2]

However, there is no absolute dichotomy between these two

worlds. Whereas for Kant the inner reality was so different from its phenomenon that it could not be known, for Hegel the appearance manifests its essence, and the essence is the truth of its appearance. The distinction cannot be 'substantively fixed'; it is 'inner distinction', 'self-repulsion of the self-same as self-same'. 'Thus the super-sensible world, which is the inverted world, has at the same time reached out beyond the other world and has in itself that other; it is to itself conscious of being inverted, i.e. it is the inverted form of itself; it is that world itself and its opposite in a single unity.'[3]

In this way Hegel reached the 'distinction *per se*', in the 'form of Infinity', or 'absolute motion'. This is the 'ultimate nature of life, the soul of the world, the universal life-blood' which is itself 'every distinction that arises, as well as that into which all distinctions are dissolved'.[4] Ultimately, therefore, the internal distinction is self-identity and self-consciousness. But if this is so, the distinction between appearance and inner reality in the natural world is nothing but a reflection of the distinction in self-consciousness – materiality itself becomes the inverted appearance of self-consciousness. The distinction between consciousness and its object is thus eliminated. As Marx formulated it in his criticism of Hegel, 'The main point is that the *object* or *consciousness* is nothing else but *self-consciousness*, or that the object is only *objectified self-consciousness*, self-consciousness as object.'[5] In the process of dividing itself, of repelling itself from itself, self-consciousness establishes the object as the reverse of itself. Inversion, therefore, is the result of the alienation of self-consciousness.

It is worth noting that Hegel identified alienation with objectification in so far as, by producing the object, consciousness recognises itself as absolutely alien to itself, as an object devoid of meaning. Objectivity itself is therefore alienated self-consciousness. This means that for Hegel the overcoming of alienation, the reappropriation of self-consciousness, is necessarily the transcending of objectivity. But this is a process which takes place in consciousness, for Hegel has identified reality with con sciousness. Hence the overcoming of alienation, and the inversion it entails, is seen as a mere recognition by consciousness that objectivity is its own inverted creation. As Marx put it, 'the appropriation of man's objectified and estranged essential powers is therefore firstly only an *appropriation* which takes place in *con-*

sciousness, in pure thought'.[6] Both alienation and inversion are therefore inherent conditions of self-consciousness and are given in its necessary division between object and abstract thought. The notion of inversion is thus defined in epistemological terms as the natural result of the process of production of thought which is simultaneously the process of production of reality as its opposite.

Although Marx took the notion of inversion from Hegel, he understood it in a different manner. For a start, inversion is not necessarily given in all processes of objectification. By means of their conscious practice, humans necessarily produce an 'objective power' which is the conjunction of relations of production and productive forces existent at any time in a society. This objectification of human practice is not of itself alienating. Alienation arises out of individuals' lack of control of that objective power. It is only then that objective conditions, which are practically produced, can govern their producers instead of them governing their products. It is here that Marx located the problem of alienation, in a particular *kind* of objectification which is inhuman because men and women do not control its results, but are controlled by them. For Hegel the problem is different: 'It is not the fact that the human essence *objectifies* itself in an *inhuman* way, in opposition to itself, but that it *objectifies* itself in *distinction* from and in *opposition* to abstract thought.'[7] So, for Hegel, inversion is necessarily given in the division of self-consciousness, whereas for Marx inversion is the hallmark of a particular and specific social condition.

In the second place, for Marx it is not the alienation of consciousness that generates an inverted objective reality, but an inverted reality that generates an inverted consciousness. If religion is an inverted consciousness of the world, it is because the state and society that produced religion are an inverted world. Certainly, Hegel conceives of religion as self-alienation as well as a world constructed 'in the ether of pure consciousness' in opposition to the actual world in which the Idea has alienated itself.[8] But it is self-consciousness that produces both worlds, and so the inversion is reputedly abolished when religion, as much as the objective world, are recognised as projections of self-consciousness. This is why Marx criticised Hegel by saying that 'having superseded religion and recognised it as a product of self-alienation, he still finds himself confirmed in *religion* as *religion*. Here *is* the root of Hegel's *false* positivism or of his merely *appar-*

ent criticism.'[9] The same result occurred with, for example, the Prussian state and all other objectifications: as self-consciousness can only manifest itself through them, they become the self-realisation of the Idea and in this way they became justified.

In making these criticisms, which are the direct antecedents of the concept of ideology, Marx turned around Hegel's notion of inversion. The conception of real history and objective reality as the inverted appearances of self-consciousness is, in its turn, an inversion of reality because human activity 'appears as the activity and product of something other than itself',[10] and consciousness, being a product of man's head, appears as the producer. This is the inversion which Marx and Engels extensively criticised in *The German Ideology* as the inversion of the order of determination between consciousness and material conditions. The German ideologists explained material practice from ideas instead of explaining consciousness from practice; they fought against illusions of consciousness, which they believed constituted the real chains for men and women, instead of fighting against German political and social reality.

But Marx simultaneously affirmed that this kind of inversion is not a mere epistemological distortion produced by consciousness in an arbitrary manner. The origin of this inversion is in reality itself, which is upside down. Hence the religious inversion corresponds to an inverted world, and 'if in all ideology men and their circumstances appear upside-down as in a *camera obscura*, this phenomenon arises just as much from their historical life-process'.[11] This means that Marx proposed the existence of two kinds of inversion – the inversion of consciousness and the inversion of objectified social practice. The former he treats as ideology, the latter as alienation. Ideology conceals alienation, it constitutes an inverted reflection of an inverted reality which results in the negation of the latter inversion. For Hegel there could be only one kind of inversion, for the inversion of consciousness *was* the objectified social reality. Such a distinction between ideology and alienation would not make sense in the Hegelian perspective. Everything is subsumed under the alienation of the Idea.

Up until the end of the second stage of his intellectual development Marx worked with this scheme of a double inversion. But as I have already shown, the sphere of objectified social practice which constitutes the field of alienation was still depicted in very simple terms. When Marx initiated a more detailed analysis of the capitalist forms of social practice he discovered that their reality is not transparent and that the basic inversion contained in them was able to negate itself by presenting itself under the guise of its opposite. In other words, capitalist reality itself is divided in such a way that what occurs at the level of production is denied at the level of circulation. Marx's appropriation of the notion of inversion had not, until this point, taken into account the context within which Hegel developed it, namely the distinction between inner reality and its appearance. Now, in trying to dissect the capitalist forms of economic practice and having returned once more to Hegel's *Logic*, Marx discovered that this distinction allows the interplay between production and circulation to be explained. What had been the simple 'inversion of the world' unfolds itself into two connected inversions. One of them evokes the Hegelian distinction: the appearances of the circulation process are the reverse of the inner reality of the productive process. But this is so because the very essential relations at the productive level are, in their turn, twisted and inverted.

As I have already said, Marx defined this basic real inversion in capitalism as alienation. But from this point he was able to make precise its specific nature. As he noted:

> to the extent that, from the standpoint of capital and wage labour, the creation of the objective body of activity happens in antithesis to the immediate labour capacity – that this process of objectification in fact appears as a process of dispossession from the standpoint of labour or as appropriation of alien labour from the standpoint of capital – to that extent, this twisting and inversion is a *real* (*phenomenon*), not a merely *supposed one* existing merely in the imagination of the workers and the capitalists.[12]

Alienation, therefore, is not merely objectification, but a kind of objectification which occurs in antithesis to the labourer, and results in his or her dispossession. The very relationship of labour to the conditions of labour is 'turned upside-down so that it is not the worker who makes use of the conditions of labour, but the conditions of labour which make use of the worker'.[13] Or, as Marx explained, 'this relation is an inversion – personification of the thing and materialisation of the person',[14] it is an 'inversion of subject and object that takes place . . . in the process of production'.[15] Man as a producer is converted in a product and his products take the form of producers. 'As in religion, man is governed by the products of his own brain, so in capitalistic production, he is governed by the products of his own hand.'[16]

This basic inversion at the level of production is nevertheless concealed at the level of circulation by 'the final pattern of economic relations as seen on the surface' which shows the opposite; this determines the emergence of ideology because 'the distorted form in which the real inversion is expressed is naturally reproduced in the views of the agents of this mode of production'.[17] Thus there exist three kinds of inversions: alienation or the basic inversion of subject and object whereby live labour is subordinated to dead labour; the market and the process of circulation which inverts the former inversion and presents it as a natural process of objectification realising freedom and equality; and finally ideology which reproduces the level of appearances in the mind, thus inverting the inner 'twisted' relations. One must not conceive of these three inversions as entirely distinct phenomena which correspond to three separate layers of reality. They are of course analytically distinct, but they belong to the same process whereby human practice objectifies itself, and to that extent they are mutually inclusive. This process can be represented diagrammatically (see Figure 4.1).

Figure 4.1

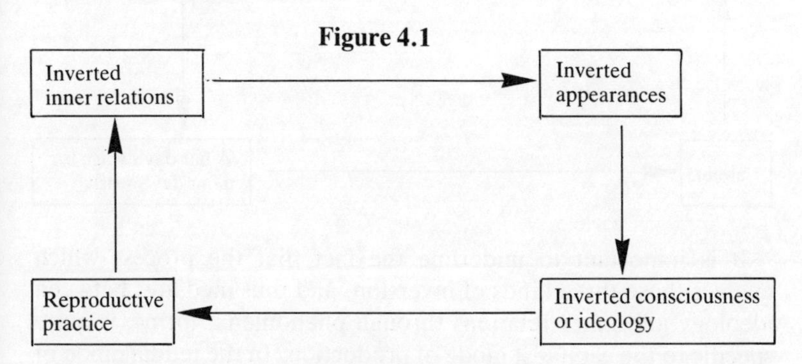

Let us take, for example, reproductive practice, or labour under the capitalist mode of production. The labourer sells his or her labour-power in the market for its value, or, in other words, sells a certain length of working day for a wage. On the surface it is obvious that the wage pays for all the labour done within the working day. What happens beneath this surface appearance is quite different. The value of the labour-power sold proves to be only a fraction of the value which the labour-power produces. This means that the labourer is paid only for a fraction of the working day, for the time necessary to reproduce himself or herself, and the rest constitutes unpaid labour which is appropriated by the capitalist. This, however, is concealed by the wage form which was agreed as payment for the whole working day. This appearance shows the direct opposite of the inner relation and is naturally reproduced in the minds of both capitalist and worker as the idea of an equitable exchange. So the inner inverted relation (the capitalist expropriating part of the value produced by labour-power without pay) appears reversed both in the wage form and in the ideological consciousness of capitalists and workers. This ideological consciousness, in its turn, is a necessary element in the social reproduction of this whole process. It is a condition for the labourers to go to the market and sell their labour-power for less than they produce. In terms of our former diagram the process can be represented as shown in Figure 4.2.

Figure 4.2

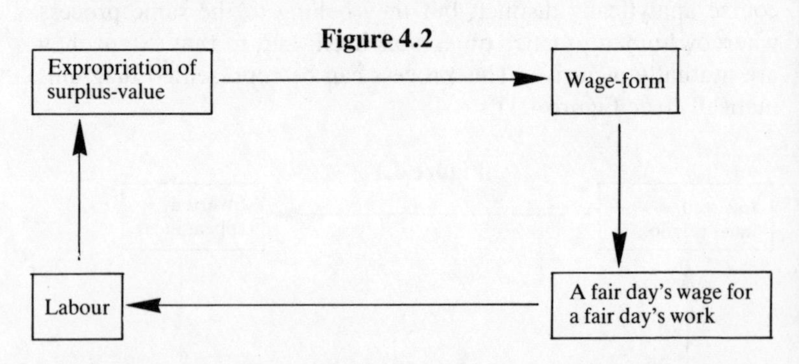

It is important to underline the fact that the process which evolves these three kinds of inversion, and thus mediates between ideology and inner relations through phenomenal forms, is quite specific to the capitalist mode of production. In the feudal mode of production, 'for the very reason that personal dependence forms the ground-work of society, there is no necessity for labour and its products to assume a fantastic form different from their reality'.[18]

We have already seen that personal dependence produced the appearance of 'purely personal relations', whereas in fact it was based on objective social relations. But no surface appearance emerged which concealed the very nature of the production process. As Marx perceived, 'in the corvée, the labour of the worker for himself, and his compulsory labour for his lord, differ in space and time in the clearest possible way'.[19] It is only in the capitalist mode of production that this distinction between paid and unpaid labour is obliterated by the wage form, thus constituting a specific source of ideological consciousness.

From inversion to contradiction

From its inception in Hegel, the notion of inversion was related to the idea of contradiction. In portraying the opposition between inner reality and appearance as an inversion between two poles of a single unity, Hegel hoped to avoid any fixed distinction. This was only possible by conceiving them in movement, as absolute opposition. As he put it:

> from the idea, then, of inversion which constitutes the essential nature of one aspect of the supersensible world, we must dissociate the sensuous idea of keeping distinctions substantively fixed in a different element that sustains them; and this absolute notion of distinction must be set forth and apprehended purely as *inner* distinction, self-repulsion of the self-same as self-same, and likeness of the unlike as unlike. We have to think pure flux, opposition within opposition itself, or Contradiction.[20]

This means that everything that exists contains an opposition in itself, that its being consists in its relation to its opposite. Hence Hegel could affirm that 'contradiction is the very moving principle of the world: and it is ridiculous to say that contradiction is unthinkable'.[21]

In this Hegel opposed the Aristotelian logical tradition which denied the possibility of contradictions in reality, only accepting contradictions as logical mistakes. The distinction between logic and reality does not make sense in Hegel's conception because the production of thought is simultaneously the process of production of reality. Contradiction is inherent in the process of the self-alienation of consciousness, which in turn is the process of creation of materiality and objectivity. It is not possible, therefore, to distinguish logical contradictions from real contradictions; or, in other terms, the contradiction in consciousness *is* the real contradiction. Just as inversion is necessarily given in the process of objectification, so too is contradiction, for as Marx pointed out, 'it is not the *particular* character of the object but its *objective* character which constitutes the offence and the estrangement as far as self-consciousness is concerned. The object is therefore negative, self-superseding, a *nullity*.'[22] Inversion and contradiction are therefore inherent in the very essence of all that exists, because all that exists is the contradictory opposite of self-consciousness or, rather, all that exists is self-consciousness as the opposite of itself.

The consequence of conceiving contradiction as given in objectivity as such is not merely the ontological pervasiveness of negativity but also the illusory way in which that negativity is superseded. As self-consciousness recognises itself in the object it reaffirms itself as alienated, it confirms itself in contradiction with itself or, as Marx put it, it 'claims to be at home in his other-being as such'.[23] So the solution of the contradiction is not in the supersession of the inverted pole but in the recognition or knowledge of itself as in contradiction with itself. This is why Marx says that 'in Hegel, therefore, the negation of the negation is not the confirmation of true being through the negation of apparent being. It is the confirmation of apparent being or self-estranged being in its negation.'[24] This means that every alienated or contradictory aspect of reality is superseded only in abstract, in the knowledge of self-consciousness, while in practice it is confirmed as a manifestation of self-consciousness. Hence religion, the state, civil society and ultimately the Prussian state itself are confirmed as moments of self-consciousness moving towards absolute knowledge. Hegel's idealism thus leads to the paradoxical conclusion that the solution of contradictions lies in their recognition, or, what is the same, in their confirmation as contradictions.

Marx's concept of contradiction is also related to the notion of inversion. Just as in Hegel, contradiction appears as the dynamic aspect of inversion. That is to say, the inverted opposites cannot be conceived as substantive elements which can exist on their own, but their being is intelligible only in relation to each other and as the negation of each other. However, since for Marx inversion is not a result of the process of objectification of practice as such, but the result of men and women's inability to control it (alienated objectivity), contradiction cannot be conceived as the universal essence of reality but only as the condition of specific social situations where this basic inversion occurs. This coincides with what Marx calls the pre-history of man, that is to say, the history of class societies. So contradiction is not constitutive of all things but the hallmark of a historical situation in which men and women are divided into classes which they do not choose, and in which they are dominated by the products of their practice. The connection between inversion and contradiction within the concrete historical situation of capitalism is summarised by Marx as follows:

> The barrier to *capital* is that this entire development proceeds in a contradictory way, and that the working-out of the productive forces, of general wealth, etc., knowledge, etc., appears in such a way that the working individual *alienates* himself; relates to the conditions brought out of him by his labour as those not of his *own* but of an *alien wealth* and of his own poverty. But this antithetical form is itself fleeting, and produces the real conditions of its own suspension.[25]

For Hegel 'contradiction is the root of all movement and vitality' and he could argue that 'our consideration of the nature of contradiction has shown that it is not, so to speak, a blemish, an imperfection or a defect in something if a contradiction can be pointed out in it'.[26] For Marx, on the contrary, contradiction stems from imperfection; it is the result of human inability to control the 'objective power' which they themselves have produced by means of their practice. Contradictions may be inevitable and necessary while men and women are still struggling to control nature and while productive forces are still developing within a restricted framework of social relations. But their necessity is historical, not absolute.

This is a consequence of the character of the inversion which lies behind this process. As I said above, for Marx the real capitalist inversion was not given in the process of objectivation of practice as such, but in the fact that the objectivation meant the dispossession of the labourer and the appropriation of alien labour by the capitalist. This is why he can say that

> obviously this process of inversion is a merely *historical* necessity, a necessity for the development of the forces of production solely from a specific historic point of departure, or basis, but in no way an *absolute* necessity of production; rather, a vanishing one, and the result and the inherent purpose of this process is to suspend this basis itself, together with this form of the process.[27]

Marx conceived of contradictions as historical phenomena which emerge, develop and vanish, and which, after capitalism, will eventually disappear altogether. This is the sense of the classless society he advocated.

The consequence of understanding contradictions in historical terms is not only that they can be concretely transcended but also that they have within themselves the immanent mechanism of their destruction, or, as Marx conceived it, the very antithetical forms themselves produce the conditions of their own supersession. Whereas for Hegel contradictions were solved in abstract in such a way that the negation of the inverted pole was simultaneously its confirmation, for Marx contradictions can only be solved in concrete historical situations in such a way that the negation of the inverted pole entails its destruction. While for Hegel supersession occurred by the recognition of the contradiction, for Marx supersession can only occur by the practical alteration and destruction of the contradiction. This means that the central preoccupation for Marx was historical, real contradictions as opposed to the formulation of logical contradictions. Hegel's idealism, on the contrary, could not perceive any distinction between them, so that the contradiction involved in the self-alienation of consciousness became *the* real contradiction.

Logical and real contradictions

That Marx distinguishes between logical and real contradictions is shown by his differentiated use of the term in a single context. For instance, in the *Grundrisse* he affirms that

> it is not at all contradictory, or, rather, the in-every-way mutually contradictory statements that labour is *absolute poverty as object*, on one side, and is, on the other side, the *general possibility* of wealth as subject and as activity, are reciprocally determined and follow from the essence of labour, such as it is *presupposed* by capital as its contradiction and as its contradictory being, and such as it, in turn, presupposes capital.[28]

Elsewhere Marx states that 'classical political economy occasionally contradicts itself in this analysis', but further below he adds that 'the development of political economy and of the opposition to which it gives rise keeps pace with the *real* development of the social contradictions and class conflicts inherent in capitalist production'.[29] When Marx says that 'it is not at all contradictory' at the beginning of the first quotation, or that classical political economy 'contradicts itself' in the second quotation, he is clearly referring to logical contradictions which he rejects as unsound reasoning. In the first case he actually argues that there is no logical contradiction in accepting contradictions in reality; in the second case he condemns the logical contradictions of classical political economy while accepting that its development keeps pace with the development of real contradictions.

Marx sees no conflict in upholding the logical principle of non-contradiction and propounding the existence of real contradictions.[30] Ideology has to do with the concealment of real contradictions and not necessarily with the existence of logical contradictions, although, of course, a logical contradiction can be used to conceal a real contradiction, in which case it becomes ideological on top of being logically false. But the source of the criticism must be kept separate. When Marx says that classical political economy occasionally contradicts itself, he does not necessarily mean to criticise an ideological distortion. In fact, when he explains the cause of these logical contradictions he adds that 'this is however a necessary consequence of its analytical method, with which criticism and understanding must begin'.[31] Further below, however, he shows by contrast the real source of ideological distortions when he says that 'the position is quite different as regards vulgar political economy' in so far as it 'deliberately becomes increasingly *apologetic* and makes strenuous attempts to talk out of existence the ideas which contain the contradictions'.[32] That these contradictions exist in reality and not merely in consciousness is strongly emphasised when Marx discusses the ideological approach of vulgar economy to crises. In order to deny crises apologists

> assert unity where there is conflict and contradiction. They are therefore important in so far as one can say they prove that there would be no crises if the contradictions which they have erased in their imagination, did not exist in fact. But in reality crises exist because these contradictions exist. Every reason which they put forward against crisis is an exorcised contradiction, and, therefore, a real contradiction, which can cause crises. The desire to convince oneself of the non-existence of contradictions, is at the same time the expression of a pious wish that the contradictions, which are really present, *should not* exist.[33]

The question arises, nevertheless, as to whether it is possible to conceive the existence of contradictions in reality. The Aristotelian logical tradition denied the possibility of real contradictions by basing itself on the principle that everything was identical with itself, and that therefore a thing could not, be and not be at the same time and from the same point of view. Hence, by definition, a contradiction was a logical mistake. Kant upheld the same principle and introduced a distinction between 'real opposition' and 'contradiction'. The former could be found in reality because it did not entail contradictoriness: both extremes were real and positive and their being was not dependent on each other's existence. The antagonism between two real opposites was quite common, 'a fact which is constantly brought before our eyes by the different antagonistic actions and operations in nature', and entailed a real negation in that 'one reality united with another in the same subject annihilates the effects of the other'. But this kind of opposition was different from contradiction, which was a logical opposition between extremes which could not be conceived as existing on their own. That was why 'realities (as simple affirmations) never logically contradict each other'.[34]

By following this line of reasoning Eugene Dühring made a strong attack on 'the actual absurdity of contradictions in reality', having in mind both Hegel's and Marx's dialectic. His argument restated the view of traditional logic as follows:

> The first and most important principle of the basic logical properties of being refers to the *exclusion of contradiction*. Contradiction is a category which can only appertain to a combination of thoughts, but not to reality. There are no contradictions in things, or, to put it another way, contradiction accepted as reality is itself the apex of absurdity.[35]

This and other attacks prompted Engel's reply in *Anti-Dühring* which quickly became the standard point of view of orthodox Marxism. Plekhanov, for instance, used similar arguments in his polemic against Zhitlovsky.[36] But the preoccupation with the impossibility of conceiving real contradictions did not remain the exclusive domain of pre-Marxist philosophies or anti-Marxist theoreticians. Recently Lucio Colletti has reopened the question from a Marxist point of view and has been joined in Britain by contributions from Roy Edgley and Scott Meikle.[37] Apart from Meikle's standpoint, the drift of the discussion seems to challenge the apparently strong case presented by formal logic in such a way as to save Marx's notion of contradiction without denying its logical character.

In the main three positions develop. Two of them try to make compatible the logical character of contradiction with Marx's viewpoint, and the other, represented by Engels and Plekhanov and later followed by Lenin and Mao, argues along Hegelian lines in favour of real contradictions. This latter is the orthodox approach. In essence, Engels contends that Dühring's argument is only valid as long as we consider things at rest. 'But the position is quite different as soon as we consider things in their motion, their change, their life, their reciprocal influence on one another. Then we immediately become involved in contradictions. Motion itself is a contradiction.'[38] Then he goes on to list a series of examples mostly taken from mechanical change, organic life and mathematics. In all of these spheres of real life contradiction is objectively present. One can see, therefore, that Engels's argument closely follows Hegel's refutation of traditional logic. It was Hegel who first argued that everything was inherently contradictory and that things could move only in so far as they had a contradiction within them. He also argued that something could be alive only in so far as it contained contradiction within it, and gave examples drawn from chemistry and physics.[39]

The problem with this line of argument is not so much that there is something inherently mistaken in conceiving movement and life as the result of contradiction, as the fact that it misses the specificity of Marx's notion of contradiction. For Marx contradiction was not a metaphysical principle present in all existence, but the historical result of men and women's 'limited material mode of activity' which objectifies itself in social relations which human beings do not control. Marx's point was precisely to investigate and propose the possibility of transcending the contradictory form of society so as to replace it by one in which men and women gain mastery over their own social relations. Marx clearly saw the difference between this kind of contradiction, which needs to be overcome by means of revolutionary practice, and other processes of natural movement. As he put it, 'universally developed individuals, whose social relations, as their own communal relations, are hence also subordinated to their own communal control, are no product of nature, but of history'.[40] Thus Marx was not really concerned with an objective dialectics of nature, but with social contradictions which can be historically and effectively destroyed.

True, Plekhanov could argue that he expressly pointed to the differences between Hegel's dialectic and Marx's dialectic when he stated that

> with Hegel, *dialectic* coincides with *metaphysics*. For us, *dialectic* is built on the *doctrine of Nature*. With Hegel, the *Absolute Idea* was, to use Marx's expression, the demiurge of reality. For us, the absolute idea is merely an *abstraction of motion*, which latter is the cause of all *combinations and states of matter*. With Hegel, thinking progresses in consequence of the uncovering and resolution of the *contradictions* inclosed in *concepts*. According to our doctrine – the *materialist* – the contradictions embodied in concepts are merely reflections, *translations into the language of thought*, of those contradictions that are embodied in *phenomena* owing to the contradictory nature of their common basis, i.e. *motion*.[41]

Thus, he concluded, materialism places the dialectic the right side up. However, Plekhanov failed to realise that simply by 'inverting' the Hegelian dialect he had not escaped from metaphysics. He has substituted the notion of Nature for the notion of Absolute Idea, but contradiction remains the ontological principle of all beings. Both the Absolute Idea and the 'doctrine of Nature' remain in a metaphysical world which fails to appreciate the specificity of the historical social world.

Engels's and Plekhanov's recourse to Hegel's inverted dialectic committed them to a conception of dialectic which missed the essential character of the Marxist contradiction, namely its social and historical character. This can also be said of Lenin and Mao, who saw contradictions primarily as natural phenomena. Lenin explicitly subsumed social contradictions in nature when he said that one has to recognise contradictions 'in *all* phenomena and processes of nature (*including mind and society*)'.[42] The argument which seeks to prove the existence of contradictions in reality is not necessarily mistaken so long as one is able to make precise the kind of reality one is talking about. As far as Marx was concerned, one is certainly not talking about the relationship between oxygen and hydrogen in water or about the connection between the negative and the positive pole in electricity. Contradiction for Marx exists in reality, but he was only concerned with social reality. Of course, this argument does not of itself prove that there can be contradictions in social reality, for the objection of formal logic still applies to this sphere of reality, as much as to any other. But before trying to solve this problem let us have a look at the two other alternative solutions.

By starting from Kant's distinction between 'real opposition' and 'dialectical contradiction', Colletti assumes that in the real world one can only find the former but not the latter. In other words, all contradictions can only be logical contradictions. But as he is aware of the fact that Marx spoke of dialectical contradictions in the capitalist mode of production, he is driven to qualify the character of capitalist reality. Capitalism 'is not reality *sic et simpliciter*, but the realisation of alienation. It is not a positive reality, but one to be overthrown and negated', 'it is a reality that is upside-down, that is stood on its head'.[43] The problem is this. As Colletti does not accept the existence of contradictions in reality he must implicitly affirm that the fact that capitalist reality is inverted makes this reality somehow 'unreal'. And it is only because capitalism is not fully real that it can be contradictory. In this way he resolves the existence of contradictions in capitalism with his belief that only logical contradictions can exist. In short, capitalism is not full reality but alienated reality and this is why it is contradictory.

There is an aspect in Colletti's argument which is certainly true: if capitalism is contradictory, it cannot be a 'positive reality'. But he makes the mistake of confusing and identifying a 'negative reality' with lack of reality, or simply unreality. There is no doubt that for Marx capitalist reality is contradictory as it is an alienated reality. But this does not prevent it from being 'fully' real. There is no way in which one can affirm at the same time that capitalism is contradictory and that there are no real contradictions unless, of course, one denies the reality of capitalism. But this is not possible even if one considers capitalist reality to be upside down. To think otherwise is arbitrarily to restrict the concept of reality to an ideal situation which is yet to be achieved. Colletti is right in arguing against the Hegelian identification of contradiction and reality, but he is wrong in identifying contradiction with non-reality, particularly if he still wants to affirm the contradictory character of capitalism. He goes from one extreme to the other and does not realise that reality can be contradictory at one point in history and non-contradictory at another. Whereas for Marx the historical process should go from a contradictory to a non-contradictory reality, for Colletti the historical process progresses from unreality to reality.

Roy Edgley proposes a third solution to the problem. He starts from Colletti's main assumption that dialectic and contradiction are essentially logical in character. But as he realises that to deny the reality of capitalism is an untenable position – 'capitalism seems to be only too bloody real'[44] – he propounds the idea that the logical contradictions exist in reality and that we must abolish the dichotomy between logic and reality. As he puts it, 'Logic must become ontologic.'[45] Edgley wants to deny the belief that ideas and judgements are not part of reality and therefore he rejects Kant's distinction between contradiction and real opposition. It may be true that not all real conflicts are logical contradictions, 'but it is also true that a contradictory or logical opposition can be a perfectly real conflict: as, for instance, when, on that question of whether the Earth moves, Copernicus and Galileo contradicted the Church'.[46]

I am sympathetic to an argument which rejects the dichotomy between consciousness and reality. This was the position that

Marx adopted in the first thesis on Feuerbach when he criticised the old materialism for conceiving reality only in the form of the object, not subjectively, as practice. But Edgley misses the point when he tries to derive from this the idea that logical contradictions exist in the world outside consciousness. A logical contradiction may be real in the sense that it really exists in someone's consciousness, but it cannot exist outside the mind. Edgley's own example shows that he is talking about something different. The idea that the sun moves around the earth does indeed contradict the idea that the earth moves around the sun. But it is not possible to say that this contradiction *is* the real conflict between Galileo and the Church, even if this conflict was *about* that contradiction. The earth cannot in reality move, and not move, around the sun; whereas Galileo and the Church are two poles which in reality may or may not oppose each other over that issue.

Hence Edgley's example presents two problems. First, the contradiction between the sun moving around the earth and the earth moving around the sun can only exist in consciousness. Even if the conflict between Galileo and the Church is about that contradiction, it is not the same contradiction. The two opposed terms have changed. Second, if one accepts that in order for a contradiction to exist the two opposite terms cannot stand without each other's existence – that they necessarily entail a relation to each other – then the conflict between Galileo and the Church is not a contradiction. So it does not seem that Edgley's attempt to demonstrate the existence of logical contradictions in the real world has succeeded. His solution, although different from Colletti's, is undermined by the same premise, namely that contradiction has an essentially logical character. Can one expect to find a better answer?

A more substantial attempt to justify the existence of logical contradictions in reality is carried out by Elster. According to him, 'the term "contradiction" is basically a logical one, and should not be extended in a way that is totally divorced from the primary meaning'.[47] Consequently, he distinguishes contradiction from conflict or struggle. But he thinks it is possible to argue that logical contradictions are real, for they can be found in both mental and social phenomena. Mental contradictions arise at the level of the individual who may entertain contradictory beliefs and contradictory desires. For instance, in the master–slave relationship the master may desire both the respect of the slave and the satisfaction of having absolute power over him. But this, Elster argues, is like trying to have your cake and eat it.[48] Social contradictions are connected with the 'fallacy of composition', which entails that what is possible for any individual is also possible for a whole category of individuals. For example, the 'essential paradox of capitalism' according to Keynesian economics is that 'each capitalist wants low wages for his own workers (this makes for high profits) and high wages for the workers of all other capitalists (this makes for high demand)'.[49] Of course, this is possible only for an individual capitalist but it is not possible for all capitalists. If all capitalists act upon the premise that this is possible for all of them, some unintended consequences arise which Elster calls 'counterfinality'. According to him, Marx thus explained the fall in the rate of profit: individual capitalists cut down on labour in order to increase their rate of profit, but when all capitalists do that the unintended result is a reduction of aggregate surplus-value and a fall in the rate of profit.[50]

It seems to me that, despite some differences, Elster's account of the relationship between logic and reality is essentially Hegelian. For Hegel the notion of contradiction was inherent in the development of consciousness, but as the self-alienation of consciousness was simultaneously the process of production of reality, there was no possible distinction between logic and reality. Elster, more cautiously, derives from Hegel the limited thesis that 'there are situations in reality that can only be described by means of the concept of a logical contradiction'.[51] But ultimately the whole of his analysis of contradictions is reduced to the effects of unintended results which mental contradictions have in society. It can be argued that Elster considers not only mental contradictions but also social contradictions. Yet the difference between them is tenuous: in the final analysis Elster's contradictions, whether mental or social, are all based on the individual consciousness and its intended or desired goals. Counterfinality seems to apply to all of them, too.

In effect, for Elster there is no real contradiction between the bourgeoisie and the working class or between masters and slaves. The 'real' contradiction exists 'within the mind of the master' and 'within the working class',[52] or, for that matter, within the minds of capitalists and slaves. In all these cases intended results are negated by unintended outcomes. True, Elster treats the contradictory expectations of the master as a mental contradiction, yet immediately after claiming that the master tries to have his cake and eat it he adds 'the master disappears from the history as a blind alley and the slave becomes (for a while) the carrier of the further development'.[53] Is this not a case of counterfinality even though it is not based on the 'fallacy of composition'?

The only difference between the intended desire of the master and the intended desire of the capitalist is that the former cannot be realised even at the individual level, whereas the latter can be hypothetically realised at the individual level. Yet the difference evaporates when one sees that the aggregate outcome of the desires of individual capitalists makes the individual expectations impossible. In other words, Elster's social contradictions presuppose a conception of the social as the unintended result of the simple addition of individual intentions and, conversely, Elster's mental contradictions can also produce unintended results which go beyond the individual. What this boils down to is sheer idealism: the logical produces the real; the expectations of individual consciousness are supposed to produce social results. The truth is, on the contrary, that the real social contradictions between master and slave and between capital and wage-labour account for the expectations and contradictions of the individual consciousness. Counterfinality is not the cause but a mere effect of social contradictions which have been previously constituted.[54]

On the character of historical contradictions

From this discussion it appears that the definition of contradiction in terms of a purely logical opposition does not allow us to posit the existence of contradictions within the capitalist system. But of course this does not necessarily mean that therefore there cannot be real contradictions within capitalism. The question can be put in the following terms: is there a compelling reason for restricting the concept of contradiction to the sphere of logic? Let us examine Colletti's definition of contradiction in order to see whether its essential features effectively rule out its existence in social reality. According to Colletti, a contradiction 'is the instance in which one opposite cannot stand without the other and vice versa'. Each opposite is nothing for itself:

> it is the negation of the other *and nothing else* . . . if in fact we wish to know what one extreme is, we must at the same time know what the other is, which the first element is negating. Each term, therefore, to be itself, implies a relation to the other term; the result is unity (the unity of opposites). Only *within* this unity is each term the negation of the other.[55]

Why cannot contradiction exist in the real world outside consciousness? Because in reality the opposites are not negatives in themselves but positive. As Colletti puts it; 'in a real opposition or relation of contrariety, the extremes are both positive, even when one of them is indicated as the negative contrary of the other'.[56] Opposite physical forces can annul each other, but this is a negation of a kind different from contradiction. Most of the time real opposites have nothing in common with each other, they do not form a unity, and they do not need each other to exist. There is no doubt that Colletti's argument is correct when it refers to conflicts between natural forces. If one accepts the above-mentioned features of contradictions, then the opposition between physical objects or things is not of a contradictory nature. But is this also necessarily true of all conflicts in social reality? The answer cannot be given in principle but has to emerge from the analysis of the object itself. If one identifies social phenomena with things, or natural forces, then clearly there cannot be contradictions in social reality either. But such identification is a mistake. If one looks more closely, one can see that there are in society certain objects or social entities whose essential reality is given by a relation of opposition. These entities are different from things in that they cannot stand on their own without the reference to their opposite. If this is so, then contradictions do exist in social reality.

Let us see the way in which Marx presents the most basic of these contradictions within the capitalist mode of production:

> Proletariat and wealth are opposites; as such they form a single whole. They are both creations of the world of private property. The question is exactly what place each occupies in the antithesis. It is not sufficient to declare them two sides of a single whole. Private property as private property, as wealth, is com-

> pelled to maintain *itself*, and thereby its opposite, the proletariat, in *existence*. That is the *positive* side of the antithesis, self-satisfied private property. The proletariat, on the contrary, is compelled as proletariat to abolish itself and thereby its opposite, private property, which determines its existence, and which makes it proletariat. It is the *negative* side of the antithesis, its restlessness within its very self, dissolved and self-dissolving private property.[57]

This formulation of the contradiction by the young Marx is repeated in a different but equivalent form by the mature Marx:

> within this process the worker produces himself as labour capacity, as well as the capital confronting him, while at the same time the capitalist produces himself as capital as well as the living labour capacity confronting him. Each reproduces itself, by reproducing its other, its negation. The capitalist produces labour as alien; labour produces the product as alien. The capitalist produces the worker, and the worker the capitalist, etc.[58]

If one compares Marx's description of the opposition between capital and labour with Colletti's definition of contradiction, it is possible to see that the former fulfils all the requirements of the latter. There are two opposites, capital and labour, which cannot stand without each other. Each term, to be itself, implies a relation to the other term; capital cannot exist without labour and vice versa. Capital and labour constitute a single whole within which each is the negation of the other. So it appears that there is a relationship of a contradictory kind between capital and labour, and yet this relationship is not logical but real. In other words, there is no logical contradiction in affirming the existence of a real contradiction between capital and labour. This means that Colletti's definition of contradiction is not the specific definition of logical contradiction but the definition of contradiction in general which by itself cannot determine the precise mode of existence of the opposite terms involved, but only fixes the formal requirements of their relationship.

In this way it is possible to distinguish, as Marx does, between logical and real contradictions. The specific nature of a logical contradiction is given by the fact that the opposite terms are *propositions*, the result of which is that only one of them can be true. A logical contradiction, therefore, can only exist in consciousness and is possible only as the result of deficient reasoning. The specific nature of a real contradiction is given by the fact that the opposite terms are not propositions but social entities existing in social reality. While the logical contradiction is static and cancels itself out once it is recognised as such in consciousness, the real contradiction 'is nothing but the movement of both its sides'[59] and is only solved when its negative side succeeds in destroying it. This is not a process of the mind, but a practical, historical struggle. Whereas in a logical contradiction the place each of its opposite terms occupies in the antithesis is important from the point of view of the truth-value of its terms (but immaterial from the point of view of the drive to solve the contradiction) in a real contradiction the place each term occupies in the antithesis is crucial in order to determine which of them benefits from the maintenance of the contradiction, and which benefits from its supersession. In the case of the contradiction between capital and labour, for instance, 'the private property-owner is . . . the *conservative* side, the proletarian, the *destructive* side. From the former arises the action of preserving the antithesis, from the latter the action of annihilating it.'[60]

This feature of the real contradiction underpins the crucial role of ideology for the positive side of the contradiction. By concealing the very existence of the contradiction, ideology helps preserve the antithesis and checks the destructive action of the negative side of the contradiction. This means that the adequate or distorted perception of a contradiction and the true or inadequate recognition of its character are indispensable elements of its development and have a bearing upon its eventual supersession. The evolution and possible solution of social contradictions are not blind, predetermined processes which occur despite human activity and ideas, but processes which necessarily involve men and women's conscious practice. However, the kind of consciousness that arises from the contradiction is, in its turn, essentially conditioned by the very existence and degree of development of the contradiction itself. In this sense ideology is both the result and the precondition of contradictions. As Marx summarised it in general terms, 'every precondition of the social production process is at the same time its result, and every one of its results appears simultaneously as its precondition. All the *production relations* within which the process moves are therefore just as much its products as they are its conditions.'[61]

Hence the contradictory whole has no preconditions for its existence which are outside the whole itself. The real contradictory unity is nothing but 'the movement of both its sides'. This is why Marx says that capitalist production, as a contradictory whole, 'is antecedent to itself' and 'the contradictory, socially determined feature of its elements evolves, becomes reality only in the process itself'.[62] However, as social contradictions emerge as part of a process which belongs to a certain specific historical period, there are historic presuppositions which are external to the contradiction itself. Thus capitalist production emerges as a result of the dissolution of the feudal mode of production, which itself was a different contradictory unity. Nevertheless,

> as soon as capital has become capital as such, it creates its own presuppositions . . . These presuppositions, which originally appeared as conditions of its becoming – and hence could not spring from its *action as capital* – now appear as results of its own realisation, reality, as *posited by it – not as conditions of its arising, but as results of its presence*. It no longer proceeds from presuppositions in order to become, but rather it is itself presupposed, and proceeds from itself to create the conditions of its maintenance and growth.[63]

Therefore, a contradiction historically comes into existence when a certain point is reached in the dissolution process of an earlier totality; but once it has emerged, it becomes its own precondition. Before the capitalist production process exists as such, the contradiction which characterises it can be said to be a *potential contradiction* which is present as a possibility in some of the forms produced by the dissolution process of the former mode of production. The potential contradiction becomes an *actual contradiction* from the moment the capitalist production process as such exists. Before the capitalist becomes a capitalist he needs an accumulation of capital created by hoarding or savings. This capital is only potentially in contradiction with labour and therefore is not really capital. It becomes so only when it is used to buy labour-power from a free worker. At the beginning of a new mode of production, its basic contradiction does not manifest itself in acute and developed conflicts or crises, and therefore it appears relatively secondary in respect to the contradictions which, concentrated and showing themselves in exacerbated struggles, bring about the dissolution of the former mode of production. Once this process of dissolution is completed the new contradiction comes to the fore and evolves until its own development (the historical movement of both its sides) erects a barrier to itself. As Marx puts it, for capitalism, 'the *real barrier* of capitalist production is *capital itself*'.[64]

Different kinds of contradiction

I have just introduced the distinction between potential and actual contradictions. In point of fact, this is one of the two explicit classifications that one can find in Marx as far as contradictions are concerned. He uses it, for example, when he describes the contradictions inherent in the commodities.[65] Another distinction occurs in Marx's writing between a *formal* and a *material* contradiction, and this is used in connection with the relationship between the deputies of civil society and their electors. The formal contradiction exists in the fact that deputies have formal authorisation by being elected; but when that authority becomes real, they are no longer authorised because they are no longer instructed by their electors. The material contradiction has to do with actual interests. Deputies formally gain their authority as representatives of the public interest, whereas in fact they represent particular interests.[66] However, there is a series of further classifications which have been introduced by later theorists. Among the most common of them one can mention the distinction between antagonistic and non-antagonistic contradictions and the distinction between principal or primary and secondary contradictions. Both these distinctions originate in the work of Mao Tse-tung.

According to Mao, a principal contradiction is that 'whose existence and development determine or influence the existence and development of other contradictions'.[67] Secondary or subordinate contradictions are therefore those which are determined and influenced by the principal contradiction. Furthermore, in any contradiction there is a principal and a secondary aspect. The principal aspect of a contradiction 'is the one playing the leading role in the contradiction',[68] but it can transform itself into the secondary aspect and vice versa. Although these distinctions seem useful, Mao's definitions of them are vague and general. This is in part the result of Mao's abstract treatment of the concept of contradiction itself. By following Lenin, Engels and Hegel he affirms that 'contradiction is present in the process of development of all things; it permeates the process of development of each thing from beginning to end. This is the universality and absoluteness of contradiction.'[69] So, again, there is no consideration of the specifically social character which contradiction has for Marx, and, in truly Hegelian fashion, contradiction becomes the universal principle of motion, the ontological constituent of all beings.

This is why the distinction between principal and secondary contradictions is located in the context of the process of development 'of a complex thing' which contains many contradictions, instead of the more specific context of a society or mode of production. It seems to me that it is at these specific levels that this distinction is most useful. Giddens, for instance, has described primary contradictions as those fundamentally involved in the system reproduction of a society, thus entering into the very structuring of the system. Secondary contradictions are 'those which are brought about through the existence of primary contradictions and which are in some sense a result of them'.[70] A similar version, which seems most appropriate, has been given by Ken Post. He has described a principal contradiction as 'that upon which the very existence of the mode of production is founded': it creates the fundamental classes, whereas a secondary contradiction is 'that which gives full shape to the formation of the principal contradiction'.[71]

If one takes these specific definitions, it is apparent that within a principal contradiction one cannot have a permutation of its principal and secondary aspects, as Mao proposes. The principal aspect of the capitalist principal contradiction is obviously capital, and wage-labour the subordinated aspect. Hence Mao's principal aspect can be equated with Marx's positive or conservative side of the contradiction, while the secondary aspect can be equated with the negative or destructive side, as long as their places are structurally determined by the mode of production and cannot be changed. When Mao gives the example of capitalism which changes its position from being a subordinate force in the feudal era to being the dominant force in the capitalist era,[72] he does not realise that there is no change of aspects within the same contradiction, for the principal contradiction in the feudal era was that between landlords and peasants. I do not deny the opposition between feudal lords and the bourgeoisie, but this is not a contradiction properly speaking because its terms are not necessary for each other's existence.

As for the distinction between antagonistic and non-antagonistic contradictions, the problem is more complex. On the one hand, Mao contends that 'some contradictions are characterised by open antagonism, others are not'.[73] This means that the methods of solving contradictions differ according to the nature of the contradiction. Some contradictions require open conflict to be resolved, others do not. On the other hand, Mao also affirms that contradictions originally non-antagonistic can become antagonistic and vice versa, as, for instance, when two contradictory classes oppose each other for a long time and coexist together until the moment their opposition 'develops to a certain stage that it assumes the form of open antagonism and develops into revolution'.[74] It is evident that there is an ambiguity in the characterisation of the distinction, for two different criteria are being used. On the one hand, contradictions are said to be antagonistic or non-antagonistic according to their very nature. On the other hand, contradictions are said to be antagonistic or non-antagonistic according to the particular phase of their development. There occurs a slippage between antagonism as an essential feature of the contradiction, and antagonism as a temporary conflictive stage of the opposition.

Various solutions have been proposed to overcome this confusion. Lucien Sève, for instance, starts from the premise that antagonism or non-antagonism are essential qualities of the whole development of a contradiction, and not historical forms it may or may not assume. Thus the contradiction between the exploiting class and the exploited class is antagonistic in its very essence all through its development, even if it is not manifest in a violent form. An antagonistic contradiction is that in which the development of one of the opposites tends to suppress the other, and whose solutions entails the creation of a new reality. A non-antagonistic contradiction, is for Sève, that in which the development of one opposite tends to the simple separation from the other, and whose solution is the fusion into a superior unity.[75] A similar distinction has been proposed by Ken Post, for whom the antagonistic contradiction is that which has the potential for self-destruction (the dominated pole cannot develop unless the contradiction disappears). Whereas for Post the non-antagonistic contradiction is that which does not abolish itself, for although the dominated pole may be impelled to reverse its status, it does not tend to abolish itself. In this case, 'the poles do not create and recreate one another but they are at least partial conditions of one another's existence'.[76] An example of this kind of contradiction would be that between employed and unemployed within the working class.

Finally, Lojkine proposes the same distinction on a different basis. For him the solution to both types of contradictions produces a new reality which is qualitatively different from the former reality from which the contradictions originally arise. But whereas the non-antagonistic contradiction does not abolish the former reality, and continues to rest upon it, the antagonistic contradiction abolishes its original social base and creates a new base. Unlike Sève, Lojkine believes that these contradictions can become transformed into one another under specific circumstances. For instance, he contends that the contradiction between fractions of the capitalist class is non-antagonistic in the early stages of capitalism, but as the principal contradiction between capital and labour develops, the secondary contradiction between monopoly capital and non-monopoly capital becomes antagonistic. Equally, today the contradiction between the state and monopoly capital is secondary and non-antagonistic, but it can become antagonistic, and even principal, in the transition to socialism.[77]

But none of these propositions really solves the problem. True, they avoid the ambiguity present in Mao's distinction and give clear-cut definitions according to a uniform criterion. But they fail to pose the key problem. This is whether or not there is any sense in the criterion of the distinction itself. In other words, the question is whether it is even possible to conceive of non-antagonistic contradictions. It seems to me that it does not make sense to speak of non-antagonistic contradictions, not just because Marx does not distinguish between antagonism (*Gegensatz*) and contradiction (*Widerspruch*),[78] but also, and primarily, because contradiction is by definition antagonistic. A contradiction necessarily entails two extremes which cannot stand without each other and which negate each other. The conflicts between monopoly capital and competitive capital, between employed and unemployed, between state and monopoly capital clearly do not entail two poles which cannot stand without each other. In other words, the so-called non-antagonistic contradiction is not a contradiction at all. It is not sufficient for one of the poles to be a partial condition of the other pole's existence, for a contradiction requires that each term is defined and becomes intelligible by its relation to the other term. It is true that to be defined unemployment requires employment, but employment does not require unemployment to exist. In short, all contradictions in society are antagonistic but not all conflicts in society are contradictions.

The principal contradiction of capitalism

Although the majority of authors agree on the value of the distinction between principal and secondary contradictions, there is hardly any agreement about the character of the main contradiction in capitalism. This situation partly arises from Marx's own treatment of contradictions, which appear in various contexts and at different levels of abstraction, without any explicit attempt to establish a hierarchy or order among them. Four candidates are frequently mentioned for the role of principal contradiction in the capitalist mode of production: the contradiction between productive forces and relations of production; the contradiction between use-value and exchange-value in the commodity; the contradiction between socialised production and private appropriation; and the contradiction between capital and labour.

The importance which Marx concedes to the contradiction between productive forces and production relations cannot be underrated. It is not only frequently referred to but also occupies a central place both in general formulations, like the 1859 Preface and *The German Ideology*, and in specific analyses of capitalism like *Capital*. The idea is that at a certain stage in the development of a mode of production the relations of production become fetters to the continuous expansion of the productive forces, thus precipitating the dissolution of the mode of production. As Marx put it in the specific case of capitalism, 'the contradiction of the capitalist mode of production, however, lies precisely in its tendency towards an absolute development of the productive forces, which continually come into conflict with the specific conditions of production in which capital moves, and alone can move'.[79] It is no wonder, therefore, that Mao, and in recent times Lojkine and Godelier, should think that this is the fundamental contradiction of capitalism. However, the last two put their cases in a different manner.

According to Lojkine, this principal contradiction 'manifests itself in the capitalist mode of production by the contradiction between capital and labour, bourgeoisie and proletariat'.[80] In other words, the contradiction between productive forces and relations determines the very existence of the mode of production. Godelier, on the contrary, distinguishes between contradictions internal to the structure of production relations, which exist from the beginning of the mode of production but do not contain in themselves the conditions for their solution (contradiction between capital and labour, for instance), and the contradiction between two structures, which is fundamental. Although the latter contradiction does not exist at the beginning, it appears at a certain stage of maturity of the system and contains in itself the condition for its solution. This is the contradiction between the structure of productive forces and the structure of the relations of production.[81] Hence the 'class contradiction' is older than the principal contradiction, but is unable to produce its own supersession, whereas the principal contradiction, in spite of not being ever present in the mode of production, manifests itself in periodic crises, and accounts for the necessity of the disappearance of the capitalist mode of production. It is also interesting to note that Godelier identifies this contradiction with that between the socialised character of production and the private appropriation of the means of production.

The problem with the so-called contradiction between productive forces and relations of production is not so much whether or not it can be considered more important than, and determinant of, the others, but whether or not it can be conceived as a contradiction at all. If one examines the two terms of this 'contradiction', one can see that they are rather heterogeneous in nature and not inherently opposed to one another, since, at least at the beginning of the mode of production, production relations stimulate the development of productive forces. There are grounds, therefore, to doubt the contradictory nature of their relationship. Two kinds of attitudes have developed with regard to this problem. Schaff recognises the existence of the problem, but instead of concluding the non-contradictory character of the relationship, he prefers to accept different meanings of the concept of contradiction so that in this case it means

> that the productive forces of society *are unable* to function within the existing relations of production; that an *incompatibility* has arisen between the productive forces and the relations of production so that the social mechanism is unable to function properly; that the social system *collapses* as a result of opposed tendencies active within it. The 'internal contradictions of the social system' mean here the state of maladjustment, of incompatibility, of the parts of the social mechanism.[82]

To accept various meanings of the notion of contradiction is obviously not a very satisfactory procedure because it induces confusion and ambiguity. For this reason I prefer the attitude taken by Bettelheim, Magaline and Echeverría, who suggest that the relationship between productive forces and production relations is better understood as a relation of *correspondence* and *non-correspondence*.[83] Schaff's description in terms of incompatibility and maladjustment would also do, as long as one keeps these notions separate from the concept of contradiction. So we must accept the fact that when Marx uses the notion of contradiction to refer to the opposition between relations of production and productive forces, he does so improperly. However, on the other hand, it is Marx himself who provides satisfactory alternative descriptions of this relationship. For instance, in the *Manifesto* he says that 'the feudal relations of property become no longer compatible with the already developed productive forces', and in the *Grundrisse* he affirms that 'the growing incompatibility between the productive development of society and its hitherto existing relations of production expresses itself in bitter contradictions, crises, spasms'.[84]

To deny the contradictory character of the relation between productive forces and relations of production means that it cannot constitute the principal contradiction of capitalism. But it does not mean that the non-correspondence between both terms is unimportant, or that it does not produce effects. However, it is not possible to conceive these effects as being determinant of the rest of the social contradictions, as Lojkine proposes, for the simple reason that the non-correspondence emerges late in the evolution of the mode of production, whereas the principal contradiction is constitutive of the system from its inception. This means that the principal contradiction of capitalism determines the emergence of this 'incompatibility' and not vice versa. The effect of the non-correspondence between productive forces and relations of production is to deepen the principal contradiction.

But which is, then, the principal contradiction of capitalism? In short, that between capital and labour, because it is constitutive of the very essence of the capitalist mode of production. We have already seen the various ways in which Marx presents this contradiction. There is no doubt that the two terms relate in a contradictory way because they presuppose and negate each other. In Marx's words, 'capital presupposes wage labour; wage labour presupposes capital. They reciprocally condition the existence of each other; they reciprocally bring forth each other.'[85] But this mutual conditioning occurs in such a way 'that the working individual *alienates* himself; relates to the conditions brought out of him by his labour as those not of his *own* but of an *alien wealth* and of his own poverty'.[86] It is this basic antagonism that determines the progress of the productive forces within capitalism during the period of 'correspondence'. The first act of capital is to gather together a number of labourers who are free to sell their labour-power. This is an innovation in the organisation of the labour-process which is prior to any technological innovation. When the manufacturers replace simple co-operation, a new form of organisation is introduced which is able to bring about a new transformation of the productive forces. So, as Magaline proposes, the relations of production materialise themselves in a system of productive forces.[87] In other words, the productive forces are the materialisation of the antagonistic social relations between capital and labour.

If one looks from the other side, to the process of dissolution of capitalism, or what Marx calls 'the real barrier' to capitalist production, the non-correspondence between productive forces and production relations is again basically determined by the contradiction between capital and labour. As Marx puts it:

> The limits within which the preservation and self-expansion of the value of capital resting on the expropriation and pauperisation of the great mass of producers can alone move – these limits come continually into conflict with the methods of production employed by capital for its purposes, which drive towards unlimited extension of production.[88]

The incompatibility between the limits imposed by the production relations and the unlimited drive of the productive forces occurs *because* the expansion of the value of capital rests upon the expropriation of labour, and this is the root cause of the barrier to the development of capital. So both the progress and the eventual limitation of the productive forces are the result of the development of the fundamental contradiction between capital and labour.

Some authors, however, believe that the principal contradiction of capitalism lies somewhere else. Colletti, for instance, affirms that according to Marx all the contradictions of capitalism are the result of the contradiction between use-value and exchange-value, between the private labour and the abstract social labour which are inherent in the commodity.[89] Meikle, arguing along similar lines, suggests that capitalist contradictions 'have at their heart the contradictions between use-value and exchange-value'.[90] The argument proposes that the contradiction inherent in the commodity between its being a particular use-value and simultaneously universal equivalent[91] is externalised as the contradiction between the commodity and money. As Marx wrote:

> the fact that the *exchange-value* of the commodity *assumes an independent existence* in money is itself the result of the process of exchange, the development of the contradiction of use-value and exchange-value embodied in the commodity, and of another no less important contradiction embodied in it, namely, that the definite, particular labour of the private individual must manifest itself as its opposite, as equal, necessary, general labour.[92]

This contradiction between the commodity and money, in its turn, develops into the contradiction between capital and wage-labour when the owner of money confronts the owner of a particular commodity, namely labour-power.

This argument is flawed, in my view, because it mistakes the historical priority of the potential contradictions inherent in the commodity for the fundamental priority of the principal contradiction. What Marx says is that the contradictions of capitalism are potentially present in the simple production of commodities, even before capitalism emerged. But in order for the contradictions inherent in the commodity to become actual and fully realised, other contradictory relations need to exist, namely the relation between capital and wage-labour. The contradictions potentially present in the commodity cannot actualise themselves, but are actualised by the capitalist mode of production which makes commodity production its exclusive basis. The actualisation of these contradictions requires that production becomes socialised and that appropriation becomes private. One cannot derive the capital–labour contradiction from the contradictions immanent in commodities; on the contrary, the emergence in history of the capital–labour contradiction is the precondition for the actualisation of the potential contradictions inherent in commodities. As Marx argued:

> simple circulation of money and even the circulation of money as a means of payment – and both come into being long *before* capitalist production, while there are no crises – are possible and actually take place without crises. These forms alone, therefore, do not explain why their crucial aspect becomes prominent and why the potential contradiction contained in them becomes a real contradiction.[93]

As for the contradiction between the socialised character of production and the private character of appropriation, it has also been judged to be the principal contradiction of capitalism. Engels, for instance, says that 'this contradiction, which gives to the new mode of production its capitalistic character, *contains the germ of the whole of the social antagonism of today*'.[94] Giddens takes the same view and argues that this is the principal contradiction because it presages a new social system, socialism.[95] We have already seen that Godelier thinks this is the fundamental antagonism of capitalism, though he identifies it with the contradiction between productive forces and production relations. Marx formulates this contradiction in the following terms:

> The contradiction between the general social power into which capital develops, on the one hand, and the private power of the individual capitalists over these social conditions of production, on the other, becomes ever more irreconcilable and yet contains the solution of the problem, because it implies at the same time the transformation of the conditions of production into general, common, social conditions.[96]

The relationship of this contradiction with the capital–labour contradiction is analysed by Engels and Magaline. For Engels the antagonism between capital and wage-labour is a manifestation of the contradiction between socialised production and capitalistic appropriation,[97] whereas for Magaline this latter contradiction is nothing but a different and more ambiguous formulation of the essential antagonism between capital and wage-labour.[98] It seems to me that neither of these accounts is satisfactory and that the contradiction in question is a secondary contradiction which depends on the capital–labour contradiction. In effect, the very terms of the contradiction suppose the existence of a previous contradiction between capital and wage-labour. In order for capital accumulation to grow, and hence become a social power opposed to the private power of the individual capitalist, a previous process is required whereby the surplus-value that is accumulated is produced in the first place and extracted from wage-labour. So the labour–capital relation is not really a manifestation of the socialised character of production, but the latter depends on the former.

It should not be difficult to see that the principal contradiction between capital and wage–labour is crucial in order to understand the origin and role of ideology in the capitalist mode of production. Marx analyses this mode of production not as a ready-made result – the independent, social power of capital – but as a contradictory process of reproduction in which capital, its positive side, is compelled to reproduce itself by reproducing its opposite, wage-labour. For Marx reproduction is not mainly the reproduction of material means and material wealth, but the reproduction of the principal contradiction and its social conditions. As he puts it, 'Capitalist production, therefore, under its aspect of a continuous connected process, of a process of reproduction, produces not only commodities, not only surplus-value, but it also produces and reproduces the capitalist relation; on the one side the capitalist, on the other the wage-labourer.'[99] And it is basically this contradictory process that lies at the origin of, and needs to be concealed by, ideology so that it can continue to reproduce itself. In so far as the secondary contradictions are dependent upon, and contribute to shape, this principal contradiction, they too become the object of ideological distortions. Ideology is therefore both the result and the condition of the reproduction process of the contradiction between capital and wage-labour.

The way in which ideology is produced as part of the process of reproduction of the principal contradiction can only be explained by looking at the way in which the two terms of the contradiction relate to each other. Although the production and appropriation of surplus-value occurs at the level of production, capital and labour first come into contact through the market. As Marx analysed it, 'it is the process itself that incessantly hurls back the labourer on to the market as a vendor of his labour-power, and that incessantly converts his own product into a means by which another man can purchase him'.[100] And as we have already seen, this contact through the market appears perfectly equitable, for capital and labour exchange equivalent values. So the process of production and extraction of surplus-value, which forms the basis of the contradictory opposition between capital and labour, is concealed by the operation of the market, which in turn becomes the source of ideological representations. In Marx's terms, the labourer's 'economic bondage is both brought about and concealed by the periodic sale of himself, by his change of masters, and by the oscillations in the market-price of labour-power'.[101] Because the exchange of equivalents by free individuals in the market is seen on the surface of society and conceals the hidden process of production, it naturally tends to be reproduced in the minds of both capitalists and labourers as equality and freedom, the lynchpins of capitalist ideology.

Contradictions, class struggles, conflicts and crises

There has been an endemic lack of clarity within Marxism about the relationship between contradictions and other phenomena like economic crises, class struggles and various kinds of social conflicts such as racial conflicts, men–women conflicts, student conflicts which, in spite of showing a certain similarity, cannot be simply identified with them. The problem has its origins in Marx's own treatment of some of these phenomena, which omits an explicit discussion of their hierarchy and mutual relationship. A good example is the absence of any elaborated formulation of the connections between contradictions and class struggle. There are of course certain scattered comments in Marx's work which can contribute some understanding on these relations. But on the whole the field is open for new theoretical developments. Giddens, for instance, has introduced a distinction between contradiction and conflict which is useful in some respects, though I fundamentally disagree with its formulation in terms which deny the contradictory character of the labour–capital relationship.[102] It is beyond the scope of this book to go into the specific analysis of the various kinds of social conflicts and their relations to contradictions, but there are some general relations which are worth while outlining in so far as they have a bearing upon the understanding of ideology.

The contradiction between capital and wage-labour, we have seen, is constitutive of the very essence of the capitalist mode of production, and it is always present for as long as capitalism subsists. However, because this contradiction arises in the inner relations of capitalism, it cannot be seen on the surface by itself, but manifests itself through other phenomena. In order to show how this contradiction appears on the surface, I propose distinguishing between its form (the kind of social relation) and content (what the social relation is about). This is an analytical distinction. By its form, the capital–labour contradiction is a social relation between two classes. By its content, this contradiction is the extraction of surplus-value by means of the production of commodities. The contradiction is shown on the surface at these two levels. By its form, it manifests itself as class struggle; by its content, it shows itself as economic crises in the production of commodities and the realisation of surplus-value.

According to Marx, 'the crises are always but momentary and forcible solutions of the existing contradictions. They are violent eruptions which for a time restore the disturbed equilibrium',[103] or, as he puts it elsewhere, 'in the crises of the world market, the contradictions and antagonisms of bourgeois production are strikingly revealed . . . the world trade crises must be regarded as the real concentration and forcible adjustment of all the contradictions of bourgeois economy'.[104] Althusser has successfully transposed this idea of a concentration of contradictions, 'fusion' as he calls it, into the sphere of political crises: in a revolutionary situation, contradictions may 'fuse' or 'condense' to produce a revolutionary rupture.[105] Marx, nevertheless, limited his analysis of crises in *Capital* to the economic level. The formal possibility of a crisis is already given in the separation between purchase and sale which money allows in the exchange of commodities; for one commodity can be turned into money, but the money thus obtained need not be immediately turned into another commodity, and in this way some commodities may not find a buyer, from which emerges a disjunction between production and circulation.[106]

However, Marx is quite clear that the contradiction between sale and purchase present in the simple exchange of commodities (and therefore existent long before capitalist production) creates only the possibility of a crisis. It does not actually produce crises itself. In fact, former modes of production dependent on some commodity production did not experience crises similar to those in capitalism. The cause of crises must be sought in the specific character of the capitalist mode of production. The capitalist mode of production tends continually to expand production; but in order to achieve this it cannot avoid depreciating existing capital, reaching a point where some capitals are displaced from the market. This manifests itself as an overproduction of means of production and increased stocks which cannot be sold. The consequence is that capital cannot realise the surplus-value incorporated in these commodities and this results in bankruptcies and unemployment. The solution to the crisis is the destruction or withdrawal of some capitals, thereby allowing part of the depreciated capital to recover its value.[107] The crisis of overproduction is therefore a direct expression of the contradiction between the tendency of production to expand and the need to maintain the value of capital. And at the same time it actualises the potential contradiction present in the commodity exchange between sale and purchase. As the need to preserve and expand the value of capital rests on the expropriation of labour, crises are ultimately an expression of the fundamental contradiction between capital and wage-labour.

Crises manifest a series of capitalist contradictions, but at the same time are a provisional solution to these contradictions. As Marx commented, 'crisis is the forcible establishment of unity between elements that have become independent and the enforced separation from one another of elements which are essentially one'.[108] By forcibly uniting and separating elements of the circulation process in relation to elements of the production process, crises within capitalism represent a necessary, though temporary, adjustment of its contradictions. It is not possible to think that an economic crisis is by itself capable of bringing about the destruction of capitalism. Nevertheless, it goes almost without saying that the concentration of contradictions creates favourable conditions for an intensification of class struggles and other political conflicts which may eventually produce social transformation. In this sense Althusser's fusion of accumulated contradictions into a ruptural unity appears as the effective combination of an acute economic crisis with exacerbated class struggle.

This brings us to class struggle, which is the other expression of the principal contradiction of the mode of production. In one of the few places where Marx establishes this relationship he says that 'In Germany, therefore, the capitalist mode of production came to a head, after its antagonistic character had already, in France and England, shown itself in a fierce strife of classes.'[109] According to Marx, the class struggle, as an expression of the principal contradiction of a mode of production, has different phases in its development. It can be more or less intense and it can also manifest itself sporadically during certain periods, or can become a frequent occurrence during other periods. When sketching the evolution of political economy, Marx refers to these phases in the following terms: 'Political Economy can remain a science only so long as the class-struggle is latent or manifests itself only in isolated and sporadic phenomena'; 'the class-struggle between capital and labour is forced into the background, politically by the discord between the governments and the feudal aristocracy gathered around the Holy Alliance on the one hand, and the popular masses, led by the bourgeoisie, on the other; economically by the quarrel between industrial capital and aristocratic landed property'; 'in France and in England the bourgeoisie had conquered political power. Thenceforth, the class-struggle, practically as well as theoretically, took on more and more outspoken and threatening forms.'[110] Although in rough terms one can see a certain historical progression from the initial latency to the most threatening forms, it is also true that these phases evolve in cycles. There are alternate periods of latency and periods of acute struggle, even in the most advanced forms of capitalism. In general Marx proposes the idea that the development of class struggle keeps pace with the development of industry, and that in the early stages of the latter class struggle is quite undeveloped, which contributes to the emergence of utopian socialism.[111]

It is interesting to note that when Marx refers to the class struggle 'practically as well as theoretically', he considers class struggle as a manifestation of the principal contradiction at both the political level and the level of consciousness. As Marx and Engels stated in the *Manifesto*, 'every class struggle is a political struggle',[112] but there is no struggle without certain forms of consciousness, without certain intellectual apprehension of the issues at stake. This is what, within Marxism, has been traditionally called 'ideological struggle'. I would prefer to call it 'class struggle on the terrain of ideas'. Although the expression is not as neat as 'ideological struggle', it is theoretically more precise in that it recognises that struggle does not only involve ideological forms of consciousness, in the restricted sense I give to this expression, but involves all forms of ideas.

The way in which the fundamental contradiction of a mode of production manifests itself in class struggles is not uniform, in at least two senses. First, within a mode of production the principal contradiction directly manifests itself in the actual struggle of both its sides. For instance, in the feudal mode of production, peasants were in constant struggle with their landlords, and in the capitalist mode of production the proletariat confronts the bourgeoisie. But the principal contradiction also indirectly manifests itself in the struggle between fractions of these classes or between one of the principal classes and a new class which, although it is not one of the sides of the main contradiction, is derived from the actual struggle of its sides. For instance, in medieval Germany the contradiction between serfdom and overlordship indirectly manifested itself in fractional struggles between the monarchy and the landlords, and between the princes and the landlords.[113] But more important, it also indirectly manifested itself in the decisive struggle between the bourgeoisie and the overlords. As Dobb and others have argued, the emergence of the bourgeoisie was the direct result of the peasant struggles for emancipation which created a class of petty-commodity-producers and which gradually expanded into a wealthy, independent bourgeoisie.[114] In the beginning the bourgeoisie became an ally of the feudal lords, but in the final and last stages, when the lords were debilitated by internal strifes and by their struggle against the peasants, the bourgeoisie, leading the popular masses, overthrew them. One cannot properly speak of a contradiction between the bourgeoisie and the feudal lords because these two poles do not necessitate each other, but their struggle as classes was overdetermined by, and indirectly manifested, the main contradiction of feudalism which underlay the dissolution of the mode of production.

Second, if one compares the feudal mode of production with the capitalist mode of production, one can see that their respective principal contradictions manifest themselves in class struggles which have a different degree of complexity and a different political potentiality. Although the contradiction between lords and serfs is at the basis of the dissolution of feudalism, it cannot succeed in overthrowing the lords through the direct political struggle of the peasantry, because serfs were dispersed and disunited as a class. The contradiction operated indirectly through the self-differentiation of the peasantry into a new class which led the struggle and completed the task.[115] The essential contradiction between capital and wage-labour, on the contrary, can express itself in a class struggle between its two sides, whereby the political organisation of the proletariat is directly capable of accomplishing the political overthrow of the capitalist class. The principal capitalist contradiction also manifests itself indirectly in the internal struggles between fractions of the capitalist class, and the proletariat: for instance, between monopoly capital and small capital, or between industrial workers of multinational concerns and workers of traditional industries in decline.

Apart from certain cases where there is total confrontation – for instance, in general uprisings and revolts – classes are rarely seen acting as united agents on the political and cultural field. Most of the time their struggles are partial and show themselves in various kinds of political conflicts and theoretical disputes. The discrete and partial character which class struggle frequently assumes, coupled with an often ideological understanding of the real motives and interests behind the struggle, make it more difficult for it to be recognised for what it is. In this sense political confrontations between parties and intellectual disputes are not just an expression of the class struggle but also veil its existence or true character. According to Marx and Engels, 'all struggles within the state, the struggle between democracy, autocracy and monarchy, the struggle for the franchise, etc., etc., are merely the illusory forms in which the real struggles of the different classes are fought out among one another'.[116] But the real character of these struggles is not easily discerned.

Marx gave a very clear example when he analysed the French parliamentary republic from 28 May 1849 to 2 December 1851, when the Legislative National Assembly was dispersed. Looked at with the eyes of democrats, Marx insisted that this period was concerned with

> the simple struggle between republicans and royalists. The movement itself, however, they sum up in the one shibboleth: '*reaction*' . . . and, to be sure, at first sight the party of Order reveals a maze of different royalist factions, which . . . unite in common hatred of, and common onslaughts on the 'republic'. In opposition to this royalist conspiracy the *Montagne*, for its part, appears as the representative of the 'republic' . . . If one looks at the situation and the parties more closely, however, this superficial appearance, which veils the *class struggle* and the peculiar physiognomy of this period, disappears.[117]

And Marx went on to show how the two factions of the party of Order represented the two bourgeois interests of landed property and capital, and how the *Montagne*, in its turn, represented a coalition of workers and petty bourgeois controlled by the latter. While the party of Order represented the only possibility for the two bourgeois factions to exercise an unrestricted domination, the *Montagne* looked to political solutions which could apparently *reconcile* capital and labour.

This shows the role of ideology in a new light. We have already generically established that the effect of ideology is to conceal contradictions. We can see now that the result of this concealment is twofold. On the one hand, it helps prevent the contradictions from manifesting themselves in active struggle. Although this is never totally successful, ideology seeks to block the realisation of any basic opposition of interests which may lead to open struggle. Giddens has pointed to two other factors which inhibit actual class struggle, namely the dispersion of contradictions and direct repression.[118] But repression itself can be considered a form of class struggle, in fact the most successful form of class struggle – at least in the short term – waged by the ruling class, because it suppresses the main, but never all, forms of struggle of the dominated classes. It is worth noticing, however, that not all the struggles of the dominated classes are against the interests of the ruling class. The state, as the crucial instance for the organisation and reproduction of the ruling-class hegemony, achieves domination not only by reconciling and compromising with various fractions in the power bloc, and not only by compromising with sections of the dominated classes, but also by regulating conflicts and by disorganising, dividing and promoting conflicts among the various dominated classes and their fractions. On the other hand, by concealing contradictions, ideology veils the character of class struggles, and it does so by providing mystified motives and 'banners', the misplaced phrases and principles which appear as the cause and purpose of the struggle.

Marx and Engels gave numerous historical examples of this phenomenon. In the German peasant rebellions the intellectual justification of the struggle was almost always religious in nature. Thus Thomas Münzer's revolutionary programme was couched in theological terms and Luther 'donned the mask of the Apostle Paul, the Revolution of 1789 to 1814 draped itself alternately as the Roman republic and the Roman empire, and the Revolution of 1848 know nothing better to do than to parody, now 1789, now the revolutionary tradition of 1793 to 1795'.[119] In the capitalist mode of production the particular dependence of ideology upon the sphere of circulation – that 'very Eden of the innate rights of man' where freedom, equality, property and Bentham rule supreme – provides the battle-cries and conscious motives for many political struggles. By basing itself on the principles which are seen to operate at the level of commodity exchange, ideology does not only conceal the underlying contradiction between capital and labour, but also disguises the true character of its necessary expressions – class struggles – presenting them as if they were arbitrary conflicts between different political ideals.

Nevertheless, it is important to emphasise that it is only through class struggle that the working class can penetrate the veil of ideology and become conscious of the real contradictions which need to be practically overcome. The working-class consciousness of its common interests, free from ideological distortions, does not spring automatically from the material conditions of class relations, for these conditions are bound to reproduce the fundamental contradiction, and ideology, as one of its results and presuppositions. It is only through political struggle that the class can become 'for itself'. As Marx puts it:

> economic conditions had first transformed the mass of the people of the country into workers. The domination of capital has created for this mass a common situation, common interests. This mass is thus already a class as against capital, but not yet for itself. In the struggle, of which we have pointed out only a few phases, this mass becomes united, and constitutes itself as a class for itself. The interests it defends become class interests. But the struggle of class against class is a political struggle.[120]

In this sense it is possible to affirm that the fundamental contradiction of capitalism does not only reproduce itself, and reproduce ideology, as its own result and precondition, but also, by necessarily manifesting itself in class struggle, it produces the conditions for overcoming ideology and its own abolition as contradiction. However, one must not underestimate the difficulties which the working class experiences in advanced capitalism to become a class for itself, united and conscious of its real interests. The partial character of some struggles and the ideological concealment of the real significance of some confrontations – especially through their regulation and manipulation by the bourgeoisie – constitute major obstacles to class consciousness.

Laclau has theorised the variety of class struggles by means of a distinction between 'class struggle' and 'classes in struggle'. By class struggle he understands the struggle which constitutes classes as such at the level of the mode of production. By 'classes in struggle' he understands the struggle between classes which are already constituted at the level of the social formation. Whereas in the former 'the production relation which constitutes its two poles as classes is an antagonistic relation', in the latter the two poles are not in confrontation as classes because 'their insertion in the production process is relatively external to the confrontation itself'.[121] From here he derives the existence of two kinds of contradictions which are expressed at the ideological level by different 'interpellations'. The first contradiction is expressed in the interpellation of the agents as a *class* and constitutes the sphere of *class struggle*. The second contradiction is expressed in the interpellation of the agents as *the people* and constitutes the sphere of *popular-democratic struggle*. The relationship between these contradictions is such, according to Laclau, that 'not every contradiction is a class contradiction, but every contradiction is overdetermined by the class struggle'.[122]

It seems to me that Laclau confuses contradiction with class struggle. He does not realise that whereas the contradiction is a permanent underlying feature of the mode of production because it is constitutive of its very essence, class struggle is a variable manifestation which possesses different degrees of intensity and generality, and which may be periodic, sporadic, or latent for long periods. The basic contradiction of a mode of production is defined by the inclusive opposition of its two sides which subsist only by producing each other. Class struggle exists only at the level of the social formation when there is active struggle between the two sides. Even when temporarily there is no active struggle, the underlying opposition of interests and the reciprocal reproduction of both sides remain as the underlying contradiction. On the other hand, there seems to be little point in denying the character of class struggle to the confrontations between feudal lords and the bourgeoisie just because their antagonism does not constitute them as classes. A more correct solution, in my view, is to say that although there is class struggle between them, there is no contradiction between them. As I have already argued, following Dobb, the basic contradiction behind the dissolution of feudalism is that between serfdom and overlordship.

Another consequence of Laclau's confusion between contradiction and class struggle is that by distinguishing two kinds of struggle he is compelled to recognise as well two kinds of contradictions, namely class contradiction and 'the people–power bloc' contradiction. The distinction between class struggle and 'classes in struggle' may seem odd within the Marxist tradition but it does not necessarily contravene the notion of class struggle. But when one speaks of contradictions such as these the situation is rather different because by definition an antagonism between two sides is a contradiction *only if* both sides are constituted by their opposition and reproduce one another. So the opposition between 'the people' and 'the power bloc', which is not intelligible at the level of the mode of production and which does not constitute its two sides, *cannot* be a contradiction. Laclau therefore not only conflates contradictions with class struggle but also fails to understand the nature of contradictions.

Thus Laclau's statement that 'not every contradiction is a class contradiction, but every contradiction is overdetermined by the class struggle' must be rejected. It is not possible to accept two kinds of contradictions, one of which does not constitute its two terms as the negation of each other. What can be affirmed instead is, rather, that not all conflicts or struggles in society are a direct expression of the basic contradiction, but all conflicts are conditioned by it and may be articulated with class struggles. The principal contradiction which constitutes the mode of production as such, I have argued, manifests itself in crises and class struggles. However, there appear to be in society other conflicts which cannot be reduced to these expressions and which are not the direct manifestation of the underlying contradiction. I think, for instance, of racial conflicts, student conflicts and men–women conflicts. Although these conflicts do not directly manifest the basic contradiction, they cannot exist totally apart from it and are determined by it. The oppression of women by men, for example, exists in different modes of production, but assumes forms which are specific to and determined by the fundamental contradiction developed by each mode of production. At the same time these specific forms of conflict may be articulated with concrete class struggles as, for instance, in advanced capitalism in Britain, where there is an obvious articulation between the massive entry of women to work in factories – with all the related problems at home, discrimination in salaries, etc. – and the general issues of the exploitation of the working class as a whole.

In so far as ideology is concerned, it is necessary to draw attention to the ambiguous character of these conflicts. If they are not understood in connection with the main contradiction of society – even if one allows for their specific and irreducible character – they may be judged to be paramount, and to this extent they may contribute to conceal and obscure the main contradiction. These conflicts can therefore perform the ideological task of covering up and deviating the attention from a more fundamental opposition of interests. In this sense, for instance, the role which racial conflict may play in dividing and alienating the political practice of the working class should be clear. The ideological role of these conflicts comes under what I described in Chapter 1 as one of the forms of concealing contradictions by means of their displacement. However, on the other hand, these conflicts can also be articulated with forms of class struggle in such a way that they help reveal rather than conceal the main contradictions. Thus there is a great deal of difference between student movements as a substitute for an allegedly passive and incorporated working class – as some members of the Frankfurt School propose – and student movements liaising with the struggle of the working class, as some aspects of May 1968 showed in France.

5

Ideology, Superstructure and Determination

Ideology and superstructure

One of the ambiguities in Marx's and Engels's treatment of ideology which I pointed to in Chapter 2 was the fact that they did not adequately separate the discussion of ideology, as a particular form of distorted consciousness, from their discussion of the general principle of the social determination of ideas. As a consequence, questions arose about the extension of the concept of ideology. I have already examined this ambiguity in connection with the emergence of a positive concept of ideology. But I mainly focused on one aspect of the positive version, the notion of ideology as the political ideas or, more generally, the world-view of a class. I want to focus now upon a different aspect of the positive version which links ideology with the totality of forms of consciousness produced in a society. In this version ideology appears as an objective level or superstructure which corresponds to, and is determined by, a different level of the social totality, the economic base. In short, I want to discuss the relationship between ideology and the base–superstructure metaphor.

I intend to do this in three stages. First, I consider Marx's and Engels's views on this issue and pinpoint some difficulties implicit in their approach. Second, I propose a possible solution to these difficulties which keeps the essentials of Marx's conception of both ideology and the base–structure relationship. Third, I examine this solution and the general idea that the forms of social consciousness can be conceived as a superstructure.

The orthodox interpretation of Marx and Engels, from Plekhanov and Kautsky onwards, takes it more or less for granted that the founders identify ideology with an all-encompassing superstructural level determined by the economic base. This view is confidently advanced even by independently minded authors like

Althusser: 'Marx has shown that all social formations constitute an 'organic totality' which comprises three essential "levels"; the economy, politics and *ideology or the forms of social consciousness*'.[1] This objective 'level', which Althusser simply calls ideology, is rendered in other versions as the 'ideological superstructure'. Does the evidence from Marx's and Engels's work support this interpretation?

For a start one has to say that any answer should take into account differences between Marx and Engels. Yet even if one takes them as a unity, the evidence is not at all conclusive in favour of identifying ideology with the totality of forms of consciousness. Nevertheless, there are three or four places in their writings where expressions such as 'ideological superstructure', 'idealistic superstructure' or 'ideological spheres' are used. In *The German Ideology* Marx and Engels state that 'the great revolution of society brought about by competition . . . destroyed for the proletarians all naturally derived and traditional relations, e.g. family and political relations, together with their entire ideological superstructure'.[2] Elsewhere in the same work they affirm that 'civil society as such only develops with the bourgeoisie; the social organisation evolving directly out of production and intercourse, which in all ages forms the basis of the state and of the rest of the idealistic superstructure, has, however, always been designated by the same name'.[3]

Whereas the context of the first quotation does not seem to indicate an intention of establishing a general proposition, but rather confines the reference to the proletariat, the second quotation has wider implications and can be considered to be the first formulation of the base–superstructure thesis. As for Engels's writings, the expression 'ideological superstructure' appears once in *Anti-Dühring*[4] and a similar formula, 'ideological spheres', is used in a letter to Schmidt.[5] The problem which these expressions pose is obviously their apparent incompatibility with a negative concept of ideology: if ideology entails distorted forms of consciousness and the 'ideological superstructure' encompasses all forms of social consciousness, this means that the totality of ideas of a society, including Marx's, are necessarily impaired; unless, of course, as some authors suggest, science should be excluded from the ideological superstructure.[6] But then this objective level would not be all-encompassing. The problem is therefore that either the totality of forms of social consciousness is distorted, which is manifestly absurd, or science is not considered to be a form of consciousness, which is also absurd.

I do not think that the use of these expressions provides conclusive evidence that Marx and Engels believed ideology to be equivalent to the totality of forms of social consciousness. The references to the negative character of ideology in their writings are so numerous,[7] and the contrast they made between their own position and ideology is so clear, that it is difficult to believe that Marx and Engels identify ideology with the entirety of consciousness. One need only remember the passage in *The German Ideology* where they state that 'where speculation ends, where real life starts, there consequently begins real, positive science . . . we shall select here some of these abstractions, which we use in contradistinction to ideology, and shall illustrate them by historical examples'.[8] Besides, the few quotations about an 'ideological superstructure' are relatively obscure in comparison with better-known passages in which this equation is not present.

In *The Eighteenth Brumaire of Louis Bonaparte*, Marx used the term superstructure to refer to the 'distinct and peculiarly formed sentiments, illusions, modes of thought and views of life' which 'the entire class creates and forms . . . out of its material foundations',[9] but he does not add the term 'ideological' to it. Just as in the only passage of *The German Ideology* where the expression 'ideological superstructure' appears, the notion of superstructure seems to refer to the consciousness or world-view of a class, and not to a global societal level. Similarly, in the 1859 Preface Marx referred to the 'forms of social consciousness' which correspond to the economic structures,[10] but he does not equate them with ideology, nor does he use the term superstructure to refer to them. None the less, in a subsequent passage Marx affirmed that 'a distinction should be made between the material transformation of the economic conditions of production, which can be determined with the precision of natural science, and the legal, political, religious, aesthetic or philosophic – in short, ideological forms in which men become conscious of this conflict and fight it out'.[11]

Marković believes that this passage marks the beginning of the use by Marx of the term ideology in a broader sense; that is to say, he surpassed the notion of ideology as inadequate, mis-shapen consciousness to propose ideology as 'the totality of the forms taken by the superstructure of an historical period'.[12] I do not see how Marković can read this much into the passage. I would have thought that Marx suggests the opposite in so far as he contrasts the material transformation of the economy, which can be determined with the precision of natural science, to ideological forms in which men and women become conscious of this transformation. Science is separated and excluded from ideological forms. By distinguishing science from the legal, political and other forms Marx implicitly asserts that such ideological forms are inadequate for gaining a true consciousness. This is why he adds further below that 'we resolved to work out in common the opposition of our view to the ideological view of German philosophy'.[13] The negative sense of ideology is obviously maintained throughout the passage.

The problem arises as to whether the distinction between ideological and non-ideological forms simply opposes science to philosophy, aesthetics, politics, jurisprudence and religion as if they were, as a whole, and always, necessarily ideological. It seems to me that the text is open to two interpretations. The comprehensive view holds that *all* philosophical, political, legal, etc., forms are ideological, though this is not said in so many words. The restrictive interpretation holds that only those philosophical, political, legal, etc., forms *which are ideological* can be opposed to science, without implying that they are always necessarily so. I think this interpretation is more consistent with Marx's other tenets, but one has to accept that an ambiguity exists in Marx's text.

At any rate, despite the fact that the evidence does not seem to support an identification between ideology and the totality of forms of social consciousness, expressions such as 'ideological superstructure' or 'idealistic superstructure', in so far as they entail a necessary negative connotation and in so far as they mean to include all forms of consciousness – which is not always the case – remain contradictory. Yet even if one considers them as aberrations, there is still need to clarify the relationship which ideological and non-ideological forms of consciousness have with the notion of superstructure. If one wants to uphold both a negative concept of ideology and the idea of an all-encompassing level of consciousness, then the solution is to propose a superstructure of ideas or 'ideational superstructure' which contains both non-ideological and ideological forms of consciousness.[14] The superstructure of ideas refers to a global societal level of consciousness, whereas ideology is only a restricted part of the superstructure which includes specific forms of distorted consciousness.

In the superstructure of ideas of any class society, the ruling ideas are the ideas of the ruling class; but this does not make all of them ideological. The distinction between ideology and superstructure of ideas means that the class character of ideas is not a sufficient condition to make them ideological, and that not all errors or distortions are necessarily ideological. This is why Marx considered that bourgeois classical political economy was a science and showed his appreciation of Smith's and Ricardo's scientific achievements, even though he submitted them to a thorough and lifelong critique. Classical political economy was a science in so far as it surpassed appearances: as Marx put it, 'to examine how matters stand with the contradiction between the apparent and the actual movement of the system. This then is Ricardo's great historical significance for science.'[15]. This does not mean that Ricardo's method was adequate: 'the historical justification of this method of procedure, its scientific necessity in the history of economics, are evident at first sight, but so is, at the same time, its scientific inadequacy'.[16] However, this inadequacy was not necessarily ideological in its own time to the degree that it was conditioned by the undeveloped character of capitalist contradictions themselves. It became ideological when capitalist contradictions developed as predominant in the social formation at a later date. Marx never condemned the whole of bourgeois thought as ideological. That the distinction between ideology and the superstructure of ideas has a firm basis in Marx's thought is shown by a passage in the *Theories of Surplus-Value* where Storch is criticised for not conceiving material production as historical. Storch, Marx says, '*deprives himself of the basis on which alone can be understood partly the ideological component parts of the ruling class, partly the free spiritual production of this particular social formation*'.[17] Here a distinction is clearly drawn between ideological and non-ideological ideas at the level of intellectual production of a society.

The problem of the spatial image

Although the notion of a superstructure of ideas, as different from ideology, eliminates the contradiction inherent in the concept of 'ideological superstructure', it is not itself exempt from serious problems. The question we must address is whether the representation of consciousness as a superstructure of ideas determined by the base is adequate. In other words, the traditional spatial representation of base and superstructure must be examined in relation to the products of consciousness. Although the 1859 Preface seems to restrict the use of the term superstructure to the legal and political level, other texts like *The German Ideology* and *The Eighteenth Brumaire of Louis Bonaparte* subsume both politics and consciousness under the term superstructure. The spatial image of base and superstructure intends to convey the idea that the forms of social consciousness are not autonomous and that they do not emerge out of themselves, but that they have a foundation in the social relations of production. Max Adler pointed out that the building-like simile was mainly directed against spiritualist metaphysics and idealism which confirmed a belief in the self-development of the idea.[18]

It is not difficult to see that some of the connotations of the spatial image may induce confusion and indeed create the very opposite of its intended meaning. On the one hand, to distinguish the superstructure from the base or foundation from which it rises may lead us to believe that consciousness is a secondary phenomenon, a mere reflection whose reality is ultimately to be found in the production relations. Consciousness is emptied of its specific content and significance, and reduced to economic relations. An example of this extreme reductionism is provided by one of Lenin's first theoretical analyses in which he maintains that in *Capital* Marx explained the economic structure only in terms of the relations of production and yet, in doing so, always accounted for the corresponding superstructures.[19] It is as if one did not need to analyse the superstructures themselves. This is in stark contrast to the importance and autonomy which Lenin later attributed to the political and 'ideological' spheres.

On the other hand, the spatial image may induce the opposite idea such that the base and the superstructures are seen as separate and self-sufficient totalities – the economy, the state and ideology – which combine in certain fashion to produce a 'mode of production' and which reciprocally affect each other in a specific way. The relationships between these totalities are conceived as external influences of already constituted instances which hold different degrees of effectivity. The base and the superstructures, therefore, become substantialised as if they were relatively autonomous spheres, one of which has the ultimate determining primacy. I think it is this conception, typical of some forms of structuralism, which Hindess has in mind when he criticises the notion of 'relative autonomy' and argues that '*either* we effectively reduce political and ideological phenomena to class interests determined elsewhere (basically in the economy) . . . *or* we must face up to the real autonomy of political and ideological phenomena and their irreducibility to manifestations of interests determined by the structure of the economy'.[20] The problem is that in this issue, as in many others, Hindess is only too ready to take the Althusserian positions as the truly Marxist ones and thereby his criticisms are mistakenly addressed to Marxism instead of the structuralist interpretations of it.

The least one can say is that the base–superstructure image is not a happy one, for it does not succeed in conveying a precise or adequate meaning. It can be interpreted either in a reductionist fashion or as a theory of consolidated elements which reciprocally and externally influence each other. In both cases, however, the economic base appears as the objectified determining factor. The various 'levels' of society are taken as given entities and there is no explanation as to how the social totality emerges. The base–superstructure image tends to turn social reality into a reified world of objects, some of which are supposed to determine others. But if one poses the problem in these terms, the notion of determination becomes impossible: how can the economy as an objective instance produce theory or art as a different objective instance? What the spatial image fails to convey is the crucial fact that both the economy and theory are produced by human practice and that, therefore, the concept of determination makes sense only within a perspective which does not reduce reality to the form of the object.

However, the reification of 'instances' or 'levels' of society is not merely the product of a misinterpretation of a simile, but is prompted by the very character and development of the capitalist mode of production.[21] This is the case in at least two senses. On the one hand, the fetishism of commodities and of capital is a specific historical feature of capitalism in which social relations between individuals are disguised as social relations between things. The reification of the economy is not a mere illusion, but the result of the social appearances of capitalism impressed upon uncritical consciousness. On the other hand, capitalism replaces the feudal relations of personal dependence by an 'objective restriction' which allows a greater autonomy and specialisation of economic and cultural production. Both the economy and culture cease to be directly controlled by the exercise of direct personal power by the landlord and church representatives and develop their own material apparatuses. This new material independence contributes to the image of self-sufficient totalities related externally.

It can be argued that it is only with the end of the feudal mode of production that the 'politico-juridical' and 'ideational' superstructures constitute themselves as distinguishable aspects of society based upon advanced institutional differentiation. The modern state is born when the juridical and repressive 'personal' relationship between serf and overlord is abstracted and concentrated in a series of distinctively political apparatuses which govern society as a whole. Intellectual production, in its turn, had been carried out under the patronage of the church and the aristocracy during medieval times, in such a way that intellectuals were hardly independent from the landlords. Capitalism ends the direct tutelage upon intellectual production, creating a new institutional space which can be distinguished from economic and political institutions. This is what Bourdieu has called the 'intellectual field', which becomes increasingly independent from external influences and whose internal relations are governed by a specific logic.[22]

This process of differentiation brought about by capitalism has nevertheless a different character according to each superstructure. While in the political sphere the scattered relations of authority become monopolised by the state, in the sphere of ideas the monopoly control of intellectual production is dissolved. Whereas the state acquires its self-identity by centralisation, the superstructure of ideas acquires specificity from decentralisation and competition. In this sense it can be argued that there exists a homology between the changes which occur at the economic level and the changes which occur at the ideational level: economic competition among a variety of economic units, freely deciding what to produce and trade, corresponds to the intellectual competition for recognition and legitimacy among contending intellectual positions which freely decide what to think and propose to 'the public'. Mannheim has described this change in the intellectual life as the movement from the monopoly position of the church to an atomistic competition between a variety of groups.[23] Capitalism therefore centralises authority in the state, but frees economic and intellectual production.

Raymond Williams has explored the changes in the conception and practice of art which the industrial revolution brought about in England. He mentions the creation of a middle-class reading public and the formation of commercial publishing and of the literary market. The production of art, he maintains, 'was coming to be regarded as one of a number of specialised kinds of production subject to much the same conditions as general production'.[24] It was in this specific context that the ideas of art for art's sake and of the individual genius of the artist first evolved. Commercial publishing specialised the function of the intellectual as a producer for the market within a net of relationships which included a series of mediating agents such as publishers, critics, art dealers, journalists, academics, etc. According to Bourdieu, some of these agents or groups of agents defined by the position they occupy in the intellectual field can impose their cultural norms in other sections of the field.[25] But his main point is that the intellectual field has an entity, a specific weight of its own. This can also be seen at the level of political ideas. Habermas has pointed to the emergence of a 'public sphere' which follows the development of capitalism in the eighteenth century. This is a realm where 'public opinion' is formed by means of public discussion and debate of political life which freely proceeds without reference to dogma or tradition. An important part of this public sphere is a privately owned press which channels public discussion.[26]

It seems, therefore, that the distinction between separate and autonomous spheres of society implicit in the simile of base and superstructures has a firm basis in the reality brought about by the capitalist mode of production. Still, the problems involved in such conception remain, particularly in regard to the notion of determination, which is especially difficult to conceptualise adequately. How can one resolve this paradox? I think part of the problem stems from the traditional attempt to enclose the contents of each superstructure or level according to oversimplified criteria of what constitutes the economic, the political or the ideological, so that within these closures heterogeneous elements coexist. For instance, the ideational superstructure is supposed to encompass all forms of social consciousness plus a series of institutions and apparatuses like education, media, churches, etc. The political superstructure is supposed to enclose political apparatuses like parliament, the judiciary, the police, but also laws and regulations and more general power relations. The economy must accordingly encompass material relations of production, economic units and institutions, means of production, but also other productive forces like technology and science.

One can immediately see that this conception of the base–superstructure distinction presents many difficulties. Is it not true that science is a form of social consciousness and yet also a productive force? Is it not equally true that jurisprudence, laws and codes are also cultural products or forms of consciousness? Can political discussion through journals and newspapers be reduced to either the superstructure of ideas or to the political superstructure, to the exclusion of each other? Can one really reduce the problematic of power to the political superstructure, or are there also problems of power within economic, or academic, institutions, and so forth? Putting the questions in more general terms, can one conceive any economic or political act in which consciousness is not involved? As the obvious answer is negative, it seems that there is no sense in characterising consciousness as a specifically separated superstructure. The forms of social consciousness permeate the whole social structure. Of course, one can distinguish specific forms of consciousness which are present at certain levels. Thus the economic structure works by means of scientific and technological knowledge and the state functions by means of laws and political ideologies (in a positive sense). But at the same time both law and scientific knowledge are important parts of the educational apparatus. In general, therefore, the forms of social consciousness cannot be located in one separate level. This is so in at least two senses: (i) there is no superstructure of ideas separate from the actual functioning of the political and economic spheres; and (ii) there are no ideas which can only be conceived as operating at one particular level, and not in others.

In my view, therefore, the traditional distinction of three levels – the economic base and the political and ideational superstructures – only has sense in terms of institutions and material organisations which are specific to these levels and which indeed have become differentiated and specialised with the development of capitalism, thereby creating a distinct 'field' of practices. I am not proposing a distinction between material and ideal aspects of society. What Marx called 'forms of social consciousness' have also a material entity: they come in books, are communicated through language by means of 'agitated layers of air', etc. There is no such thing as a purely ideal form of consciousness in society. Yet the materiality in which ideas are embedded must be distinguished from the organisational materiality of the various apparatuses which specialise in different practices. Whereas the former is not necessarily affected by the political, ideological or economic character of ideas, the organisational materiality of political, economic or ideational apparatuses is specific to each level. All material apparatuses at any level of society work by ideas, but the ideational apparatuses (education, media, etc.) specialise in the production and transmission of ideas as their dominant aim. This is why the 'intellectual field' can be distinguished from the 'political field' and from the 'economic field', as the latter two are mainly devoted to the exercise of state power and the production and distribution of capital and consumer goods.

The base–superstructure image has traditionally had to perform two simultaneous tasks. It has had to describe the development of three specialised spheres which have been brought about by capitalism. And it has had to explain how two of these spheres are determined by the third. To my mind the spatial image can only adequately perform the first task; it can help describe the existence of institutional differentiation and of specific 'fields' of practice presided over by specialised apparatuses. But it cannot explain the determination of social consciousness, nor can it account for the emergence of each level as part of the social totality. The spatial image is inevitably static and makes sense only in terms of a description of the differentiated institutionality in which the capitalist social practice crystallises. It does not and cannot explain dynamic elements such as consciousness, practice, class struggle unless they are *reduced* to one specific level. The spatial image has to take the levels as already given, but cannot explain their practical formation. So the determination of the superstructures by the base necessarily becomes an external mode of causation, whereby a dead economic objectivity is assumed to be able to produce specific forms of consciousness. Consciousness is thus reduced to its material conditions.

Determination in the last instance

The base–superstructure image seems to face a narrow choice. By 'solidifying' various levels of society it can either propose a pluralist understanding of their reciprocal interaction, which leads to functionalism; or it can put forward the idea of mechanical causality whereby one level is supposed to be the cause and the others its effects, which leads to reductionism. However, the Marxist tradition has refused to accept this narrow choice and has endeavoured to find a solution which, although keeping the base–superstructure model, may avoid those two extremes. This effort can be traced back to Marx himself. In answering the objection that the determination of the superstructures by the economic base may be true for capitalism but not for feudalism or classical antiquity where Catholicism or politics reigned supreme, Marx replied that 'the middle ages could not live on Catholicism, nor the ancient world on politics', and went further by stating that 'it is the mode in which they gained a livelihood that explains why here politics, and there Catholicism, played the chief part'.[27]

The sense of this remark is not entirely clear but it seems to suggest that the determination by the base may be compatible with, and indeed the cause of, one of the superstructures playing the predominant role in certain types of societies. In other words, the determination by the economy would not only not suppress the effectivity of the superstructure, but it would condition that effectivity to become the most important aspect of social practice. Structuralist authors like Althusser, Balibar and Poulantzas find in this passage the justification for a distinction between the 'determinant level' and the 'dominant level' of a social formation, seeming to avoid both reductionism and a pluralist interactionism. The distinction supposes that although the economy is always determinant in the last instance, this does not mean that it is always dominant. The economy may determine that other levels – the political or 'ideological' – may be dominant. It is only within capitalism that the economy is both determinant and dominant.[28]

Jacques Texier opposes this interpretation and holds that for Marx the economy does not only determine in the last instance but also necessarily dominates. According to Texier, the structuralist authors misunderstand the passage in question: 'For Marx the economic conditions of feudalism explain why Catholicism plays the principal role *within the ideological sphere of society*, but this does not mean that "the ideological instance" dominates all the other instances in the social totality.'[29]

Both these interpretations attempt to read too much into a passage which, after all, is taken from a brief and unelaborated footnote in *Capital*. The distinction between determinant and dominant levels is not spelled out with the clarity and generality the structuralists would have us believe. Nor is Texier's interpretation that the chief role of Catholicism during feudalism refers to a dominance within the superstructure of ideas and not within the social formation as such directly supported by the text. Besides, this interpretation cannot be applied to 'politics' in the ancient world. This obliges Texier to provide a separate, complicated and not altogether convincing explanation which makes his version even less plausible. In effect, Texier argues that 'politics' in the ancient world cannot be adequately distinguished from 'economics' in so far as 'the ancient commune is a social form of appropriation, a property relationship'.[30] This may be so, but then the sense of the thesis of the determination and domination by the economy, which he wants to uphold, becomes unclear. Both interpretations coincide in that the text seeks to explain determination in the context of the base–superstructure paradigm. I have already argued that this is problematic. Yet at least the passage suggests that the determination by the economy is more complex than it may seem. It has to be recognised, however, that this suggestion is no more than an initial clue which needs to be elaborated.

As I have already shown in Chapter 2, Engels, in his turn, attempted in the 1880s to find a solution in a series of letters which sought to reconcile the struggle against mechanistic conceptions with the commitment to a dialectical notion of causality. Engels's key notion was that of 'determination in the last instance', which has enjoyed an immense prestige among Marxists ever since. Althusser and other structuralists have made it a central plank of their conceptions. Briefly, Engels's solution was that the economic base was ultimately decisive in shaping the superstructures, but this did not exclude the superstructures in their turn from being determining factors which, as secondary causes, could produce effects and 'react' back upon the base. Engels accepted the cause–effect explanation but rejected what he called an 'undialectical' conception of it. What mechanical viewpoints forgot was that 'once an historic element has been brought into the world by other, ultimately economic causes, it reacts, and can react on its environment and even on the causes that have given rise to it'.[31] Engels's point was therefore that if the economy were ultimately the determining factor in history, it was not, nevertheless, the only one. And to emphasise this, he added 'neither Marx nor I have ever asserted more than this. Hence if somebody twists this into saying that the economic factor is the *only* determining one, he transforms that proposition into a meaningless, abstract, absurd phrase.'[32] I have already shown some of the problems which derive from Engels's solution, particularly the fact that he understood the relationship between primary and secondary causes as the relationship between the necessary and the accidental. As Althusser has rightly pointed out, the problem is that 'the elements of the superstructure do have an effectivity, but this effectivity is *in some way dispersed into an infinity*, into the infinity of effects, of accidents, whose inner connection may, once this extremity in the infinitesimal has been reached, be regarded as *non-existent*'.[33]

Nevertheless, Althusser wants to keep the essential of Engels's formulation – that is, the economy determinant in the last instance and the superstructures imposing some determinations – so that there occurs an 'accumulation of effective determinations'. Yet Althusser goes further. He too hastily associates Engels's view with the distinction between determination and dominance. Thus he maintains that

> determination in the last instance by the economy is exercised precisely in the permutations of the principal role beween the economy, politics, theory, etc. Engels saw this quite clearly and pointed it out in his struggle with the opportunists in the Second International, who were awaiting the arrival of socialism through the action of the economy alone.[34]

In fact, Engels nowhere proposed 'permutations of the principal role'. For him economism meant simply that the economic factor was taken to be the only determining instance, and not that the economic factor was taken to be dominant. Althusser's struggle against economism entails the abandonment of the idea of the necessary dominance of the economy, but this cannot be found in Engels.[35]

Althusser also explicitly deals with and rejects the passivity of the superstructures which economism certainly entails. This is expressed in his belief in an 'accumulation of effective determinations'. One way of understanding the specific effectivity of the superstructures is expressed in his concept of overdetermination which constitutes a valuable contribution to the Engelsian tradition: the effects produced by the economy are 'overdetermined' by the superstructures. However, in order to understand the relationships between the various effective determinations, Althusser also proposes a new concept of causality which departs from the Engelsian model, and which he names *structural causality*. According to Althusser, classical philosophy proposes two notions of causality: first, mechanical or transitive causality, of Cartesian origin, whereby a determinate effect is related to an object-cause which is a different phenomenon; second, expressive causality, of Leibnizian and Hegelian origin, whereby the whole is reduced to an inner essence whose elements are but the phenomenal forms of expression. The inner essence is present at each point in the whole, each element is expressive of the entire totality.

In Althusser's view these two notions are inadequate. Mechanical causality cannot think the effectivity of the whole on its elements; and expressive causality, although it makes it possible to think the effectivity of the whole on its elements, can only accomplish this in such a way that each element expresses the entire totality, and this can only be true of a spiritual whole.[36] In contrast to these notions, structural or metonymic causality conceives the whole as structured so that the structure is a cause immanent in its effects. The whole existence of the structure consists in its effects, and the structure, as a specific combination of its elements, is nothing outside its effects.[37] In applying this concept of causality to the Marxist totality, Althusser says:

> it is a whole whose unity, far from being the expressive or 'spiritual' unity of Leibniz's or Hegel's whole, is constituted by

> a certain type of *complexity*, the unity of a *structural whole* containing what can be called levels or instances which are distinct and 'relatively autonomous', and coexist within this complex structural unity, articulated with one another according to specific determinations, fixed in the last instance by the level or instance of the economy.[38]

However, these instances or levels are not articulated once and for all according to a pre-set hierarchy. In Althusser's view:

> it is economism that identifies eternally in advance the determinant-contradiction-in-the-last-instance with the *role* of the dominant contradiction, which for ever assimilates such and such an 'aspect' (forces of production, economy, practice) to the principal role, and such and such another 'aspect' (relations of production, politics, ideology, theory) to the secondary *role*.[39]

It is by no means clear that Althusser has succeeded in surpassing the notion of expressive causality. The least one can say is that the difference between expressive and structural causality is not as clear cut as Althusser would have us believe. One wonders whether an inner essence expressed in each of its effects and a structure immanent in its effects are not more or less the same thing. Why should not an inner essence be structured and complex? As Hindess and Hirst have pointed out, if one is to find a difference between both kinds of causality, that could be the fact that the Hegelian essence contains the principle of its own transformation, whereas the Althusserian structure contains no such principle. According to Hindess and Hirst, the Althusserian structure is the essence of an eternity, and therefore structural causality precludes any conception of transition from one mode of production to another.[40]

However, I think the real problem lies elsewhere. The essence of what Engels and Althusser contend is that the superstructures have an effectivity of their own and that in conjunction with the determination in the last instance by the economy they overdetermine social phenomena. Whether the relationship between these effective determinations is to be understood in terms of structural causality or in terms of expressive causality matters less than explaining what the determination by the base in the last instance means. And this crucial issue is not really tackled by Engels or Althusser. They state that determination by the economic structure does not preclude the relative autonomy of, and the overdetermination by, the superstructures; but they do not explain what determination is. Their solution is therefore achieved only by displacing the problem. They give an answer to reductionism and economism but they do not really explain the character of determination. We are informed that economic determination is not the only form of determination but we are not informed about its meaning. By confining their analysis to the narrow limits of the base–superstructure image, Engels and Althusser have indeed made more difficult the task of understanding its nature. For as I said before, how can the economic structure – conceived as an objective level – 'determine' consciousness? Does this mean that determination must primarily be understood as conditioning; that is to say, as the setting of limits?

Epistemology and determination

Before going into the analysis of this problem it is perhaps worth while considering in greater detail the critique and the solutions which Hindess and Hirst have put forward. In their first book they proposed the concept of material causality in opposition to expressive and structural causality.[41] Although the context in which this material causality appeared was not directly concerned with the base–superstructure relationship, but rather with the conditions which made possible the transition from one mode of production to another, one can see its relevance for our problem. By material causality they understood the specific agency of concrete social struggles and practices. Whereas teleological conceptions of causality were unlineal and deterministic, the authors could only understand the transition from one mode of production to the other in terms of specific struggles. Teleological conceptions negated both the crucial role of class struggle and the necessity for the concrete analysis of the current situation: the transition was the expression of an inner principle, not the outcome of class struggle. If one extrapolates this notion and applies it to determination, one can see that determination is not just the setting of limits by passive structures, but requires agency and class practices. Had Hindess and Hirst pursued this line, they would have perhaps produced a more satisfactory concept of determination.

But they did not. On the contrary, their critique of determination in the last instance led them to abandon the concept of determination altogether. The gist of their critique is as follows: if political and ideological forms are determined in the last instance by the economy, then their essential features can be deduced directly from the concept of the economy. The concept of the object 'relations of production' has necessary consequences for the conceptualisation of political and legal objects. However, to say that capitalist relations of production presuppose a legal system is merely to specify some abstract and general conditions which such a system must meet if it is to be compatible with capitalist production. The concept of capitalist relations of production itself does not tell us in what precise form the legal system will be secured. Hence the problem with determination in the last instance is that it implies that certain specific social relations are capable of producing their own conditions of existence. Instead, Hindess proposes

> to conceptualise the connections between relations of production and political, legal and ideological or cultural forms and relations in terms of *conditions of existence*. This means that while, for example, certain legal forms may be necessary as conditions of existence of capitalist relations of production, their existence is not secured by capitalist relations of production themselves.[42]

There is implicit in Hindess's account a circularity of conditions, the mutual setting of limits among the three levels in such a way that only certain forms of political and ideological structures are compatible with the relations of production. But there is no way in which these particular relations of production could, of themselves, secure specific political and ideological structures. So they cannot provide their own survival. Whether or not the conditions for their survival are met depends on the specific form of those conditions as determined by class struggle. So far so good. The problem emerges when Hindess discovers an ambiguity in the Marxist notion of class. On the one hand, politics and ideology are effects of class determinations, but on the other hand they are not, because a class defined at the level of social relations of production does not necessarily correspond with class political positions. For Hindess this situation is tantamount to recognising and denying the autonomy of politics, and so he concludes that '*either* we effectively reduce political and ideological phenomena to class interests determined elsewhere . . . *or* we must face up to the real autonomy of political and ideological phenomena and their irreducibility to manifestations of interests determined by the structure of the economy.[43]

In other words, Hindess has abandoned the idea of determination as material causation by class struggle. Now classes remain at the economic level, defined only in terms of their structural interests, and cannot determine legal and ideological forms. If Hindess had previously mentioned class practices, he no longer does so: classes are reduced to the economic level and no political consequences can be derived from their structural configurations. By focusing upon class structural interests and no longer upon class practices, politics becomes totally detached from economics. It is of course true that the political positions of classes can be at variance with their class interests. But it is a mistake to think that they can be separated from concrete class practices. By reducing classes to the level of the economy, Hindess is again trapped by the base–superstructure image which divides society in separate compartments. As he refuses to reduce the superstructures to the base, his only alternative is to accept the other extreme: the three levels as absolutely autonomous. Hindess and Hirst believe that in order consistently to avoid reductionism one should accept the existence of 'non-class forms of politics and of ideology'.[44] that is to say, the total autonomy of politics and ideology from any class determination. Hindess and Hirst's mistake is to confuse the separation between politics and class interests with a separation between politics and class practices. The former is possible; the latter does not make sense within Marxism.

But this is not all. Hindess and Hirst want to give a more profound foundation to their critique of determination in the last instance. According to them, the central problem of the notion of determination is an epistemological one, namely the transposition of a certain type of relation between concepts on to a relation of determination between objects specified by those concepts. But this is not an exclusive problem of determination; it is the hallmark of all epistemologies in so far as they separate the realm of discourse from the realm of independently existent objects, and postulate a certain correspondence between these two realms which is secured by an epistemologically privileged form of discourse. Epistemology is therefore essentially dogmatic in that it posits a privileged form of discourse which is not supposed to be demonstrated, but which is assumed to be the absolute criterion that can guarantee a correspondence between objects and knowledge.

Hindess and Hirst want to escape from this dogmatism and propose that 'entities referred to in discourse are constituted solely in and through the forms of discourse in which they are specified'.[45] So objects do not exist independently from, and cannot be specified without, a form of discourse, and consequently there can be no privileged form of discourse which can guarantee that certain concepts represent the real itself. This means that epistemology as such is to be rejected. In so far as determination is concerned, Hindess and Hirst's argument goes as follows. Because there is no privileged form of discourse there can be no privileged basic concepts of any discourse. If there are no privileged concepts, then a discourse cannot be derived as a simple deduction or extension of these privileged concepts; no concept can serve as absolute criterion for the formation of others. Therefore, from the concept of relations of production (the economy) one cannot derive the concept of political and ideological forms. Hence determination is not longer valid.

Hindess and Hirst's analysis poses very serious problems. At first glance one can detect an obvious pitfall in their attempt to escape epistemology. In their attempt to abandon the 'epistemological enterprise' they try to put themselves beyond the limits of current theorisation, be it Marxist or empiricist. Almost *a priori* one has the suspicion that such an attempt is impossible and doomed to failure. However, the claim that they can abandon the 'dogmatic' terrain of epistemologies has to be scrutinised. Let us examine first the consequences of their position – assuming that theirs is a logically tenable position – and second, whether such a position can be maintained without contradiction. According to Hindess and Hirst, the root cause of epistemological dogmatism is the separation between discourse and its objects. So they propose to consider objects as constituted through discourse, thus abolishing the distance between knowledge and reality. To deny the sharp separation between consciousness and reality may seem a perfectly sound claim within a Marxist perspective. After all, did not Marx himself propound this idea in the 'Theses on Feuerbach'?

It is true that Marx did not want to consider reality only in the form of the object. But he did not dissolve reality into consciousness. The unity between consciousness and reality was never an identity but a result of that reality being constructed by human practice. So the separation between consciousness and reality was not bridged by dissolving reality into consciousness, as idealism propounded, but was bridged by practice. Whereas for idealism the processes of consciousness and discourse became the speculative production of reality, for Marx reality was produced by material practice. Hindess and Hirst's proposition that objects have no independent existence from discourse borders, therefore, on idealism, for reality becomes a function of knowledge and nothing else. In this respect Hindess and Hirst do little more than pursue Althusser's logic to the end – despite the fact that they criticise him for his 'rationalist epistemology'. It was Althusser who held that science created its own objects and that the objects of knowledge were not the objects in external reality. But Hindess and Hirst accuse Althusser of inconsistency, of having accepted that the objects of knowledge are produced through knowledge, and yet having maintained the existence of a world of real objects which has an essential homology with the world of discourse. So Althusser reintroduces the distinction and correspondence which Hindess and Hirst reject.

The problem with Hindess and Hirst's position is that, even if it could be upheld, it would not permit them to think the way in which the objects produced in and through discourse are adequate to understand reality. If objects have sense only within the discourse that constitute them, there is no guarantee that they accurately depict what actually goes on outside that discourse. If there is no guarantee, if there is no privileged form of discourse, then there is no way of knowing the truth. The individual dogmatism of epistemologies is apparently gone, but at the cost of making every discourse, including Hindess and Hirst's, a closed world which cannot be properly measured against any external yardstick. Hence any position would be true or false according to its internal logic, according to the coherence with which the discourse has created its objects. But contrary to what Hindess and Hirst claim, there would be no way of comparing various positions. Paradoxically, therefore, it may be that theories are no longer foreclosed by a sole, immune epistemological criterion, but they are certainly foreclosed by the lack of any criterion. What Hindess and Hirst do not realise is that the so-called 'dogmatism' can be arrived at, not only through the individual claims of particular epistemologies, but also through the elimination of all particular claims. For there is no way of disproving a discourse which has created its own objects.

Furthermore, Hindess and Hirst's claim that they are not assuming another epistemological position is contradictory. What they have done, without recognising it, is to constitute their own discourse as the privileged discourse against which all epistemologies are judged. Their own discourse is as dogmatic as an epistemological discourse because it is posited as the ultimate point of reference against which the claims of epistemologies are measured. True, they maintain strongly that there is no privileged form of discourse, but surely they hold this with the exception of their own discourse. If they did not consider their own discourse as privileged, they could not possibly criticise the closure of epistemologies. By criticising them, they implicitly erect their own discourse as *the* criterion which is never demonstrated and which admits no discussion. Where is one to find any justification for the principle that 'objects of discourse cannot be specified extra-discursively'? Why should this principle be less dogmatic than the principle which maintains the opposite? Hindess and Hirst are unavoidably trapped in this paradox. They seek to end dogmatism, but they create a new one. They want to abandon epistemology, but they erect a new one. They criticise undemonstrated epistemological principles which are assumed to be self-evident, but they put forward undemonstrated principles which are not subject to discussion.

Hindess and Hirst cannot escape from epistemology. By denying the validity of epistemologies they constitute a new world of separate objects, the knowledge of which they measure against their own discourse. So they cannot avoid the separation between discourse and objects. What their conception boils down to is this: there is an epistemological discourse and its object is a particular relationship between discourse and object. The epistemological discourse misjudges its object; that is, it misinterprets the relationship between discourse and object. Hindess and Hirst's discourse has the same object: a particular relation between discourse and object. But their discourse understands well that relation. So their discourse is to be preferred because it properly effects the correlation between discourse and object (see Figure 5.1).

Figure 5.1

Discourse		*Object*
Epistemological	wrong understanding of →	discourse/object relationship
Hindess and Hirst	right understanding of →	discourse/object relationship

So, in effect, Hindess and Hirst have not avoided positing a distinction between two realms and a particular correspondence between them as secured by their own discourse, and hence, in contradiction to their own claim, they are involved up to their necks in what they call an 'epistemological enterprise'. By rejecting epistemology as such they contradict themselves, because the very logic of that rejection makes it impossible to compare one discourse with others. If one rejects epistemology because it erects a self-sufficient and undemonstrable discourse as a touchstone for measuring claims to knowledge, one is unwittingly condemning one's own rejection of epistemology. If there is no privileged discourse, there is no way of deciding whether Hindess and Hirst's position or the traditional epistemological positions are better. There are no grounds for rejecting or approving anyone. Any rejection of epistemology constructed upon this feeble base leads into plain relativism or self-contradiction.[46]

What to say then of Hindess and Hirst's critique of 'determination in the last instance'? Is it essentially vitiated as a result of their having failed to get rid of epistemology? I do not think so. Some elements of their critique indeed seem pertinent. For instance, it is quite true that capitalist relations of production cannot on their own tell us in what specific form the legal system will exist. But this is not very new, as Marx himself acknowledged that capitalist relations of production on their own could not even determine in what specific form the economic base will exist. As he put it:

> it is always the direct relationship of the owners of the conditions of production to the direct producers . . . which reveals the innermost secret, the hidden basis of the entire social structure, and with it the political form of the relation of sovereignty and dependence, in short, the corresponding specific form of the state. This does not prevent the same economic basis . . . due to innumerable different empirical circumstances, natural environment, racial relations, external historical influences, etc., from showing infinite variations and gradations in appearance, which can be ascertained only by analysis of the empirically given circumstances.[47]

This conception does not do without the concept of determination, nor does it emerge from the abolition of epistemology, as Hindess and Hirst would have us believe. The problem with 'determination in the last instance' does not derive from the dogmatism of epistemology, but derives from a certain conception of determination.

In certain respects Hindess and Hirst do help us understand the problems of the current conception of determination. I think an important clue is given when they state that 'we must therefore distinguish between conditions of existence and the social relations and practices which provide them. The first can be inferred from the concept of determinate relations of production but the second cannot.'[48] By distinguishing between general conditioning and specific forms of practice, Hindess and Hirst implicitly show the insufficiency of any concept of determination which remains solely at the first level. Their mistake is to confine the concept to that level, with the result that they have to abandon it because it is clearly insufficient. They do not realise that perhaps the concept of determination should be understood in a different manner, that it must be applied also and preferentially to the provision of specific forms of politics and consciousness by class practices. But as they reduce classes to a separate economic level, they are unable to do this. By reducing determination to the general conditioning by the economy they are led to acknowledge the conditioning by politics and ideology in equal terms, and no instance may have primacy: relations of production impose definite constraints on the type of legal system compatible with them, but also the legal system is a condition of existence of those relations of production. So there follows a circular process of conditioning. My point is, on the contrary, that there is no need to restrict the concept of determination to this reciprocal conditioning and that what Hindess and Hirst call the provision of specific forms of political and ideological elements by class practices is at the centre of the Marxist concept of determination.

Material and intellectual production

Implicit in what I have said so far is the idea that the concept of determination is multidimensional. This is true from at least two points of view. On the one hand, determination involves both the idea of conditioning and of production. As conditioning, determination means the setting of limits, the imposition of certain constraints by objectified forms of practice (apparatuses, institutions, organisation of the field, etc.). This is the sense in which Marx says that

> men are not free to choose their productive forces . . . for every productive force is an acquired force, the product of former activity. The productive forces are therefore the result of practically applied human energy; but this energy is itself conditioned by the circumstances in which men find themselves, by the productive forces already acquired, by the social form which exists before they exist, which they do not create, which is the product of the preceding generation.[49]

This means that as far as social consciousness is concerned, not just economic apparatuses but also political arrangements and the specific organisation of the intellectual field are determinant in the sense of setting the context within which consciousness emerges. This context is given, historically specific and limited.

As production, determination is a dynamic process whereby social consciousness and social institutions are practically brought to life. Men and women come to know reality through their own practice which is increasingly differentiated. As men and women produce their material life, they produce also their forms of consciousness. This is a collective process which does not entail a priority in time – men and women anticipate practical results in consciousness – but which entails a fundamental priority derived from the practical need for reproducing material existence. Because this process of reproduction necessarily involves the division of labour and class differentiation, the active dimension of determination can be said to be accomplished by class practices. If one conceives the class structure as a given phenomenon derived from certain relations of production, one can say that this structure conditions and sets limits to certain political or ideological forms, which are not specified. Various forms are compatible. But if one conceives of classes as practically involved in struggles and productive practices, they do specify particular ideational and political forms through their struggles and practices. Determination concerns both aspects.

On the other hand, determination affects both social consciousness and the intellectual field: that is, the conjunction of apparatuses and the system of relationships which are specifically evolved for the creation and communication of various forms of social consciousness. The determination of consciousness refers to the character and content of ideas; the determination of the intellectual field refers to the structure of relations and material organisation of apparatuses which specialise in the production and transmission of ideas. The determination of consciousness by material practices is mediated by the character and organisation of the intellectual field. I have already shown that, historically, the organisation of the capitalist intellectual field followed the pattern of the organisation of the economy. While in medieval times the production relations based on personal dependency corresponded with the church's particularised monopoly of intellectual production, the capitalist revolution meant a liberalisation of both levels. To the new 'freedom' of the worker and his or her separation from the means of production, a new 'intellectual freedom' corresponded which separated intellectual production from church tutelage. In both levels a 'free market' is created which allows the circulation of commodities, in one case purely material goods, and in the other material goods which carry explicit ideas and messages (books, films, etc.).

To this extent, a Marxist concept of determination must be historical and specific. It is true that Marx proposed general and abstract formulae such as 'life is not determined by consciousness but consciousness by life' or 'it is not the consciousness of men that determines their being, but, on the contrary, their social being that determines their consciousness'. These formulae seem to be concerned more with the universal applicability of a principle than with the specific analysis of historical forms of consciousness. However, in my view these statements have sense in the context of a polemic with idealism and cannot exhaust the meaning of determination. Marx clarifies this not only when he carries out concrete analyses and specifies what 'life' and 'social being' mean for each historical period, but also in a theoretical formulation:

> In order to examine the connection between spiritual production and material production it is above all necessary to grasp the latter itself not as a general category but in *definite historical* form. Thus, for example, different kinds of spiritual production correspond to the capitalist mode of production and to the mode of production of the Middle Ages. If material production itself is not conceived in its *specific historical* forms, it is impossible to understand what is specific in the spiritual production corresponding to it and the reciprocal influence of one on the other.[50]

The correspondence between material and intellectual production can be described in terms of homology as distinct from analogy. This distinction has been elaborated by Rossi-Landi to account for the relationship between linguistic and material production. His thesis is that there is a relative 'sameness' between two social processes, namely the production and circulation of goods as commodities and the production and circulation of sentences as messages. Rossi-Landi maintains that 'when goods circulate in the form of commodities they "are" messages; and that when sentences circulate in the form of verbal messages they "are" commodities'.[51] This is justified by the fact that these two processes originate in the same practical activity whereby human beings produce and reproduce themselves. While analogy reunites what is divided by comparing processes which are originally separate, homology recognises the original unity of what appears to be divided.[52] By introducing this distinction to our topic one can see that there is a homology between intellectual and material production in so far as they are united in practice. It is in the production of material life that consciousness is also produced. This is why determination is not merely the setting of limits by given structures and apparatuses but also, and mainly, the production of consciousness by/in practice. The fact that the reproduction of material life implies increasingly differentiated forms of practice, and the separation of manual and intellectual labour, does not affect the basic principle that the forms of social consciousness cannot be conceived apart from those practices. Nevertheless, a distinction should be drawn between consciousness as produced by an intellectual stratum which makes its living by producing or transmitting ideas, and consciousness as produced by individuals in their productive practices of everyday life. Although both are mediated by the intellectual field and must be conceived in connection with social practice, the former adds an element of critical and rigorous reflexivity upon the more or less spontaneous and common-sensical forms of the latter.

The emergence of this intellectual stratum as separated from the church is one of the specific features brought about by capitalism. For as long as the bourgeoisie struggled in order to secure political power, the intellectual production of this stratum was highly politicised and critical. But once the bourgeoisie achieved the political control of society, the separation between the state and the economy, between political and civil society, was increasingly transposed into a depoliticised kind of consciousness which was no longer concerned with the problem of domination but fixed its attention on the 'private' problems of the individual. As civil society became the sphere of the 'liberated' individual and (generally) his or her private decisions, the content of intellectual production and art too became fixed in the sphere of privacy. The kind of instrumental reason which rules over the production of material commodities came also to be applied to intellectual production and hence an intellectual industry was created which has to produce for the market and make profits.[53] This situation affects radical thinking as much as conservative thinking. As Benjamin has pointed out, 'the bourgeois apparatus of production and publication is capable of assimilating, indeed of propagating, an astonishing amount of revolutionary themes without ever seriously putting into question its own continued existence or that of the class which owns it'.[54]

Hence intellectual production under capitalism is not merely depoliticised, but also depoliticising in that it succeeds in turning all forms of consciousness, even revolutionary ones, into objects of consumption, entertainment and amusement. It is not by pure chance that a poster of Che Guevara has become a best-selling decorative object. The bourgeois system of cultural production recuperates and dilutes revolutionary themes by making of them a fashion which is only an object of contemplation or admiration but never a 'compelling motive for decision'.[55] The system desensitises by overexposure and commercialisation. However, just as the field of material production is the focus of contradictions and class struggles, the intellectual field is never the monolithic expression of the ruling class and is also pierced by those very contradictions. In this sense educational apparatuses, media, churches, etc., are deeply divided and also express, although in a subordinated manner, the positions of dominated classes. The homology between material and intellectual production is also illustrated by this fact.

Determination, class character and validity

I have argued that determination goes beyond the mere setting of limits by objective conditions and that it primarily concerns the practical production of material life, which is at the same time the source of intellectual production. It is by/in practice that men and women – as divided into classes – produce social reality and the forms of consciousness which seek to represent that reality. It is important to understand that those forms of consciousness are not merely a representation of an already constituted social reality, but also contribute to produce that very reality. They have, to that extent, an irreducible entity which enables them to survive the destruction of that particular social reality which originally produced them. Hence the forms of social consciousness are determined in the sense that they have been produced in the process of production of social reality, but not in the sense that their scope and validity is inexorably tied up with that reality. Marx realised that this is the most difficult aspect of his conception of determination and expressed it in relation to ancient Greek art: 'The difficulty lies not in understanding that the Greek arts and epic are bound up with certain forms of social development. The difficulty is that they still afford us artistic pleasure and that in a certain respect they count as a norm and as an unattainable model.'[56]

Unfortunately, Marx did not elaborate on this, and the few

comments which follow concerning the inherent charm of the historic childhood of mankind are clearly insufficient. As Kosik has pointed out, the problem is more general and concerns the distinction between the genesis and the validity of ideas and art works.[57] In a different context Marx implicitly acknowledged this distinction when he discussed Ravenstone's critique of Ricardo, and – more generally – of capitalism. Ravenstone's point is that machinery, luxury products, the development of natural sciences and the literary and artistic productions brought about by capitalism have emerged in opposition to the interests of the workers, as a result of the leisure of the non-workers, and that therefore an egalitarian society would have to do without them. Marx criticised those who think along these lines by saying that

> they share the narrowmindedness of the economists (although from a diametrically opposite position) for they confuse the *contradictory form* of this development with its content. The latter wish to perpetuate the contradiction on account of its results. The former are determined to sacrifice the fruits which have developed within the antagonistic form, in order to get rid of the contradiction.[58]

This statement implicitly recognises that, however contradictory the genesis of works of art or theories may be, and whatever their class origin, their validity as fruits of a necessary process of development cannot be put in question. It would indeed be narrow-minded to sacrifice them in the attempt to eliminate the contradiction. This is in accordance with what Marx had anticipated in 1846 when writing about 'the fruits of civilisation' and productive forces: 'men never relinquish what they have won, but this does not mean that they never relinquish the social form in which they have acquired certain productive forces'.[59] This terminology, 'the fruits' of social development or civilisation, 'what men have won', shows that Marx firmly believed that ideas and works of art may survive beyond the society, class and time in which they were produced. This means the character of theories and works of art cannot be exhausted by an investigation about their social origins. It means also that the forms of social consciousness cannot be reduced to their social background and that, as part of social reality themselves, they may have the same durability as other material products of practice.

The consequence of this is that the validity of socially determined ideas is not totally external to them, is not to be found solely in the social situation within which they originated. But neither is it entirely immanent, that is to say, inherent in the ideas themselves as an autonomous reality separate from the rest of social reality. As Kosik has suggested, a work of art is, of course, a witness of its time, a document which somehow represents the social situations within which it was produced.[60] But it is not just that. Because it is itself part of that social situation and contributes to produce it as such, one cannot reduce it to that situation. It can perfectly well become an element of a new social reality, it can be articulated to a new context where it becomes constitutive of a new social reality. This is why determination cannot be conceived of as a single causative act. Determination is a permanent process of production and reproduction of ideas or works of art, within new contexts and practices which give to them a renewed sense. A work of art survives not because it contains within itself, as a totally autonomous being, a universal validity, but because it can be inserted in, and assume meaning for, the practice of new generations. In this sense a work of art or a theory is independent of the author's intentions.

Hadjinicolaou has argued that paintings which pass the test of time change their nature and become the source of new values which are determined by the interests of the new critics and observers. Consequently he maintains that there is no aesthetic effect which is definable by itself. It is always referred to a particular historical period and the concrete appreciation of people. In the case of paintings, the aesthetic effect relates to the pleasure which the expectator experiences by recognising himself or herself in the imaged world-view of the painting in question.[61] Of course, this is not a purely arbitrary process. There must be something in the work itself which allows the actualisation of its multiple potentialities. But as Kosik has pointed out, the efficacy of a work of art is not a physical property of the work itself, but its specific mode of existence as social reality, its continuous reanimation, its continuous interaction with mankind.[62]

Because ideas and works of art outlive the situation in which they were formed, they become forms through which men and women can live their problems and struggle for their resolution. Marx implicitly refers to this fact when he writes that

> the tradition of all dead generations weighs like a nightmare on the brain of the living. And just when they seem engaged in revolutionising themselves and things, in creating something that has never yet existed, precisely in such period of revolutionary crisis they anxiously conjure up the spirits of the past to their service and borrow from them names, battle cries and costumes in order to present the new scene of world history in this time-honoured disguise and this borrowed language.[63]

It is a common occurrence that in order to represent to themselves their own practices, men and women resort to old formulae and ideas, and reformulate their practices in terms of past representations and images. This fact may have an ideological meaning, if the conjuring up of the past has the purpose (conscious or unconscious) of concealing from the actors the class limits and contents of their struggle. This is the context in which Marx referred to it. But it can also have a different meaning when the reappropriation of the past seeks to recognise a historical orientation and to express a collective will (in the Gramscian sense) with which the present struggle hopes to be closely associated. In any case it is the demands of the present struggle that give sense and validity to past representations.[64]

This is why determination must be understood as a continuous process of reanimation of ideas in the context of new practices. In so far as the original context and the original process of production imprint a certain character upon ideas or works of art, they become witnesses to their time and can be best understood in connection with their original background. In so far as the same ideas or works of art articulate something within new contexts and practices, they become 'overdetermined' by them. Hence determination has to do with both these phenomena, and not just with the genesis of forms of consciousness. These two aspects cannot be separated at will. The original determination of a work does limit the number of interpretations which are possible within new determining contexts. Thus the process of continuous reanimation of the work cannot be a totally arbitrary assignment of new meanings to a supposedly neutral content in order to suit different interests. This is the problem of those conceptions which, in order to avoid reductionism, sharply separate the form from the content of ideas, and confine determination to the former.

In effect, Laclau has proposed an understanding of determination which exemplifies the problem of the form–content distinction.[65] He accepts the class determination of 'ideological elements' (his terminology uses ideology or 'ideological' in a general positive sense as ideas or systems of ideas such as nationalism, liberalism, etc.) but seeks to avoid a reductionist interpretation of it. By 'reductionism' he means the claim that every ideological element has a necessary class belonging in which, for instance, liberalism is supposed to be a bourgeois ideology, Marxism the ideology of the proletariat, and militarism deemed to be a feudal ideology. In order to avoid this reductionism, Laclau introduces the distinction between the form and the content of an ideology and proposes that 'the class character of an ideology is given by its *form* and not by its *content*'.[66] This means that the content of ideological elements has no necessary class connection and that class determination is 'conferred' upon them by means of an articulating principle. For example, nationalism is not a feudal, bourgeois or proletarian ideology. In itself it has no class connotation. The class character of nationalism derives from its form, from its specific articulation with other ideological elements. Hence the bourgeoisie may link nationalism to the struggle against the particularism and regionalism of the feudal lords, but the proletariat can also link nationalism to the struggle against an internationalised and dependent bourgeoisie. So by their contents, ideological elements are not bound to any class, but they are open to articulation to various hegemonic principles.

The problem with Laclau's solution is that it requires the existence of non-class contents or neutral contents which can be articulated to different class interests. One may ask where these supposedly neutral contents come from. It is true that some ideological elements or ideas are not necessarily bound to a particular class in the sense that they can be articulated to or used by other classes. But this does not mean that they must be considered as non-class contents. In practice they are necessarily attached to the perspective of a class, though their validity and function cannot be confined to that class. Moreover, to hold that the validity of certain elements cannot be bound to one particular class does not mean that the content of those elements is totally free from class determination. According to one of Laclau's examples, liberalism was the ideology of the European bourgeoisie during the period of competitive capitalism, and yet it was also the ideology of feudal landowners in Latin America. It seems to me very difficult to argue that the same content of liberal ideology was shared by the British bourgeoisie and the Latin American landowning aristocracy. It may be that the same label was used, but the contents were quite different – as indeed one would have expected in two different modes of production, with different class formations.

Laclau may object that, indeed, liberalism is not exactly the same in both cases, and that his point is precisely to determine where the difference is supposed to lie. In his own words he may ask: is it the case that liberalism 'refers to such diverse contents that it is not possible to find a common element of meaning in them all? Or rather is it that certain common nuclei of meaning are connotatively linked to diverse ideological articulatory domains?'[67] Of course, one would have to agree that there does exist at least certain common elements, even if superficial and limited. Otherwise there would seem to be little sense in adopting the same label. We have to assume that the common element in Laclau's example is the belief in free trade. One cannot properly argue, however, that the belief in free trade is equivalent to liberalism. It is only one element in a complex system of ideas. Of course, the belief in free trade can be articulated to the bourgeois liberal outlook as much as to the semi-feudal exporting ideology of Latin American landowners. But this does not mean that, therefore, the content of liberalism is neutral, for liberalism is far more complex than the idea of free trade. My point is that the class character of liberalism is not just given by the mere articulation of that limited abstract common element to a particular class ideological domain, but it is mainly given by the specific content which the European bourgeoisie originally gave to the term.

I accept that the specific content of liberalism as elaborated by the European bourgeoisie can be reinterpreted and adapted to new circumstances which are not exactly those of nineteenth-century Europe. But in the case of the nineteenth-century Latin American landowners, I cannot agree that theirs was a genuine liberalism, apart from the obvious interest in free trade and in the use of the same label. In this sense I fully agree with Mouzelis that 'if there is no one-to-one correspondence between classes and ideological themes, neither is there a completely arbitrary relationship between the two' and that when classes are conceptualised, not in an abstract manner but in historically specific terms, 'then it becomes obvious that there are strict limits to the types of content that their ideological discourse can have'.[68] Neither classes nor ideological contents can be conceived as abstract entities which subsist quite apart from each other and which, nevertheless, can freely combine without limits. Such a conception is ahistorical and formalist. Determination is always a historically specific process which involves both the form and the content of ideas. True, Laclau has a good point when he argues against a reductionist conception of determination which confines ideological contents to a particular class and makes impossible a common framework of meaning. But his formalist account of determination is just another extreme whereby 'articulation' totally displaces the class production of specific contents. If 'articulation' seems a particularly apt term to describe a dynamic process of determination, then one has to understand it not as the integration of neutral contents into a class discourse, but as the integration of class-produced or class-reworked contents into the class discourse.

6

Critique of Ideology or End of Ideology?

Some assumptions of the critique of ideology

The idea of a critique of ideology involves different connotations depending on whether one holds a positive or a negative concept of ideology. Whatever the kind of positive concept one adopts, be it an objective level of society, the world-view of a class, or a body of political ideas orientated to action, ideology does not of itself pass judgement upon the ideas involved. Ideologies may be true or false, they may serve this or that class and they may represent a variety of interests without losing their character as ideologies. It is not of the essence of ideology to be a distortion or an adequate representation of reality. As I pointed out in Chapter 3, this does not necessarily mean that those who hold a positive concept are prevented from taking an evaluative stand concerning ideologies. But the assessment can hardly be made upon the basis of elements inherent in the concept of ideology itself. So, very often, the emphasis is displaced towards other criteria which have to do with the nature of the class or interests behind the ideology or with the 'scientificity' of ideology.

In effect, a common version within orthodox Marxism distinguishes between 'ascendant' and 'descendant' classes. Revolutionary classes are supposed to have interests which coincide with the trend of social development so that their consciousness is a true reflection of reality. Descendant or conservative classes, by opposing social development in defence of their interests, are supposed to blind themselves to the truth.[1] However, to sustain a critique of ideology upon this basis seems problematic. For a start the criterion appears rather extrinsic in that it does not take into account the intellectual contents of ideologies. This may induce the mistaken idea that the mere ascription of thought to a class suffices to validate it or falsify it. Besides, the criterion begs the question, for new criteria are required to decide what is the trend of social development or which are the progressive interests. The criterion of 'scientificity' which Lenin introduced[2] at least considered the contents of ideologies in order to pass judgement upon them; but apart from the obvious difficulty of determining what can be considered 'scientific', the problem remains that the critique of ideology would be carried out in terms which are also applicable to all other forms of knowledge. There would be nothing in the notion of ideology itself which can sustain a specific kind of critique.

The negative concept of ideology, on the contrary, is in itself critical because it alludes to a certain distortion of thought. However, the traditional negative definition of ideology as false consciousness can also be accused of lack of specificity and vagueness because it does not determine which sort of falsity ideology is concerned with. Hence all kinds of errors can appear as ideological. Consequently in this perspective the critique of ideology is not entirely different from that which invokes the criterion of 'scientificity', only that the criterion here is even more abstract, namely the opposition truth–error, and ideology appears exclusively as representing error. In fact, the criterion of 'scientificity' is also explicitly invoked by negative conceptions in order to sustain a critique of ideology. This is, for instance, of paramount importance in Althusser's concept of ideology, despite the fact that somewhat contradictorily he also describes ideology as an objective and eternally necessary level of society and strongly opposes the idea of false consciousness. Although ideology is identified with the pre-scientific or the non-scientific, it is also considered as the raw material which by means of theoretical practice is supposed to be transformed into science.

As far as Marx's concept of ideology is concerned, a distinction should be introduced between the practical resolution of ideology and the critique of ideology. For Marx the overcoming of ideology could be accomplished only through practice, by solving in practice the contradictions which give rise to the ideological form. Revolutionary practice is supposed to transform in reality those contradictions which ideology attempts to solve in consciousness. By doing so, the real base of ideology is eliminated, and hence ideology cannot arise. Yet for Marx a transforming practice is not a blind, deterministic process, but on the contrary it is a conscious practice which entails the comprehension of contradictions and the anticipation of their solution. It is in this sense that Marx affirms that ideological distortions first collapse in theory, before the existing conditions of society collapse in practice.[3]

The critique of ideology therefore plays an important role in the real solution of contradictions, though by itself critique cannot resolve them. At the same time, Marx does not exempt the critique of ideology from social determination. Just as the evolution of the theory of political economy was shaped by the development of capitalist contradictions, so the evolution of the critique of political economy develops in accordance with a similar pattern of contradictory social development. For Marx, classical political economy could develop as a science only in so far as the potential contradictions of capitalism did not become actual. From the moment contradictions appeared on the surface, vulgar political economy adopted an increasingly apologetic role.[4] Similarly, Marx described the initial failure of the critique of capitalism in terms of the incomplete development of the social contradictions. Thus the appearance of the utopian socialists was connected to the backwardness of productive forces and the lack of development of the working class. As Marx put it, the theoreticians of the proletariat at first appear as

> merely Utopians who, to meet the wants of the oppressed classes improvise systems and go in search of a regenerating science . . . So long as they look for science and merely make systems, so long as they are at the beginning of the struggle, they see in poverty nothing but poverty, without seeing in it the revolutionary, subversive side, which will overthrow the old society. From this moment, science, produced by the historical movement and associating itself with it in full recognition of its cause, has ceased to be doctrinaire and has become revolutionary.[5]

Nevertheless, Marx was far from believing that the emergence of a revolutionary critique which was no longer doctrinaire is the automatic result of class struggle. Although the very evolution of capitalist contradictions facilitates its emergence, it cannot guarantee its adequacy. The comprehension of contradictions is not reducible to a more advanced stage of the class struggle. Take, for instance, Marx's analysis of Sismondi. Contrary to Ricardo, to Marx he appeared 'profoundly conscious of the contradictions in capitalist production . . . he is particularly aware of the fundamental contradiction .... he forcefully *criticises* the contradictions of bourgeois production but does not *understand* them, and consequently does not understand the process whereby they can be resolved'.[6] This is also the case with Ravenstone, Hodgskin and the anonymous pamphleteer who 'seize on the mysteries of capitalist production which have been brought to light in order to combat the latter from the standpoint of the industrial proletariat'.[7] But as they do not *understand* the contradiction they describe, they mistakenly propose to abolish the cultural and material benefits which capitalism had brought about because they had originally been produced in opposition to the workers.[8]

For Marx the critique of ideology is neither a 'pure science' separated from class struggle, nor the automatic result of that struggle. The unity (not the identity) of class practice and the theoretical comprehension of contradictions constitute the basis upon which Marx based his critique. In this context Marx distinguished the role of intellectuals from the 'active agents' of the class.[9] Intellectuals may even be former members of the dominant class who have gone over to the dominated class and who 'have raised themselves to the level of comprehending theoretically the historical movement as a whole'.[10] In this Marx implicitly acknowledged the fact that science does not grow spontaneously out of the practice of the active members of the dominated class, and also that there is a specific role to be fulfilled by the intellectuals of the class. However, ideology does not disappear as a result of the critique developed by intellectuals; only the practical solution of contradictions through political struggle can achieve that. These two related aspects, the critique of ideology and the end of ideology, are at the centre of many debates concerning the validity of the Marxist position. They will be explored in the rest of the book.

The critique of ideology and dogmatism

One of the most important questions which arises in the context of a negative concept of ideology is whether the critique of ideology, and particularly Marx's critique, is inherently one-sided and dogmatic, and whether it is bound to claim a vantage-point which is assumed to be beyond criticism. Mannheim's classic objection to Marxism was formulated in these terms. Marxism, he believed, had criticised all other points of view as ideological, but had refused to subject itself to the same critique. Since there cannot be a privileged vantage-point from which one position can pass judgement upon all others without being itself called into the question, Marxism, according to Mannheim, must undergo the same critique and should therefore be considered as another ideology. Because Marxism is socially determined it cannot lay claim to exclusive validity and can only be understood as one partial point of view among a variety of others.[11]

For Mannheim, Marxism represented a decisive step in the development of a 'total' conception of ideology,[12] but it had only managed to reach a 'special formulation' of this total conception. This 'special formulation' was characterised by a one-sided attitude which meant that, while considering opponents' ideas as ideological (a mere function of the social position they occupy), Marxism regarded its own position as absolute. The total conception of ideology reaches its 'general form' – via Mannheim, of course – only when the critic has the courage 'to subject not just the adversary's point of view, but all points of view, including his own, to the ideological analysis'.[13] In other words, Marx did not surpass the one-sidedness which he had criticised in bourgeois thought. He discovered the connection between bourgeois thought and its social basis, but did not apply the same method to his own thought. More recently, Seliger has formulated a similar objection and accused Marx of dogmatism because he failed to reconcile his claim to 'positive science' with the proposition that thought is distorted because it is socially determined.[14]

Mannheim's criticism is based upon a displacement of the negative character of ideology. As I have already shown in Chapter 1, the negative character of ideology had for Marx a very precise and specific meaning which I identified with the concealment of contradictions. Mannheim, on the contrary, identifies the negative connotation of ideology with the social determination of knowledge; all standpoints are limited, partial and therefore ideological precisely because they are socially determined. In distinguishing ideology from determination, Marx proposed that the latter does not entail any necessary negative effects on consciousness. Of course, ideology, too, is socially determined. But it is not the general fact of determination that constitutes the distortion of ideology. Moreover, it is a mistake to believe that Marx perceived the social determination of knowledge only in the case of his opponents. As I have shown in the last section, he accepted the determination of his own thought by linking it to the emergence and development of contradictions in capitalism and by explicitly taking the side of proletarian interests. However, the point is that because Marx did not identify the distorted character of ideology with determination, and in recognising his own 'determinateness', he had no reason to call his own theory an ideology.[15] Nor did he think that all other theories, including some bourgeois theories, were necessarily ideological.

The partiality and one-sidedness which Marx criticised in bourgeois thought was not due to the simple fact of it being class-determined thought, in general. Had this been the case, it would have been difficult for him to maintain that his own thought could be exempted from the same accusation. The criticism was rather that bourgeois thought did not recognise *any* determination, and thus could not properly understand the past or its own 'determinateness'. Marx recognised the principle of social determination of consciousness in general and his own determination in particular. So in this respect his position can claim not to be partial or one-sided. Still, the question remains as to the foundation of Marx's own thought, for to say that he recognises his own determination is not a sufficient proof of the validity of his own position. Is it possible to keep a critical concept of ideology if one is unable to prove the scientificity of one's own point of view?

Raymond Williams has pointed to the problems involved in a negative concept of ideology and has tried to show that the distinction between ideological and non-ideological forms of consciousness is a tempting path which should not be followed far 'because there is a fool's beacon erected just a little way along it. This is the difficult concept of "science".'[16] In effect, in *The German Ideology* Marx seems to oppose ideology to 'real, positive science'.[17] According to Williams, this contrast depends on a knowable distinction between these two forms of knowledge, but this is made impossible by the *a priori* assumption of a 'positive' method. This position, he claims, is 'either a circular demonstration or a familar partisan claim (of the kind made by almost all parties) that others are biased but that, by definition, we are not. That was the fool's way out of the very difficult problem.'[18]

The question arises as to the exact meaning of Williams's warning, for there are at least two different conceptions of dogmatism which could be drawn from it. On the one hand, dogmatism can be conceived of as a position which refuses to examine its own premises and/or give reasons for its tenets. On the other hand, dogmatism can be conceived as the position which purports to have the truth, to the exclusion of other positions. Implicit in this version is the claim that a knowable distinction between science and ideology is impossible. I fully agree with the first definition of dogmatism. But then one must point out that it cannot possibly be applied to Marx because he did not want to exclude his method from scrutiny and, whatever one thinks of his claim to positive science, he certainly tried to substantiate his theory by means of concrete analyses and by proposing specific explanations of its formation. Marx did not just 'assume' he had a truly scientific approach, he also tried to justify it by tightly argued discussion. One may disagree with his arguments, but it does not make sense to accuse him of dogmatism in the first sense.

As for the second definition of dogmatism, I cannot agree with it. The implication is that a knowable distinction between science and ideology is impossible, or even, in some extreme cases, that all claim to truth is inherently dogmatic. One is here on the terrain of a relativist objection. Although this does not seem to be Williams's intention, one has to deal with its implications for a negative concept of ideology. For a start I would like to make two preliminary observations. First, as I have already shown, Marx did not conceive of the relationship between science and ideology as the opposition between truth and error. But even if this is clear, one cannot escape from the fact that any negative concept of ideology is bound to be presented as different from science, or, at the very least, presupposes the possibility of a non-ideological point of view. Second, it is true that Marx's conception of science at the stage of *The German Ideology* was somewhat limited. In trying to emphasise that he started from the opposite end to the young Hegelians, he assumed an oversimplified notion of material reality, as if it were just a matter of summoning it up and empirically verifying its true character. There is no trace yet of the distinction which Marx later introduced between the phenomenal forms or appearances and the essential or inner relations of material reality. Such a distinction demands a different, more sophisticated, concept of science which, by means of abstraction, penetrates appearances to uncover their inner relations.[19]

However, the relativist objection has not yet disappeared since it is still possible to question whether any particular position can successfully claim that it has penetrated the appearances of reality. This is a difficulty which Lazar has recently raised. The problem for him is that 'both ideologists and scientists claim to capture the essence of reality', and therefore the crucial question is 'how are we to discriminate between unjustifiable and justifiable claims to scientific status?'[20] It seems to me that it is a mistake to search for a guarantee or abstract principle which can, *a priori*, help us discriminate between science and ideology. The problem is that, ultimately, in the social sciences one can give reasons for holding a position, but there cannot exist final guarantees which could convince everyone of a certain position. More often than not this is not even possible in natural sciences.[21] The search for an abstract guarantee of scientificity is in vain, and as problematic as the dogmatic assumption of scientificity. Yet from this fact one cannot then deduce that science is impossible, or that there is no way of distinguishing between science and ideology. Relativism and scepticism are self-defeating and contradictory, for they implicitly postulate the absolute truth of their own positions.

In fact, all positions necessarily posit a claim to validity. This is so even if one says that one's position is only relatively valid, for in the end one has to accept a proposition which is not relative, namely that one's position is only relatively valid.[22] To this extent the position that denies the distinction between truth and error is bound implicitly to reintroduce the same distinction. One cannot therefore criticise Marxism for dogmatism because it claims to have the truth. This is an *a priori* of all positions. One can criticise the specific way in which a claim to validity is justified, but not the fact that that claim is posited. Marxism can be proved wrong or right on specific propositions, or even on the whole of its approach. But this must be shown by a concrete analysis of the substance of its arguments. To raise, as an objection of principle to Marxism, the fact that it implicitly lays claim to validity, and yet cannot give a final guarantee, is also a fool's way out of a very difficult problem.

The truth: epistemological or ontological reality?

None the less some Marxist approaches which still want to keep a negative concept of ideology are not satisfied that Marxism itself can claim not to be ideological. Rossi-Landi, for instance, proposes a definition of ideology as false thought which he distinguishes from false consciousness by its higher level of intellectual elaboration. Thus in his view ideology is 'a discursive rationalisation and partial or total theoretical systematisation of a state of false consciousness'.[23] Now both reactionary thought and revolutionary thought are ideological in his account because they both stem from a distorted social practice. The idea that only reactionary thought is ideological seems to Rossi-Landi a dangerous illusion which is based on the 'mythical' belief that one can possess a unique revolutionary and demystifying science which fixes once and for all the road to follow. This is against the spirit of Marxism. However, when Rossi-Landi proposes that both Marxism and reactionary thought are false thought and therefore ideological, he has in mind a different meaning of falsity.

According to him, falsity can be conceived as the opposite to truth as part of an epistemological distinction which entails the existence of some criteria of truth. Yet falsity can also be conceived as a precarious or alienated situation independently from any confrontation with the truth.[24] 'False' here refers to thought that stems from a conflictive or unsatisfactory social organisation. It is in this second sense that both revolutionary and reactionary thoughts are false, for they both stem from the contradictions and limitations of the capitalist situation. In this Rossi-Landi follows the Gramscian idea that all ideologies spring from the terrain of contradictions; but whereas Gramsci abandons the use of 'falsity' as an apt description of ideologies, Rossi-Landi maintains it. However, just as Gramsci thought that Marxism was the most conscious and lucid expression of those contradictions, Rossi-Landi, too, accepts that revolutionary thought is ideological in a different manner. Reactionary ideologies tend to avoid connection with the appropriate practice, whereas the revolutionary ideology tends to seek unity with the appropriate practice.[25] All ideology is related to a false practice, but while the conservative ideology aspires to keep social practice as it is, the revolutionary ideology refers itself to a future practice which will replace the present social practice.

According to Rossi-Landi, the conservative ideologies need to present themselves as non-ideological in order to maintain an alienated social practice. Revolutionary ideologies, on the contrary, must renounce all pretence and must recognise their own ideological character, and thus become able to unmask the discourse of other ideologies which claim not to be ideological. Hence he totally reverses Marx's position, for Marx denied the ideological character of his own ideas. In the end Rossi-Landi proposes that all discourses are ideological because a precarious social reality makes them so. One of the problems of this account is, in my view, the lack of specificity of the concept of ideology. Ideology becomes so extended as to include all linguistic elaborations which spring from a contradictory society. Is it really worth while extending ideology that much? I do not believe so. Indeed, Rossi-Landi could have written his book without referring to ideology at all. It would have sufficed to introduce a distinction between theory and consciousness, and to clarify that both of them are rendered false by deficient social practice. The concept of ideology appears in this only to duplicate the role of theory or linguistic elaborations, but it adds no specific features to them. Within such a framework the utility of the concept seems questionable.

An interesting problem which arises from this conception concerns the underlying concept of truth. In describing false thought and false practice as basically alienated situations, Rossi-Landi is implicitly substituting an ontological concept of truth for the traditional epistemological concept. Whereas for Marx it was crucial to distinguish between ideological and non-ideological thought by means of an epistemological judgement, for Rossi-Landi the important thing is to focus on the basic situation of alienation, as it is the common terrain from which both Marxism and other theories emerge. Alienation involves negativity, 'a general disfunction in the development of social practice',[26] but it is not an epistemological distortion which refers to a true understanding; rather, it is a negative situation in reality which refers to a different reality which *could* (not 'ought to') be practically created. Implicitly Rossi-Landi opposes a 'true' future practice to the present false practice.

This idea of truth, I think, belongs to the best Marxist tradition and ought not to be lightly dismissed. Yet I do not believe that it can totally displace the epistemological conception of truth. In fact, it might be possible to argue that the very distinction between an ontological and an epistemological concept of truth would not have satisfied Marx. As he put it, the question concerning the truth of a theory was a practical question.[27] However, he also argued that the rational solution to theoretical problems was to be found 'in human practice and in the comprehension of this practice'.[28] Therefore, for Marx the concept of truth involved not only practice but also its comprehension. One can compare this position with other conceptions in order to explore its significance.

Idealism conceives of truth as something immanent, as the outcome of rationality in thought. There is no question of an outside reality to which thought should correspond. As Hegel put it, 'in the philosophical sense of the word . . . truth may be described, in general abstract terms, as the agreement of a thought-content with itself'.[29] Notwithstanding the emphasis on thought and the subject, Hegel's concept is not epistemological but ontological in so far as for him the rational is the real. Thus he gives the example of the 'true' friend which means a friend whose behaviour corresponds with the notion of friendship. In this sense, he goes on, untrue is equivalent to bad or self-discordant, and 'of such bad objects we may form a correct representation, but the import of such representation is inherently false'.[30] Hegel's idealism is therefore ontological, not epistemological, and this is shown by his concept of truth.

In a different manner, positivism also puts forward a conception of truth which does not depend upon the subject. It accepts the traditional epistemological definition of truth as '*adequatio rei et intellectus*', but this relation of adequacy is thought of as independent of man's knowledge of it. So a distinction is made between truth itself, which is in reality, and its verification by human beings, which could lie in the future.[31] Whereas for idealism the 'notion' was reality, for positivism reality does not include its notion at all. Marx is critical of both these ideas, as the first Thesis on Feuerbach demonstrates. Both versions presuppose that there is an absolute, ready-made truth which a special kind of knowledge can eventually grasp. For Marx there is no absolute truth waiting to be unveiled, but there is an objective historical truth which deploys itself in the historical process as men and women practically construct their social world. However, this does not mean that Marx adopts a pragmatic conception whereby truth becomes that which is useful or adaptive for the individual, nor does it mean that men and women can arbitrarily produce reality as they wish.

Truth is neither in reality itself nor in the subject conceived of as separate spheres. Truth does not pre-exist the subjects nor does it pre-exist reality. Truth is constantly being produced as the subjects build up a reality in which they themselves are an important part. However, the practical construction of reality is not carried out by a practice which is fully conscious or undetermined. This is why the products of human practice acquire independence from men and women and confront them as an objective power which they do not control. This is also the reason why reality appears external to the subjects and why the concept of truth appears independent from the subject's knowledge of it. Yet precisely because that reality has been constructed by means of practice, it can be criticised and changed. Truth therefore cannot be exhausted in the intellectual adequacy to what exists as long as what exists is contradictory and does not seem right. As Adorno expressed it, 'the idea of scientific truth cannot be split off from that of a true society'.[32]

One can say that Marx's concept of truth entails elements of the Hegelian ontological tradition in so far as he did not accept the existing state of society as an absolute norm against which the truth of a judgement should be measured. The epistemological version that truth is the adequacy of consciousness to reality is modified by Marx, for reality itself should be transformed and 'made adequate' so that it may become a 'true' reality. In this sense Marx would agree that a 'bad' state is an 'untrue' state. However, he distanced himself from the Hegelian notion that a bad state is an untrue state because it does not meet the requirements of the notion of such a state. For Marx the notion derives from the state, not the other way around. So the notion can hardly constitute a norm which is prior to, and the essence of, the state itself.

None the less Marx would not accept that a bad and contradictory reality makes 'untrue' all forms of consciousness derived from it, and so he would not have agreed with Rossi-Landi's use of 'false thought' to refer to Marxism. An ontological concept of truth cannot do without epistemological judgements. If, by false thought, Rossi-Landi means 'thought separated from a true practice', it is still necessary for him to be able to recognise what true practice is, and to comprehend the contradictions which make a practice 'bad'. Here the need arises for deciding whether the 'understanding' of practice is adequate or inadequate in an epistemological sense. This is why Marx maintained that the rational solution to theoretical problems was to be found not only in human practice but also in the comprehension of that practice. From this he claimed that his thought was not distorted and therefore non-ideological. Of course, he also accepted that both his thought and the thought of the bourgeoisie arose from the alienated and contradictory situation of capitalist society. But it is safer not to call this situation 'false' so as not to induce the mistaken idea that all knowledge produced in capitalist society is epistemologically impaired.

I have argued that for Marx ideology originates in a 'limited material mode of activity'. Rossi-Landi may respond that Marxism does so as well. He is right in the sense that the historical situation which stimulated the development of Marx's thought was an alienated situation in which men and women had lost control of their products. However, this is not the whole picture. Marx's revolutionary thought was based not merely upon a 'limited social practice' but also upon a revolutionary practice which reacted against the existing situation. This revolutionary practice was already an anticipation of the 'true practice' of the new society and did not share all the limitations of daily practice which reproduced the dominant relations of production. To this extent Rossi-Landi's idea that the unity of consciousness with a true practice can be achieved only in the future is only partially accurate. That unity will be *fully* achieved in the future; but it is already anticipated in the practice which seeks to change the existing state of society.

The foundations of the critique of ideology

In discussing ideology and utopia, Mannheim propounds at a certain point a 'quest for reality' whose motto is 'thought should contain neither less nor more than the reality in whose medium it operates'.[33] Both ideology and utopia distort reality, the former because it conceals reality, the latter because it exceeds its limits. Marxism, on the contrary, holds that reality cannot adequately be defined without exceeding its present limits. Human beings are not limited to the comprehension of what already exists, nor can they understand the present without going beyond it. However, there are two ways in which theory can go beyond the present. One is to postulate a hypothetical state of society, a perfect model which, although it is not considered to be a historical future in any sense, serves as a paradigm against which the present social reality and all claims to validity are measured. The other is to postulate that, as human beings practically produce the new, an adequate comprehension of what exists in the present can only be given by reference to a historical future.[34]

Habermas seems to take the first view. Since for him ideology in advanced capitalism performs the task of systematically limiting communication without being seen to do so,

> a social theory critical of ideology can, therefore, identify the normative power built into the institutional system of a society only if it starts from the *model of the suppression of generalisable interests* and compares normative structures existing at a given time with the hypothetical state of a system of norms formed, *ceteris paribus*, discursively.[35]

What is interesting is that this hypothetical state in which rational consensus is achieved is not only the final criterion of truth against which all claims to validity have to be measured, but it also, according to Habermas, involves some assumption about the kind of social organisation which might allow a discursively achieved consensus. The 'ideal speech situation' connects truth with freedom and justice. As this ideal state – in which truth, freedom and justice become possible – is anticipated in all speech-acts, the critique of ideology finds its normative foundation in the very structure of language.

Habermas's counterfactual model operates in a manner similar to Lukács's category of 'objective possibility', according to which

> by relating consciousness to the whole of society it becomes possible to infer the thoughts and feelings which men would have in a particular situation if they were *able* to assess both it and the interests arising from it in their impact on immediate action and on the whole structure of society.[36]

One can compare this statement with Habermas's:

> how would the members of a social system, at a given stage in the development of productive forces, have collectively and bindingly interpreted their needs (and which norms would they have accepted as justified) if they could and would have decided on organisation of social intercourse through discursive will-formation, with adequate knowledge of the limiting conditions and functional imperatives of their society?[37]

Of course, there are many differences between Lukács and Habermas, yet the similarity of approach in this context is striking. The comparison of existing structures with those which hypothetically would exist if human beings possessed adequate knowledge allows Lukács to ascertain the ideological nature of psychological class consciousness, and allows Habermas to measure the degree of ideology in a given society.

The problem with this account is that it makes the critique of ideology, and even human emancipation, dependent upon the reconstruction of a hypothetical state of perfect rationality which is totally disconnected from historical practice. Just as Lukács's 'imputed consciousness' flows from the very structure of the class being, Habermas's free and just society necessary for a rational consensus flows from the very structure of language. Ideology, therefore, is not criticised in terms of a different society which human beings can practically construct, but it is criticised in terms of an abstract, unhistorical and ascribed 'ought-to-be'. The scope of emancipation is no longer dependent upon a conscious transformative practice. It is rather the ideal model as anticipated in basic structures of language that normatively and counterfactually fixes the scope of emancipation.

However, in practice, this regulative model is too abstract to be able to provide concrete criteria which can pass judgement on specific theories and political programmes. For, as Held has pointed out, even if

> we have opted for argument, and discourse has begun, the old questions re-emerge: Does the symmetry requirement (the requirement that there should be a symmetrical distribution in chances to select and employ speech acts) set bounds on the

> kind of theoretical and practical positions that can be established? How do we judge the force of the better argument? What kinds of evidence can legitimately be employed? How do we solve disputes between competing positions claiming to establish objective moral and political stances?[38]

The very attempt to construct such a hypothetical state begs the question because it presupposes the previous existence of criteria which it itself is supposed to provide. To this extent the practical construction of an unimpeachable model is an impossible task.

As for the second view which refers the present to a historical future, I have already anticipated in the discussion of Rossi-Landi's position that there are at least two ways in which this reference to the future can be made. On the one hand, present reality can be referred to a future model, the classless society, which is conceived as its total opposite. It is a future which has no connections with present practice other than its negation. Before that model is achieved, thought is inevitably ideological in so far as it stems from a contradictory society. A non-ideological consciousness is only possible in the future but not in the present. On the other hand, the future can be conceived not as a mere negation, but as the realisation and fulfilment of elements already existent in present society by means of a conscious practice of transformation. This practice and its comprehension justifies the claim to a non-ideological thought in the present. While the former way refers a deficient practice to an absolute future model, the latter refers a possible future to present transformative practice.

Some elements of the first interpretation can be found in Gramsci and Rossi-Landi. The latter, as we have seen, maintains that 'the synthesis of consciousness and practice – the consciousness and practice that must be reunited – exists only in the future. Which means that in this moment it exists merely in thought, not as a reality outside thought.'[39] Although Gramsci, contrary to Rossi-Landi, does not accept a negative concept of ideology, he opposes the 'reign of necessity', that is, class society, the terrain of contradictions and struggles, to the 'reign of freedom', which will be free of contradictions. As Marxism is an expression of class society, of historical contradictions, it necessarily shares in the limitations of all ideologies, and will therefore disappear in the reign of freedom. Both authors consequently oppose the present to the future in such a way that a non-ideological point of view is impossible in the present. One of the problems of this position is the implicit identification of necessity with contradiction. The consequences of this are examined further below in the last section. Another problem with this conception is how to conceive the movement from the present class society to the classless society, how to overcome the illusion of a sudden leap from necessity to freedom. Gramsci states that the philosopher of praxis 'cannot escape from the present field of contradictions, he cannot affirm, other than generically, a world without contradictions, without immediately creating a utopia'.[40] When the relationship between present and future is depicted in terms of a deficient present which is confronted by a future plenitude, the question arises as to how these two worlds can bridge the enormous distance that separates them.

A temptation which Gramsci and Rossi-Landi avoid is to resort to the idea of an overall meaning of history which secures the passage from necessity to freedom, though this is one possible answer. Goldmann, for instance, draws an analogy between Marx's historical materialism and Pascal's wager. According to Goldmann, Marx has to bet on the meaningful character of history just as Pascal bets on the existence of God. While the latter is a wager upon transcendence, the former is a wager upon immanence, but both share the same Augustinian principle: *credo ut intelligam*. The beginning of knowledge is an act of faith. In order to understand human life and society, social science has to start with a double wager on the meaningfulness of history as a whole and of partial structures in particular. However, in a manner similar to the way in which Pascal's God is hidden and exists in an uncertain certainty, there can be no certainty about the meaning of history either.[41]

Less uncertain than Goldmann, Bloch asserts the existence of a meaning of history and thinks that Marx provides the notion of a final goal. The proletarian's self-creation, as the subject of history, will be fully revealed only under socialism. As Schmidt points out, Bloch comes back time and again to the idea that a more rational society is 'a realisation of the sense of the world process'.[42] If this is so, then the judgement of present reality can be made from the point of view of a future which is necessary. Utopian consciousness may be 'rectified – but never refuted by the mere power of that which, at any particular time, is. On the contrary, it confutes and judges the existent if it is failing, and failing inhumanly; indeed, first and foremost it provides the standard to measure such facticity precisely as departure from the Right.'[43] True, Bloch explicitly acknowledges a difference between the abstractions of the utopian socialists and Marx's analysis of the present as the basis for any anticipation of the future. Yet the autonomy of the future model is implicit in his conception of the meaning of history, which tends to appear as a self-reproducing principle of being. For Bloch, the overall meaning of history tends to become a substitute for human practice.

It seems to me that the conception of the future as the realisation of elements already existent in present society gives a better account. The future is not a total negation of the present but a reality which can be positively, though partially and imperfectly, found in the present. I agree with Schmidt that if one is to find a utopia in Marx's thought – because it goes beyond the limits of present society – that utopia is negative.[44] But it is negative in the sense that it avoids depicting concrete features which could give a precise idea of the content of a more rational society, not in the sense of being a reality radically discontinuous with the present. The more rational society is justified not in abstract, as a model, or as the necessary result of an overall meaning of history, but only as the legitimate possibility of changing the given social relations through a transforming practice. It is precisely because Marx refuses to give specific content to future society that he cannot conceive of it as radically opposed to the present society: he has to start from the analysis of the present. This is a point which he strongly emphasises in discussing the Paris Commune: 'The working class did not expect miracles from the Commune. They have no ready-made Utopias to introduce '*par décret du peuple*' . . . They have no ideals to realise, but to set free the elements of the new society with which the old collapsing bourgeois society itself is pregnant.'[45]

Marx does not believe in an overall meaning of history which is prior to human practice. He is highly critical of those conceptions which present history as the realisation of the Idea, Reason or Providence. Not that history is irrational. But its rationality is not predetermined in a necessary pattern, it is realised as it moves forward. The sense of history has no independent reality and must always be traced to men and women acting in accordance with their situation. Marx criticised Bauer because, for him, 'man exists so that history may exist' and hence '*history*, like *truth*, becomes a person apart, a metaphysical subject of which the real human individuals are merely the bearers'.[46] For Marx on the contrary, history is created by human beings who practically deploy themselves, and who in doing so give history its meaning. Thus Marx's theory is non-teleological. It does not propound a final goal that has to be achieved, just as it does not postulate an immanent drive which leads history towards a necessary end.[47] Marx explicitly rejected the interpretation of a critic who

> insists on transforming my historical sketch of the genesis of capitalism in Western Europe into an historico-philosophic theory of the general path of development prescribed by fate to all nations, whatever the historical circumstances in which they find themselves . . . events strikingly analogous but taking place in different historical surroundings led to totally different results. By studying each of these forms of evolution separately and then comparing them one can easily find the clue to this phenomenon, but one will never arrive there by using as one's master key a general historico-philosophical theory, the supreme virtue of which consists in being supra-historical.[48]

In going beyond the present Marx is only projecting the possibilities embedded in present society. He hoped to detect the chances of concrete freedom emerging from a world of domination. But he did not depict a 'reign of freedom' which is as bound to come as the Kingdom of God. Thus there was no need for Marx to refer to a future model in order to sustain his critique of ideology. It is the analysis of present reality itself which provided him with a basis for this critique.

Are there any guarantees that Marx's analysis is better than any others, or is itself scientifically sound? I have already argued that there can be no general guarantees. All that we can ask, in order to avoid dogmatism, is that the elements in present reality which allow the projection into the future are identified in as rigorous a manner as possible. Marx was perfectly aware of the challenge and explicitly maintained that 'if we did not find concealed in society as it is the material conditions of production and the corresponding relations of exchange prerequisite for a classless society, then all attempts to explode it would be quixotic'.[49] His critique of utopian socialists precisely stressed the point that they postulated a historical future without analysing the factors in present reality which were to surpass their present form.

Marx put forward his own analysis by contrasting it to the utopian socialists. They 'want to depict socialism as the realisation of the ideals of *bourgeois* society', they want that 'exchange and exchange-value, etc., are *originally* (in time) or *essentially* (in their adequate form) a system of universal freedom and equality, but that they have been perverted by money, capital, etc.' Marx, on the contrary, maintained that exchange-value or the money system 'is in fact the system of equality and freedom, and that the disturbances which they encounter in the further development of the system are disturbances inherent in it, are merely the realisation of *equality and freedom*, which prove to be inequality and unfreedom'.[50] What Marx intended to show was that the very relations which purport equality in fact produce inequality, and that the dominant relations of exchange set up on the basis of equivalence conceal exploitation without, however, formally violating that equivalence. This was discussed above in Chapter 1.

What is important in the present context is to underline the fact that Marx's reference to the future is based upon the analysis which shows that the equivalent exchange of values at the level of the market is contradicted by the intrinsic inequality of exchange at the level of production. It is this basic inequality concealed behind the appearances of the market which allowed Marx to present capitalist social relations as 'twisted and inverted' and which explains the emergence of contradictions and the development of class struggle. This struggle seeks ultimately to redress that basic inequality. Hence Marx does not propound a moral concept of equality to which future relations should be adapted, but simply propounds an end to the extraction and appropriation of surplus-value by the capitalist or anyone else. This is the task which is set for men and women to carry out and which projects itself into a new kind of society. The very fact that for many people this task has become conscious indicates that the conditions for its practical realisation are already present.

The end of ideology: two opposite versions

We have already seen that in order to understand Marx's concept of ideology it is necessary to distinguish between the end of ideology and the critique of ideology. The former can only be achieved through practice, by solving in reality the social contradictions which gave rise to the particular ideological form. However, Marx's idea that humankind sets itself only those tasks which it can accomplish poses the problem as to whether it is possible for men and women to build a new society which is able to eliminate all contradictions, thus abolishing the very roots of ideology and the need for its critique. Daniel Bell, for instance, thinks it is an extraordinary fact that Marx and other socialists sought to win the support of the masses for the idea of a new society and yet did not fully think out the shape of that future society and its problems. The reason for this, according to Bell, is in 'the apocalyptic belief that "the day after the revolution", rationality would make its heralded appearance on the historical scene and put all society aright'.[51] Bell is highly critical of Marx's belief in the possibility of the end of ideology. Yet he proposes a different version of the end of ideology which, in the main, announces the demise of Marxism.

Whereas Marx's end of ideology can only take place in the future, Bell's thesis is that ideology has already come to an end. Yet as they both hold radically different concepts of ideology, the respective meanings are not the same. Bell readily admits that his concept of ideology applies largely to the left-wing thought which emerged in the nineteenth century,[52] so his version of the end of ideology refers to the 'exhaustion of the nineteenth-century ideologies, particularly Marxism, as intellectual systems that could claim *truth* for their views of the world'.[53] Yet Bell emphasises not so much the intellectual power of ideology as its passion and the fact that it 'taps emotion', channelling human energy into political action. As he puts it, 'the nineteenth-century ideologies, by emphasising inevitability and by infusing passion into their followers, could compete with religion'.[54] For Bell the end of ideology means that ideology has lost its emotional appeal and its power to persuade. Marx, on the contrary, emphasised the cognitive aspects of ideology more than its passion and thought of its end not in terms of a loss of appeal but in terms of the resolution of the contradictions which gave rise to it.

However, there is one aspect of Bell's account which seems important. This is the fact that although he emphasises the emotive forces of nineteenth-century ideologies, he also suggests that these ideologies assumed 'that in the course of evolution "reason" would find its way and the perfect society would emerge'.[55] I think Bell is rash in assimilating Marx to Hegel in this context[56] because, as we have already pointed out, Marx did not believe in an overall meaning of history, nor in the Hegelian idea that history is the realisation of reason. Nevertheless, there is little doubt that Marx shared the nineteenth-century spirit which gave reason a privileged position. This is shown by the very concept of ideology which stressed the cognitive aspects more than emotive appeal. But then again, one has to bear in mind that for Marx ideology was not a belief system or an organic world-view which sought to persuade people of a final goal. Marx's concept was more restricted than Bell's because it included only distorted forms of thought. However, it is interesting to note that Bell's usage of the concept in the context of his 'end of ideology' thesis is more restricted than Marx's, for it excludes ideologies of the 'right' and considers only the exhaustion of nineteenth-century left-wing ideas. This is the main weakness of Bell's account. It is paradoxical that he should accuse left-wing ideologists of being 'terrible simplifiers' and providers of 'prepared formulae' and yet exclude right-wing ideologists from the same charge. Whereas Marx consistently applied his negative concept of ideology to all distortions which concealed contradictions, even those which appeared from within the working class, Bell unilaterally restricts his analysis of the end of ideology to left-wing systems. Ideology thus becomes negative and condemned to death – but only in the case of Marxism.

In the end, Bell's idea is that all ideology is a dogmatism in so far as 'by its nature it is an all-or-none affair'[57] demanding a blind faith in the inevitable arrival of utopia. For Bell this utopia is not possible in reality for it is only an illusion; in Herzen's words, 'an end that is infinitely remote is not an end, but, if you like, a trap'.[58] It is not that he wants to eliminate utopia or any kind of vision of the future. It is rather that he hopes to replace blind faith in a distant end by an empirical approach which specifies a possible end, how to get there, the cost of the enterprise and who is to pay. In Weber's terms, Bell wants to substitute a pragmatic 'ethic of responsibility' which seeks reconciliation as its goal for the principled 'ethic of conscience' which cannot be compromised.[59] What Bell does not seem to realise is that his pragmatic approach and his ethic of responsibility can also conceal a faith, not perhaps a faith in the future, but a faith in the status quo which assumes the same dogmatic character as that attributed to the ideologists. Bell's end of ideology is also the end of the possibility of radical change in society.

True, Bell later seems to qualify his views in a way that even allows him to speak of the persistence of ideologies. In dealing with Puritanism as an ideology, he maintains, for instance, that

> it is in the character of ideologies not only to reflect or justify an underlying reality but, once launched, to take on a life of their own. A truly powerful ideology opens up a new vision of life to the imagination; once formulated, it remains part of the moral repertoire to be drawn upon by intellectuals . . . unlike economies or outmoded technologies, they do not disappear . . . thus an ideology gnawed at, worried to the bone, argued about, dissected, and restated by an army of essayists, moralists, and intellectuals becomes a force in its own right.[60]

This new approach may lead one to believe that Bell has fundamentally modified his account of ideology. But this is more apparent than real.

In fact, as Bell himself acknowledges, 'the analysis of the "end of ideology" did not assume that all social conflict had ended and that the intelligentsia would forswear the search for new ideologies . . . the argument was also made that new ideologies would arise as a source of radicalism and that these would be third-world ideologies'.[61] In other words, Bell never wanted to deny the existence and persistence of ideologies other than Marxism. His point was that the nineteenth-century ideologies, and especially Marxism, had exhausted their appeal in the twentieth century, but not that ideology in general had perished. This point, apart from the fact that it has not been shown to be accurate in practice, highlights his unilateral analysis of the end of ideology.

At the opposite pole, Althusser puts forward the idea that ideology is an essential component part of all societies, including a future classless society. According to him,

> human societies secrete ideology as the very element and atmosphere indispensable to their historical respiration and life. Only an ideological world outlook could have imagined societies without ideology and accepted the utopian idea of a world in which ideology (not just one of its historical forms) would disappear . . . *historical materialism cannot conceive that even a communist society could ever do without ideology*.[62]

But Althusser's concept of ideology differs from Marx's and Bell's. Ideology appears as indispensable to every society because it functions as a 'cement' which unifies society and which teaches men and women how to respond to their condition; ideology is necessary because it secures the cohesion of society by adapting men and women to their roles in life. Without ideology society could not survive. Hence for Althusser ideology is neither a systematic body of ideas which fixes a social goal (Bell's concept), nor does it necessarily respond to social contradictions (Marx's concept), but it is rather a system of representations which constitutes and transforms men and women into subjects of a particular society.

For Althusser, therefore, ideology is a functional requirement for all societies and, as such, it can have no end. Despite the functionalist overtones of this conception, which seem rather odd in a Marxist theory, Althusser contrives to keep a negative concept of ideology by maintaining that ideological representations are distortions. These distortions are socially necessary because of the opaque nature of the social totality, or, as he puts it, 'the opacity of the social structure makes necessarily *mythical* the representation of the world necessary for social cohesion'.[63] In this way he conflates a functional imperative with a negative concept of ideology. The result is that ideological distortions can never be abolished, even if social contradictions disappear. Althusser's conception is therefore the opposite to Bell's. While for the latter ideology has already lost its importance, for the former ideology is a permanent and necessary feature of all societies. It is clear, however, that they are speaking of totally different concepts of ideology. None the less Althusser's position makes it easier for a Marxist to answer Bell's accusation that Marxism depends on the dogmatic belief that the day after the revolution rationality will be installed for ever. For Althusser's theory this is just an ideological belief which has nothing to do with Marxism. But it seems to me that, in its turn, Althusser's Marxism has little to do with Marx's original position.[64]

Socialism and the end of ideology

Inasmuch as Marx defines ideology in relation to social contradictions, there can be no doubt that overcoming contradiction in practice entails the disappearance of ideology. The classless society, based on a communist mode of production and anticipated by Marx, necessarily postulates the end of ideology. I have already argued, following Schmidt, that Marx's utopia is negative in that it refuses to provide a fully worked-out picture of such a society. Marx avoided the construction of an arbitrary ideal model which should be imposed upon reality like the ready-made utopias of former socialists. Nevertheless, as Schmidt also points out, a basic idea runs through the few passages in which Marx refers to this problem, namely 'the emancipation of *all sides* of human nature' or, what is the same, the establishment of the kingdom of freedom.[65] It goes almost without saying that the end of ideology contributes to that kingdom by emancipating human beings from the specific distortions produced by former contradictory relations.

Despite Marx's reluctance to specify the contents of the kingdom of freedom, there is a clear evolution in his conception of it. In his early approach Marx conceived of communism as the total and final transcendence of necessity. As he put it,

> *communism* is the *positive* supersession of *private property* as human self-estrangement, and hence the true *appropriation* of the *human* essence through and for man; it is the complete restoration of man to himself as a *social*, i.e. human, being, a restoration which has become conscious . . . it is the *genuine* resolution of the conflict between man and nature, and between man and man, the true resolution of the conflict between existence and being, between objectification and self-affirmation, between freedom and necessity, between individual and species.[66]

In *The German Ideology*, Marx even suggested that the division of labour itself is to be abolished.[67]

Later, in *Capital*, Marx realised that the total and final resolution of the conflict between necessity and freedom cannot be achieved: freedom can only expand upon the basis of necessity and, therefore, it can never be total. As he put it,

> Freedom in this field can only consist in socialised man, the associated producers, rationally regulating their interchange with Nature, bringing it under their common control, instead of being ruled by it as by blind forces of Nature; and achieving this with the least expenditure of energy and under conditions most favourable to, and worthy of their human nature. But it none the less still remains a realm of necessity. Beyond it begins that development of human energy which is an end in itself, the true realm of freedom, which however, can blossom forth only with this realm of necessity as its basis. The shortening of the working-day is its basic prerequisite.[68]

This formulation is far more cautious than the one in the *Economic and Philosophical Manuscripts*, recognising that necessity will not disappear in the realm of freedom. Additionally, as Schmidt points out, in *Capital* it is no longer the complete abolition of the division of labour which is in question. Marx refers instead to the '*abolition of the old division of labour*'.[69]

Some theorists implicitly identify the reign of necessity with the terrain of contradictions, Gramsci in particular. If it were to be shown, as Marx has, that the realm of necessity cannot be entirely dispensed with in the realm of freedom, it would follow that contradictions could not be totally eliminated and therefore ideology would not disappear. It would therefore be inconsistent to believe, like Gramsci, that 'in the reign of "freedom" thought and ideas can no longer be born on the terrain of contradictions and the necessity of struggle'.[70] But then Gramsci, unlike Marx, thought that necessity and freedom exclude one another. It seems more realistic to believe that necessity will remain at the basis of freedom. But there is no need to identify necessity with contradictions. It may well be that the former is a *conditio sine qua non* of the latter, but it is not a sufficient condition. Necessity does not of itself entail contradiction; it can be found both in a class-divided society and in a society in which associated free producers rationally regulate their interchange with nature and with one another so that there is no antagonism among them. Thus even if necessity subsists in the kingdom of freedom, ideology would disappear in so far as contradictions no longer existed.

In addition to the above-mentioned evolution in his conception of the realm of freedom Marx also conceived some necessary elements in the process of emancipation. First, Marx affirmed that 'liberation is an historical and not a mental act'[71] which 'can only take place in a practical movement, a *revolution*'. This has implications for the ideological distortions which weaken working-class politics, for, as Marx indicates, revolution is necessary 'not only because the *ruling* class cannot be overthrown in any other way, but also because the class *overthrowing* it can only in a revolution succeed in ridding itself of all the muck of ages and become fitted to found society anew'.[72]

Second, notwithstanding the necessity for the proletariat 'to organise itself as a class' and to 'make itself the ruling class' by means of a revolution, the purpose of such activity is to sweep away 'the conditions for the existence of class antagonisms and of classes generally' thus abolishing 'its own supremacy as a class'.[73] This is why Marx claimed that 'the condition for the emancipation of the working class is the abolition of all classes'.[74] Third, in so far as the state is connected with the need of a class to oppress others, the disappearance of class distinctions demands that 'the public power will lose its political character'.[75] Finally, communism must overturn 'the basis of all earlier relations of production'[76] so that the freely associated producers bring under their control society and the forces of nature. Clearly, all these elements cannot be conceived as a single act which happens overnight. This is why Marx proposed that 'between capitalist and communist society lies the period of the revolutionary transformation of the one into the other. Corresponding to this is also a political transition period in which the state can be nothing but the *revolutionary dictatorship of the proletariat*.'[77]

It is extremely important to have these elements in mind in order to evaluate any claim that contradictions have been overcome or that ideology has been surpassed. For the question which immediately arises is whether historical socialist societies are in a position to make such a claim. At least part of this claim has been explicitly made by Stalin's Soviet Constitution of 1936. This Constitution proclaimed the end of the class struggle in Russia. According to this document, different classes still exist, but no conflict emerges between them because the means of production and the production process are controlled by the 'socialist state' and, as the official version of Kuusinen puts it, 'since they jointly own social property and jointly participate in the social production process, all peoples are equal and their relations are based on the principles of comradely cooperation, and mutual assistance'.[78] Hence a 'socialist mode of production' or a 'socialist society' is supposed to have existed since 1936, under the direction of a 'socialist state' which no longer has an oppressive character because it is the 'state of the whole people'. Consequently, the 'transition from capitalism to socialism', the stage of the dictatorship of the proletariat in Stalin's terms, is over.[79] This interpretation remains the official view of the Soviet regime.

The Stalinist model conceives of ideology in positive terms and refers to 'Marxism-Leninism' as the official ideology of the Soviet state. To this extent the notion of the end of ideology is absent. Yet if one were to take ideology as a distortion which arises from and conceals contradictions, the logic of the Stalinist model would imply that ideology in this sense could no longer exist in Soviet society because contradictions have disappeared, together with the abolition of the dictatorship of the proletariat, since at least 1936. If the Soviet official doctrine does not envisage the end of ideology in a socialist society, this is not because it considers socialism as a contradictory transitional stage in which class struggle continues to exist, but simply because it holds a positive concept of ideology. Although one cannot argue against a claim which Soviet Marxism does not make (the end of ideology), it is possible to examine the basis of such a claim inasmuch as it is present in such a doctrine. This is useful because it allows us to probe further the meaning and conditions of the end of ideology. In my view, by asserting that antagonisms have disappeared from Soviet society, Stalinism does not only objectively suggest a basis for a claim to the end of ideological distortions, but also falls into the ideological trap of denying the contradictions which exist in that society.

The Stalinist conception of socialism is very different from the picture that Marx and Engels drew. Indeed, it can also be argued that it fundamentally differs from Lenin's conception.[80] Whereas for these three authors the transition from capitalism to communism requires the dictatorship of the proletariat, or socialism, Stalin proposes two separate intermediate stages: first, the 'transition to socialism' or dictatorship of the proletariat (from 1917 up to 1936); and second (from 1936 onward), a 'socialist mode of production' directed by the socialist state. Communism in this perspective comes as a third stage. This means that for Stalin in the socialist stage there are classes but no class struggles, and there is a state but not an oppressive state. The problem with this conception is that, within Marxism, it does not make sense to separate the existence of classes from class struggle or to separate the state from class oppression. To Marx, Engels and Lenin the socialist transition was precisely a period when the state existed as an expression of the ruling power of the working class. They never envisaged a 'socialist mode of production' or a 'transition to socialism', but rather a period of transition to the communist mode of production, a transition which they called socialism and which entailed the existence of contradictions, class rule and oppressive state.

There are of course many difficult problems still to be solved if one is to have a clear picture of socialist transition. For instance, how can one understand a class system in which there is no private ownership of the means of production? A discussion of this and other related issues concerning socialism is beyond the scope of this book. Suffice it to say that the survival of capitalist forms of exploitation within socialism is theoretically possible because the disappearance of the private ownership of the means of production at the juridical level does not necessarily entail a change in the economic forms of property.[81] Be this as it may, the socialist transition certainly meant for Marx, Engels and Lenin a phase of struggle between capitalist and communist elements which necessarily involved the existence of class struggle. As Balibar has pointed out, it is ironic that Stalin's declaration that class antagonisms have disappeared came 'only a few years after the collectivisation of agriculture' and, above all, 'at the very moment when there began to develop in the whole country, and among all classes, what we now know to have been a bloody mass repression, of which the great "Moscow trials" were only the visible and spectacular facade'.[82] This shows that the claim of any socialist society to having overcome all contradictions is clearly ideological

– in a negative sense. It is a claim that seeks to conceal the existence of domination.

The end of ideology, therefore, can only be achieved in the realm of freedom (communist society) but not in socialist society.[83] Hinkelammert has pointed out that the realm of freedom ought to be interpreted as a limit-concept (as counterfactual), an ideal to which society can only approximate without ever entirely achieving.[84] According to this view, socialism may *orientate* itself towards the association of free men and women that Marx envisaged as the communist society, but it will never totally reach it. This may or may not be so. But even if it is true, the very idea of a classless society without ideology performs a very important task. It functions as a constant reminder that the struggle for liberation must continue and that all attempts to claim that contradictions have already disappeared in socialist societies are themselves ideological. A critique of ideology, therefore, is a necessity not only within capitalism, but also within socialism.

Notes and References

Introduction

1. M. Seliger, *The Marxist Conception of Ideology*, Cambridge University Press, Cambridge, 1977.
2. C. Geertz, *The Interpretation of Culture*, Hutchinson, London, 1973, p.199.

Chapter 1

1. For a brief discussion of this historical material see J. Larrain, *The Concept of Ideology*, Hutchinson, London, 1979, ch. 1.
2. L. Althusser, *Lenin and Philosophy and Other Essays*, New Left Books, London, 1971, pp.151, 149.
3. Colletti has shown how Marx anticipates in his early writings many of the themes that he develops later, including the fetishism of commodities. See 'Introduction' to K. Marx, *Early Writings* (ed. L. Colletti), Penguin, Harmondsworth, 1975, p.47.
4. A particularly suggestive analysis can be found in the work of R. Echeverría, 'Marx's Concept of Science', doctoral thesis, Birkbeck College, London, 1978, which I have followed in certain aspects.
5. Ibid, ch.3.
6. See K. Marx, Letter to Ruge, September 1843, in *Early Writings*, p.209; and *Economic and Philosophical Manuscripts*, also in *Early Writings* pp.381–2, 392–3.
7. See Colletti, 'Introduction' to *Early Writings*, p.22–24.
8. K. Marx, 'Critique of Hegel's Doctrine of the State, in *Early Writings*, p.98.
9. Ibid, p.99.
10. Ibid, p.158.
11. Ibid, p.160.
12. Ibid, p.158.
13. Ibid, p.145.
14. Ibid, p.127.
15. Ibid, p.145.
16. K. Marx, 'A Contribution to the Critique of Hegel's *Philosophy of Right*. Introduction', *Early Writings*, p.244.
17. Ibid.
18. Ibid.
19. Ibid.
20. Ibid, p.251.
21. Ibid.
22. Ibid.

23. Ibid, p.257.
24. M.Löwy has shown that the distinction is drawn from Feuerbach's *Provisional Theses for the Reform of Philosophy*. See *La théorie de la révolution chez le jeune Marx*, Maspero, Paris, 1970, pp.69–75.
25. L. Goldmann, *Marxisme et sciences humaines*, Gallimard, Paris, 1970, pp.152–3.
26. K. Marx, 'Preface' to *A Contribution to the Critique of Political Economy*, in Marx–Engels, *Selected Works in One Volume*, Lawrence & Wishart, London, 1970, p.183.
27. F. Engels, 'Foreword' of 1888 to *Ludwig Feuerbach and the End of Classical German Philosophy*, in *Selected Works*, p.585.
28. See Echeverría, 'Marx's Concept of Science', p.73. See also 'La ideología capitalista y el principio de la igualdad', mimeo, Santiago, n.d., p.3.
29. J. McCarney, *The Real World of Ideology*, Harvester Press, Brighton, 1980, p.82.
30. J. Mepham, 'The Theory of Ideology in *Capital*', in J. Mepham and D.-H. Ruben (eds), *Issues in Marxist Philosophy*, 3 vols, Harvester Press, Brighton, 1979, vol. III, pp.144–5.
31. Althusser, *Lenin and Philosophy*, p.150.
32. A. Schmidt, *The Concept of Nature in Marx*, New Left Books, London, 1971, p.114.
33. See K. Marx and F. Engels, *The German Ideology*, Part I, Lawrence & Wishart, 1970, p.47. For a critique of *camera obscura*, see S. Kofman, *Camera Obscura*, Editions Galilee, Paris, 1973.
34. Marx and Engels, *The German Ideology*, p.47.
35. C. Arthur, 'Introduction' to *The German Ideology*, p.22.
36. K. Marx, 'Theses on Feuerbach', in *The German Ideology*, thesis I, p.121.
37. Marx and Engels, *The German Ideology*, p.41.
38. Ibid.
39. Ibid, p.63.
40. K. Marx, Letter to P. V. Annenkov, 28 December 1846, *Selected Correspondence*, Progress, Moscow, p.30.
41. Marx and Engels, *The German Ideology*, p.50.
42. Ibid, p.43.
43. Ibid, p.54.
44. Ibid, p.58.
45. Ibid, p.64.
46. Marx, 'Preface' to *A Contribution to the Critique of Political Economy* p.182.
47. Marx and Engels, *The German Ideology*, p.47.
48. Ibid, p.60.
49. Ibid, p.62.
50. Ibid, p.63.
51. Ibid, p.52.
52. Marx and Engels, *The German Ideology*, unabridged version in Marx–Engels, *Collected Works*, vol.5, Lawrence & Wishart, London, 1976, p.36.

53. Ibid.
54. K. Marx, *Grundrisse*, Penguin, Harmondsworth, 1973, p.831.
55. K. Marx and F. Engels, *The Holy Family*, Progress, Moscow, 1975, p.43.
56. Marx and Engels, *The German Ideology* (1970 edn), p.64.
57. Ibid, pp.65–6.
58. Ibid, p.66.
59. K. Marx and F. Engels, *Manifesto of the Communist Party*, in *Selected Works*, p.44.
60. Marx and Engels, *The German Ideology* (1970 edn), p.53.
61. Ibid, p.48.
62. *The German Ideology* (unabridged 1976 version), p.287.
63. Ibid, p.54.
64. Ibid, p.117.
65. K. Marx, 'The Paris *Réforme* on the Situation in France', in Marx and Engels, *Articles from the Neue Rheinische Zeitung*, Progress, Moscow, 1972, p.142.
66. Ibid.
67. Marx and Engels, *The German Ideology* (unabridged 1976 version), p.52.
68. Ibid, p.447.
69. Ibid, pp.193–4.
70. Ibid, p.455.
71. See Schmidt, *The Concept of Nature in Marx*, p.52, see also H. Lefebvre, *Dialectical Materialism*, Jonathan Cape, London, 1974, pp.82–3, and Echeverría, 'Marx's Concept of Science', p.92.
72. K. Marx, *Capital*, Lawrence & Wishart, London, 1974, vol. III, p.45.
73. Ibid, p.39.
74. Ibid, p.209.
75. Ibid, p.231.
76. Marx, *Grundrisse*, p.831.
77. K. Marx, *Theories of Surplus-Value*, Lawrence & Wishart, London, 1972, vol. III, p.296.
78. Marx, *Capital*, vol. III, p.168.
79. Ibid, vol. I, p.715.
80. Ibid, vol. III, p.817.
81. Ibid, vol. I, p.79.
82. K. Marx, Letter to Kugelmann, 11 July 1868, in *Selected Correspondence*, p.197.
83. Marx, *Grundrisse*, p.245.
84. Ibid, p.243.
85. Marx, *Capital*, vol. I, p.172.
86. Marx, *Grundrisse*, p.245.
87. Ibid, pp.247, 249.
88. Ibid, p.163.
89. Echeverría, 'Marx's Concept of Science', p.13.
90. Marx, *Grundrisse*, p.245.

91. Ibid, p.163.
92. Engels, *Ludwig Feuerbach and the End of Classical German Philosophy*, in *Selected Works*, p.603.
93. Marx, *Grundrisse*, p.248.
94. Marx, *Theories of Surplus-Value*, vol. II, p.500.
95. Ibid, vol. III, p.501.
96. Ibid, pp.55–6.
97. Ibid, p.260.
98. Ibid, p.261.
99. Marx, *Capital*, vol. I, p.404.
100. Marx and Engels, *Manifesto of the Communist Party*, p.61.
101. K. Marx, *The Eighteenth Brumaire of Louis Bonaparte*, in *Selected Works*, p.119.
102. Marx and Engels, *The German Ideology* (unabridged 1976 version), p.469.
103. G. A. Cohen, *Karl Marx's Theory of History; A Defence*, Clarendon Press, Oxford, 1978, p.250, and ch.9 *passim*.

Chapter 2

1. P. Anderson, *Considerations on Western Marxism*, New Left Books, London, 1976, p.75.
2. K. Marx, 'Preface' to *A Contribution to the Critique of Political Economy*, in Marx–Engels, *Selected Works in One Volume*, Lawrence & Wishart, London, 1970, p.182.
3. See on this Chapter 5 (pp.171–2).
4. See, for instance, *The German Ideology*, Lawrence & Wishart, London, 1970, p.65; 'The Class Struggle in France', in *Surveys from Exile*, Penguin, Harmondsworth, 1973, p.37; *Theories of Surplus-Value*, Lawrence & Wishart, London, 1972, vol. I, p.287; and *Capital*, Lawrence & Wishart, London, 1974, vol. I, p.420.
5. K. Marx and F. Engels, *Manifesto of the Communist Party*, in *Selected Works*, p.44.
6. K. Marx and F. Engels, *The German Ideology*, p.65 (my emphasis).
7. F. Engels, *The Peasant War in Germany*, Lawrence & Wishart, London, 1969, p.41.
8. Marx and Engels, *Manifesto of the Communist Party*, p.44.
9. Marx and Engels, *The German Ideology*, p.47.
10. F. Engels, *Ludwig Feuerbach and the End of Classical German Philosophy*, in *Selected Works*, p.584.
11. F. Engels, *Anti-Dühring*, Lawrence & Wishart, London, 1969, p.49.
12. Ibid, p.116.
13. Ibid, p.117.
14. Ibid, pp.400–1.
15. Engels, *Ludwig Feuerbach*, p.609.
16. Ibid, p.618.
17. Ibid, p.617.

18. F. Engels, Letter to C. Schmidt, 27 October 1890, in *Selected Correspondence*, Progress, Moscow, 1975, p.400.
19. F. Engels, Letter to F. Mehring, 14 July 1893, in *Selected Correspondence*, p.434.
20. G. Stedman Jones, 'Engels and the End of Classical German Philosophy', *New Left Review*, no.79, 1973, p.31.
21. F. Engels, Letter to J. Bloch, 21–22 September 1890, in *Selected Correspondence*, p.394.
22. Ibid, p.393.
23. Engels, Letter to Mehring, p.435.
24. F. Engels, letter to Borgius, 25 January 1894, in *Selected Correspondence*, p.442.
25. See on this K. Korsch, *Karl Marx*, Russell & Russell, New York, 1963, p.224; and Stedman Jones, 'Engels and the End of Classical German Philosophy'.
26. Engels, Letter to Bloch, p.395.
27. F. Engels, 'Foreword' to *The Eighteenth Brumaire of Louis Bonaparte*, in *Selected Works*, p.95.
28. Engels, *Anti-Dühring*, p.109.
29. Engels, Letter to Mehring, p.435.
30. Engels, *Ludwig Feuerbach*, p.603.
31. See on this *The German Ideology* (unabridged version) vol.5 of Marx–Engels *Collected Works*, Lawrence & Wishart, London, 1976, pp.586–7. It is worth mentioning that two of Marx's major philosophical works, namely the *Critique of Hegel's Conception of the State* and the *Economic and Philosophical Manuscripts*, were also belatedly published for the first time in 1927 and 1932 respectively.
32. F. Mehring, *On Historical Materialism*, New Park Publications, London, 1975.
33. Ibid, p.15.
34. Ibid, p.9.
35. Ibid.
36. K. Kautsky, *Etica y concepción materialista de la historia*, Cuadernos de Pasado y Presente, Cordoba, 1975, p.133.
37. Ibid, p.134.
38. See on this L. Kolakowski, *Main Currents of Marxism, vol. II: The Golden Age*, Clarendon Press, Oxford, 1978, pp.40–2.
39. F. Mehring, 'Etica Socialista', in Kautsky, *Etica y concepción materialista de la historia*, p.141.
40. K. Kautsky, *La doctrina socialista*, Fontanamara, Barcelona, 1975, p.33.
41. Ibid, pp.38–9. See also *Etica y concepción materialista de la historia*, p.124.
42. Kautsky, *Etica y concepción materialista de la historia*, p.123.
43. Kautsky, *La doctrina socialista*, p.65.
44. A. Labriola, *Essais sur la conception materialiste de l'histoire*, Gordon & Breach, Paris, 1970, p.102.
45. Ibid, p.110.

46. See on this J. Larrain, *The Concept of Ideology*, Hutchinson, London, 1979, chs 1,6.
47. Labriola, *Essais sur la conception materialiste de l'histoire*, p.116.
48. Ibid, p.124.
49. Ibid, p.139.
50. Ibid, p.226.
51. Ibid, p.122.
52. G. Plekhanov, 'For the Sixtieth Anniversary of Hegel's Death', in *Selected Philosophical Works*, Lawrence & Wishart, London, 1977, vol. I, p.420.
53. G. Plekhanov, *The Development of the Monist view of History*, in *Selected Philosophical Works*, vol. I, p.624.
54. Ibid, p.638. See also pp.624, 649.
55. Ibid, p.625.
56. Ibid, p.636. See also G. Plekhanov, *Fundamental Problems of Marxism*, Lawrence & Wishart, London, pp.60–3.
57. Plekhanov, *The Development of the Monist View of History*, p.642.
58. G. Plekhanov, 'On the Economic Factor', in *Selected Philosophical Works*, vol. II, p.272.
59. Ibid, p.275.
60. G. Plekhanov, *Socialism and the Political Struggle*, in *Selected Philosophical Works*, vol. I, p.90.
61. G. Plekhanov, *Our Differences*, in *Selected Philosophical Works*, vol. I, p.340.
62. G. Plekhanov, *A New Champion of Autocracy, or Mr L. Tikhomirov's Grief*, in *Selected Philosophical Works*, vol. I, p.400.
63. E. Bernstein, 'Das realistische und das ideologische Moment im Socialismus', in *Zur Geschichte und Theorie des Sozialismus*, Berlin and Bern, 1901, p.262.
64. Ibid, p.267.
65. Ibid, p.271.
66. Ibid, p.272.
67. Ibid, p.282.
68. G. Plekhanov, 'Bernstein and Materialism', in *Selected Philosophical Works*, vol. II, pp.326–9.
69. See on this *The German Ideology* (unabridged version), p.587, n.7.
70. Anderson, *Considerations on Western Marxism*, pp.7, 11.
71. Ibid, p.11.
72. See on this F. Castillo, 'El problema de la praxis en el teología de la liberación', Wilhelms Universität, Munster, 1976, pp.226–7.
73. I indistinctly use the terms 'positive' or 'neutral' to refer to this new concept of ideology. However, each term accounts for a different aspect of the same concept. 'Neutral' refers to the fact that this notion of ideology no longer passes judgement upon the validity or adequacy of ideas. 'Positive' refers to the fact that the same notion of ideology expresses the political ideas and interests of all classes in society, or, in other versions, the objective level of society which encompasses the totality of forms of social consciousness.

74. V. I. Lenin, *What the 'Friends of the People' are and how they fight the Social-Democrats*, in *Collected Works*, Progress, Moscow, 1960, vol. I, pp.140, 151.
75. Ibid, pp.298, 299.
76. V. I. Lenin, *What is to be done?*, Foreign Languages Press, Peking, 1975, p.48.
77. Ibid, pp.98, 37.
78. Ibid, p.37.
79. Ibid, p.49.
80. V. I. Lenin, 'Leon Tolstoy and his Epoch', in *Collected Works*, vol. XXVII, pp.83, 49–53.
81. For a good account of Plekhanov's position as developed in several articles published in *Iskra*, see H. Weber, *Marxisme et conscience de classe*, Union Générale d'Editions, Paris, 1975, pp.135–40.
82. L. Trotsky, *Nos taches politiques*, Editions Bellefond, Paris, 1970, pp.123–9. This critique seems a bit exaggerated in so far as Lenin's intention was certainly not to 'substitute' the party for the class. Trotsky abandoned it later and adopted Lenin's theory without reservation. Yet later developments within the Bolshevik party certainly approached such substitution. Bukharin's account of class consciousness theoretically expresses this evolution by seeing the class represented by the party and the party by its leaders, without any possibility of contradictions between them. As the proletariat is uneven in its consciousness, the party is needed to unify it. But as the party internally reproduces other inequalities, the leaders are necessary to unify it. Hence, 'as it is absurd to represent party and class as opposed to each other, so it is absurd to represent the party as opposed to its leaders'. See N. Bukharin, *Historical Materialism*, University of Michigan Press, 1969, pp.305–6.
83. R. Luxemburg, *Organizational Question of Social Democracy*, in M. A. Waters (ed.), *Rosa Luxemburg Speaks*, Pathfinder Press, New York, 1970, pp.112–30.
84. V. I. Lenin, *Materialism and Empirio-Criticism*, Foreign Languages Press, Peking, 1972, p.153.
85. V. I. Lenin, 'Marxism and Revisionism', in *Collected Works*, vol. XXV, p.39.
86. Anderson, *Considerations on Western Marxism*, p.12.
87. G. Lukács, *History and Class Consciousness*, Merlin Press, London, 1971, p.51.
88. Ibid, p.xviii.
89. G. Stedman Jones, 'The Marxism of the Early Lukács: An Evaluation', *New Left Review*, no. 70, 1971, pp.53–4.
90. See J. McCarney, *The Real World of Ideology*, Harvester Press, Brighton, 1980, p.44. Nevertheless, I disagree with McCarney's systematic attempt to blur the differences between Marx's concept of ideology and Lukács's.
91. Lukács, *History and Class Consciousness*, pp.258–9.
92. Ibid, p.228.

93. Ibid, p.70.
94. Ibid, pp.224–7.
95. Ibid, p.80.
96. Ibid, pp.266–7.
97. Ibid, p.79.
98. See McCarney, *The Real World of Ideology*
99. R. McDonough, 'Ideology as False Consciousness: Lukács', in Centre for Contemporary Cultural Studies, *On Ideology*, Hutchinson, London, 1978.
100. D. Adlam *et al.*, 'Psychology, Ideology and the Human Subject', *Ideology and Consciousness*, no. 1, May 1977, p.15.
101. M. Seliger, *The Marxist Conception of Ideology*, Cambridge University Press, Cambridge, 1977, p.67.
102. Lukács, *History and Class Consciousness*, p.50.
103. Engels, letter to Mehring, p.434.
104. Lukács, *History and Class Consciousness*, p.224.
105. Ibid, p.262.
106. Ibid, p.54.
107. Ibid, p.224.
108. Ibid, p.258.
109. N. Poulantzas, *Political Power and Social Classes*, New Left Books, London, 1973, p.205.
110. G. Stedman Jones, 'The Marxism of the Early Lukács', pp.48–9.
111. Poulantzas, *Political Power and Social Classes*, p.205.
112. Ibid, p.206.
113. See A. Arato and P. Breines, *The Young Lukács and the Origins of Western Marxism*, Seabury Press, New York, 1979, p.7; and McCarney, *The Real World of Ideology*, p.46. See also M. Lowy, *Marxisme et romantisme révolutionnaire*, Le Sycomore, Paris, 1979.
114. McCarney, *The Real World of Ideology*, p.49.
115. Lukács, *History and Class Consciousness*, p.304.
116. Ibid, p.262.
117. Lenin, *What is to be done?*, p.50.
118. Lukács, *History and Class Consciousness*, p.93.
119. See J. Mepham, 'The Theory of Ideology in *Capital*', *Radical Philosophy*, no. 2, Summer 1972.
120. Lukács, *History and Class Consciousness*, p. xviii. Lukács recognises that his early understanding of Marx was very much influenced by the work of Weber and Simmel (p.ix).
121. Ibid, p.205.
122. Ibid, p.262.
123. Ibid, p.169.
124. Ibid, p.259.
125. G. Lukács, 'Marx and Engels on Aesthetics', in *Writer and Critic*, Merlin Press, London, 1978, p.64.
126. Ibid, p.73.
127. Ibid, p.63.
128. Ibid, p.86.

129. A. Gramsci, *Selections from the 'Prison Notebooks'*, Lawrence & Wishart, London, 1971, p.376.
130. Ibid.
131. Ibid.
132. Ibid, p.328.
133. Ibid, p.326.
134. Ibid, p.377.
135. Lukács, *History and Class Consciousness*, pp. 65, 257.
136. Anderson, *Considerations on Western Marxism*, p.79.
137. Gramsci, *Prison Notebooks*, p.1328.
138. Ibid, p.377.
139. Ibid, p.407.
140. Ibid, p.408.
141. Poulantzas, *Political Power and Social Classes*, p.204.
142. A. Gramsci, 'Necessita di una preparazione ideologica di massa', *Scritti Politici*, p.746; quoted in J. M. Piotte, *La pensée politique de Gramsci*, Editions Anthropos, Paris, 1970, p.207.
143. See on this Piotte, *La pensée politique de Gramsci*, p.196; and M. Simon, *Comprendre les idéologies*, Chronique Social de France, Lyon, 1978, p.104.
144. Piotte, *La pensée politique de Gramsci*, p.197.
145. Gramsci, *Prison Notebooks*, p.325.
146. Ibid, p.404.
147. Ibid, p.405.
148. Ibid, p.339.
149. Ibid, p.326.
150. Ibid, p.328.
151. Ibid, p.331.
152. Ibid, p.5.
153. Ibid, p.334.
154. Ibid, p.341.
155. This expression seems better than Althusser's 'ideological state apparatuses' because it maintains the distinction between state and civil society.
156. This concept of civil society is different from Marx's in so far as it excludes the economic structure. Hence it becomes a part of the superstructure.
157. Perry Anderson has shown the existence of different connotations in Gramsci's treatment of the state which makes it difficult to ascertain its relation to civil society. See 'The Antinomies of Antonio Gramsci', *New Left Review*, no. 100, November 1976–January 1977.
158. Piotte, *La pensée politique de Gramsci*, p.204.
159. Gramsci, *Prison Notebooks*, p.366.

Chapter 3

1. See, for instance, J. Rancière, *La leçon d'Althusser*, Gallimard, Paris, 1974, p.238.

2. J. McCarney, *The Real World of Ideology*, Harvester Press, Brighton, 1980, p.22.
3. See J. Larrain, *The Concept of Ideology*, Hutchinson, London, 1979, ch. 5, s.4.
4. L. Althusser, *Lenin and Philosophy and Other Essays*, New Left Books, London, 1971, pp.151–2.
5. To mention just three of them, see P. Hirst, 'Althusser and the Theory of Ideology', *Economy and Society*, vol. 5, no.4, November 1976; Rancière, *La lecon d'Althusser*; and Larrain, *The Concept of Ideology*.
6. L. Althusser, *La Filosofía como arma de la Revolución*, Cuadernos de Pasado y Presente, Cordoba, 1970, p.55.
7. Althusser, *Lenin and Philosophy*, pp.153, 168. See also pp. 162–3 for a description of interpellation: 'ideology "acts" or "functions" in such a way that it "recruits" subjects among the individuals (it recruits them all), or "transforms" the individuals into subjects (it transforms them all) by that very precise operation which I have called *interpellation* or hailing, and which can be imagined along the lines of the most commonplace everyday police (or other) hailing: "Hey, you there!"'.
8. L. Althusser, *For Marx*, New Left Books, London, 1977, p.191.
9. Althusser, *La Filosofía como arma de la Revolución*, p.56.
10. Ibid, p.57.
11. L. Althusser, *Nuevos Escritos*, Editorial Laia, Barcelona, 1978, p.99.
12. Ibid, p.100.
13. Althusser, *La Filosofía como arma de la Revolución*, p. 47.
14. Ibid, pp.47–9.
15. Althusser, *Lenin and Philosophy*, p.150.
16. See E. Laclau, *Politics and Ideology in Marxist Theory*, New Left Books, London, 1977; P. Hirst, *On Law and Ideology*, Macmillan, London, 1979; and C. Mouffe, 'Hegemony and Ideology in Gramsci', in Mouffe (ed.), *Gramsci and Marxist Theory*, Routledge & Kegan Paul, London, 1979.
17. See N. Poulantzas, *Political Power and Social Classes*, New Left Books, London, 1973; M. Godelier, 'Fetischisme, religion et théorie générale de l'idéologie chez Marx', *Annali*, Feltrinelli, Roma, 1970; and J. Mepham, 'The Theory of Ideology in *Capital*', *Radical Philosophy*, no. 2, Summer 1972.
18. Althusser, *For Marx*, p.233.
19. R. Coward and J. Ellis, *Language and Materialism*, Routledge & Kegan Paul, London, 1977, p.67.
20. Mouffe, 'Hegemony and Ideology in Gramsci', p.171.
21. Althusser, *Lenin and Philosophy*, pp.155, 156.
22. Hirst, *On Law and Ideology*, p.38.
23. Godelier, 'Fetischisme, religion et théorie générale', p.23.
24. K. Marx, *Capital*, Lawrence & Wishart, London, 1974, vol. I, p.173.
25. See K. Marx, *The Eighteenth Brumaire of Louis Bonaparte*, in *Selected Works in One Volume*, Lawrence & Wishart, London, 1970, p.96, and 'Notes on Adolph Wagner', in T. Carver (ed.), *Karl Marx: Texts*

on Method, Blackwell, Oxford, 1975, p.201.

26. J. Mepham, 'Who Makes History', *Radical Philosophy* no.6, Winter 1973, p.24.
27. Althusser, *For Marx*, p.215.
28. Ibid, p.231.
29. L. Althusser, *Reading 'Capital'*, New Left Books, London, 1970, p.180.
30. Mepham, 'Who Makes History', pp.23–4.
31. See L. Althusser, *Essays in Self-Criticism*, New Left Books, London, 1976, p.97: 'One cannot seize (*begreifen*: conceive), that is to say, *think* real history (the process of the reproduction of social formations and their revolutionary transformation) as if it could be reduced to *an* Origin, *an* Essence, or *a* Cause (even Man), which would be its Subject . . . we are confronted with the *philosophical* petty-bourgeois communitarian *anthropology* of Feuerbach (still respected by Marx in the 1844 Manuscripts), in which the Essence of Man is the Origin, Cause and Goal of history.'
32. See K. Marx, 'Theses on Feuerbach', in C. Arthur (ed.), *The German Ideology*, Lawrence & Wishart, London, 1970, thesis 6, p.122: by resolving the religious essence into the human essence, Feuerbach is compelled to abstract from the historical process.
33. Rancière, *La leçon d'Althusser*, p.25.
34. K. Marx, *Grundrisse*, Penguin, Harmondsworth, 1973, p.83. Robinsonades are utopias on the lines of Defoe's *Robinson Crusoe*.
35. Ibid, p.265.
36. Ibid, p.712.
37. Although Hirst does not precisely define 'vulgar materialism', I take it that one can understand by it the doctrine which Marx rejected in the 'Theses on Feuerbach' and which he labelled 'old' or 'contemplative', that is to say the French and Feuerbachian materialism which does not conceive of practice and which is therefore abstract and unhistorical.
38. Hirst, *On Law and Ideology*, p.28.
39. K. Marx and F. Engels, *The German Ideology*, Lawrence & Wishart, London, 1970 pp.50–1.
40. See on this F. Rossi-Landi, *Linguistics and Economics*, Mouton, The Hague, 1975, p.58.
41. Marx, 'Theses on Feuerbach', thesis 1, p.121.
42. Althusser, *Lenin and Philosophy*, p.153.
43. F. Engels, Letter to F. Mehring, 14 July 1893, in Marx–Engels, *Selected Correspondence*, Progress, Moscow, 1975, p.434.
44. J. Habermas, 'Zur Logik der Sozialwissenschaften', Beiheft 5, *Philosophische Rundschau*, Tübingen, 1967, quoted in T. McCarthy, 'A Theory of Communicative Competence', in P. Connerton (ed.), *Critical Sociology*, Penguin, Harmondsworth, 1976, p.471.
45. See J. Habermas, 'Technology and Science as Ideology', in *Toward a Rational Society*, Heinemann, London, 1971.
46. See Larrain, *The Concept of Ideology*, ch.6.

47. See Althusser, *Nuevos Escritos*, p.86: 'the juridical ideology of the classic bourgeoisie gives way in the present to a technocratic ideology'. Nevertheless, this does not mean for Althusser that class struggle has become latent; on the contrary, the new technocratic consciousness is an adaptation of the ruling ideology to the class struggle.
48. Habermas, *Toward a Rational Society*, p.111.
49. K. Marx, *The Poverty of Philosophy*, Progress, Moscow, 1975, p.161.
50. K. Marx and F. Engels, *The Holy Family*, Progress, Moscow, 1975, p.44.
51. J. Habermas, 'What is Universal Pragmatics?, in *Communication and the Evolution of Society*, Heinemann, London, 1979, p.5.
52. J. Habermas, *Legitimation Crisis*, Heinemann, London, 1976, p.108.
53. Ibid, p.110.
54. J. Habermas, 'Vorbereitende Bemerkungen zu einer Theorie der Kommunikativen Competence' [Preparatory Remarks on a Theory of Communicative Competence], in *Theorie der Gesellschaft oder Sozialtechnologie*, p.120, quoted in McCarthy, 'A Theory of Communicative Competence', p.477.
55. Habermas, *Legitimation Crisis*, p.113.
56. J. Habermas, 'Systematically Distorted Communication', in Connerton (ed.), *Critical Sociology*, p.348.
57. See, for instance, J. Habermas, 'Appendix' to *Knowledge and Human Interests*, Heinemann, London, 1972, p.310.
58. D. Held, *Introduction to Critical Theory*, Hutchinson, London, 1980, p.277.
59. See, for instance, McCarthy, 'A Theory of Communicative Competence', Held, *Introduction to Critical Theory*, p.3; P. Connerton, 'Introduction' to *Critical Sociology*; A. Giddens, 'Habermas's Critique of Hermeneutics', in *Studies in Social and Political Theory*, Hutchinson, London, 1977; and R. Keat, *The Politics of Social Theory*, Blackwell, Oxford, 1981, esp. ch.6.
60. Held, *Introduction to Critical Theory*, p.394.
61. Giddens, 'Habermas's Critique of Hermeneutics', p.152.
62. Marx and Engels, *The German Ideology*, p.41.
63. M. Seliger, *The Marxist Conception of Ideology*, Cambridge University Press, Cambridge, 1977, p.26. I have changed past tense into present tense.
64. Ibid, p.19.
65. For an analysis of 'relationism' and Mannheim's concept of ideology see Larrain, *The Concept of Ideology*, ch.4.
66. Seliger, *The Marxist Conception of Ideology*, p.28.
67. Ibid, p.142.
68. Marx and Engels, *The German Ideology*, p.47.
69. Seliger, *The Marxist Conception of Ideology*, p.32.
70. McCarney, *The Real World of Ideology*, p.86.
71. Marx and Engels, *The German Ideology*, p.52.
72. Seliger, *The Marxist Conception of Ideology*, p.33.
73. Ibid, p.36.

74. Marx, *Capital*, vol.I, p.209.
75. Seliger, *The Marxist Conception of Ideology*, p.37.
76. See the discussion on 'dogmatism' in Chapter 6.
77. A few examples of this evidence can be found in *The German Ideology*, where Marx and Engels speak of forms of consciousness which correspond to reality; in the 1859 Preface, where Marx opposes science and ideology; in *Capital*, where Marx compares conceptions corresponding to the inner pattern with conceptions which remain trapped in appearances; in *The Theories of Surplus-Value*, where Marx distinguishes between ideology and the 'free spiritual production' of a society and where he also praises the scientific achievements of Ricardo and so on. All of these passages have been quoted at different points in this book.
78. McCarney, *The Real World of Ideology*, p.80.
79. Ibid, pp.83–4.
80. Marx and Engels, *The German Ideology* (unabridged version), in *Collected Works*, Lawrence & Wishart, London, 1976, vol.V, p.28. Although the heading comes in a passage which is crossed out, it is indicative of Marx's and Engels's position and therefore the editors have restored it to its former position. It is also worth noting that some passages in the original were crossed out by Bernstein, and the editors have tried to restore those passages wherever possible.
81. McCarney, *The Real World of Ideology*, p.84.
82. Ibid, p.89.
83. Ibid, p.91.
84. Ibid, p.92.
85. Ibid, p.109.
86. Engels, Letter to Mehring, 14 July 1893, p.434.
87. McCarney, *The Real World of Ideology*, pp.96, 97.
88. Ibid, p.110.
89. Ibid.
90. Laclau, *Politics and Ideology in Marxist Theory*, p.99.
91. Ibid, p.109.
92. Ibid, p.160.
93. Ibid, p.126.
94. Ibid, p.127.

Chapter 4

1. G. W. F. Hegel, *The Phenomenology of Mind*, Allen & Unwin, London, 1977, pp.203–4. For good commentaries on the *Phenomenology* see J. Hyppolite, *Genesis and Structure of Hegel's Phenomenology of Spirit*, Northwestern University Press, Evanston, 1974; and R. Norman, *Hegel's Phenomenology*, Sussex University Press, Brighton, 1976.
2. Hegel, *The Phenomenology of Mind*, p.205.

3. Ibid, p.207.
4. Ibid, p.208.
5. K. Marx, *Economic and Philosophical Manuscripts*, in *Early Writings* (ed. L. Colletti), Penguin, Harmondsworth, 1975, p.386.
6. Ibid, p.384.
7. Ibid.
8. Hegel, *The Phenomenology of Mind*, p.513.
9. Marx, *Economic and Philosophical Manuscripts*, p.393.
10. K. Marx, *Critique of Hegel's Doctrine of the State*, in *Early Writings*, p.98.
11. K. Marx and F. Engels, *The German Ideology*, Lawrence & Wishart, London, 1970, p.47.
12. K. Marx, *Grundrisse*, Penguin, Harmondsworth, 1973, p.831. See also *Un chapitre inédit du Capital*, Union Générale d'Editions, Paris, 1971, p.142.
13. K. Marx, *Theories of Surplus-Value*, Lawrence & Wishart, London, vol.III, 1972, p.276.
14. Ibid, vol.I, p.390.
15. K. Marx, *Capital*, Lawrence & Wishart, London, 1974, vol.III, p.45.
16. Ibid, vol.I, p.586.
17. Marx, *Theories of Surplus-Value*, vol.III, p.453.
18. Marx, *Capital*, vol.I, p.81.
19. Ibid, p.505.
20. Hegel, *The Phenomenology of Mind*, p.206.
21. G. W. F. Hegel, *Logic*, Clarendon Press, Oxford, 1975, p.174.
22. Marx, *Economic and Philosophical Manuscripts*, p.391.
23. Ibid, p.392.
24. Ibid, p.393.
25. Marx, *Grundrisse*, p.541.
26. G. W. F. Hegel, *The Science of Logic*, Allen & Unwin, London, 1976, pp.439, 442.
27. Marx, *Grundrisse*, pp.831–2.
28. Ibid, p.296.
29. Marx, *Theories of Surplus-Value*, vol.III, pp.500–1.
30. This is a point forcefully made by R. Echeverría in 'Marx's Concept of Science', doctoral thesis, Birkbeck College, London, 1978.
31. Marx, *Theories of Surplus-Value*, vol.III, p.500.
32. Ibid, p.501.
33. Ibid, vol.II, p.519.
34. I. Kant, *Critique of Pure Reason*, Dent (Everyman's Library), London, 1974, p.197.
35. Quoted in F. Engels, *Anti-Dühring*, Lawrence & Wishart, London, 1969, p.143.
36. See G. Plekhanov, *Fundamental Problems of Marxism*, Lawrence & Wishart, London, appendix, pp.89–100.
37. See L. Colletti, 'Marxism and the Dialectic', *New Left Review*, no.93, September–October 1975; R. Edgley, 'Dialectic: The Contradiction of Colletti', *Critique*, no.7, Winter 1976–7; and S. Meikle,

'Dialectical Contradiction and Necessity', in J. Mepham and D. H. Ruben (eds), *Issues in Marxist Philosophy*, 3 vols, Harvester Press, Brighton, 1979, vol.I, pp.5–35.
38. Engels, *Anti-Dühring*, p.144.
39. See Hegel, *The Science of Logic*, pp.439–43, and *The Phenomenology of Mind*, pp.204–5.
40. Marx, *Grundrisse*, p.162.
41. Plekhanov, *Fundamental Problems of Marxism*, p.96.
42. See V. I. Lenin, *Philosophical Notebooks*, in *Collected Works*, Lawrence & Wishart, London, 1972, vol. XXVIII, pp.359–60.
43. Colletti, 'Marxism and the Dialectic', pp.22, 26.
44. R. Edgley, 'Dialectic: The Contradiction of Colletti', p.48.
45. Ibid, p.50.
46. Ibid, p.51.
47. J. Elster, *Logic and Society*, Wiley, Chichester, 1978, p.3.
48. Ibid, p.72.
49. Ibid, p.97.
50. Ibid, p.113.
51. Ibid, p.70.
52. Ibid, p.72, 4.
53. Ibid, p.72.
54. See on this A. Giddens, *Central Problems in Social Theory*, Macmillan, London, 1979, pp.139–41.
55. Colletti, 'Marxism and the Dialectic', p.4.
56. Ibid, p.7.
57. K. Marx and F. Engels, *The Holy Family*, Progress, Moscow, 1975, p.43.
58. Marx, *Grundrisse*, p.458.
59. Marx and Engels, *The Holy Family*, p.43.
60. Ibid.
61. Marx, *Theories of Surplus-Value*, vol.III, p.507.
62. Ibid, p.491.
63. Marx, *Grundrisse*, p.460.
64. Marx, *Capital*, vol.III, p.250.
65. Marx, *Theories of Surplus-Value*, vol.II, p.512.
66. Marx, *Critique of Hegel's Doctrine of the State*, p.194.
67. Mao Tse-tung, *Four Essays on Philosophy*, Foreign Languages Press, Peking, 1968, p.51. For an analysis of Mao's theory of contradiction, see A. Badiou, *Théorie de la contradiction*, Maspero, Paris, 1975.
68. Mao Tse-tung, *Four Essays on Philosophy*, p.54.
69. Ibid, p.35.
70. Giddens, *Central Problems in Social Theory*, p.143.
71. K. Post, *Arise Ye Starvelings!*, Martinus Nijhoff, The Hague, 1978, pp.27–8.
72. See Mao Tse-tung, *Four Essays on Philosophy*, p.55.
73. Ibid, p.70.
74. Ibid, p.69.

75. L. Sève, 'Pré-Rapport sur la dialectique', Centre d'Etudes et de Recherches Marxistes, *Lénine et la pratique scientifique*, Editions Sociales, Paris, 1974, pp.37–42.
76. Post, *Arise Ye Starvelings!*, p.29.
77. See J. Lojkine, 'Sur l'usage du concept de contradiction dans un analyse materialiste de l'état', *La pensée*, no.197, February 1978.
78. Elster claims, on the contrary, that Marx never used *Widerspruch* to refer to the labour–capital relationship. From this he concludes that there is no contradiction between capital and wage-labour but only conflict. See *Logic and Society*, p.90, n.1. Elster's premise is mistaken, but even if we accepted that Marx did not use *Widerspruch* to refer to the labour–capital relationship, this does not of itself prove that Marx did not consider that relationship to be a contradiction. It is sufficient to have a look at Marx's and Engels's quotation from the *Holy Family* (see note 57) to realise that this relationship is the principal contradiction of the mode of production.
79. Marx, *Capital*, vol.III, p.257.
80. Lojkine, 'Sur l'usage du concept de contradiction', p.49.
81. M. Godelier, *Rationality and Irrationality in Economics*, New Left Books, London, 1972, pp.77–81.
82. A. Schaff, 'Marxist Dialectics and the Principle of Contradiction', *Journal of Philosophy*, vol.57, no.7, March 1960, p.246.
83. See C. Bettelheim, *La transition vers l'économie socialiste*, Maspero, Paris, 1974, p.23; A. D. Magaline, *Lutte de classes et dévalorisation du capital*, Maspero, Paris, 1975, p.63; and Echeverría, 'Marx's Concept of Science', p.223.
84. K. Marx and F. Engels, *Manifesto of the Communist Party*, in *Selected Works in One Volume*, Lawrence & Wishart, London, 1970, p.40; and *Grundrisse*, p.749.
85. K. Marx, *Wage Labour and Capital*, in *Selected Works*, p.82.
86. Marx, *Grundrisse*, p.541.
87. Magaline, *Lutte de classes et dévalorisation du capital*, p.56.
88. Marx, *Capital*, vol.III, p.250.
89. Colletti, 'Marxism and the Dialectic', p.25.
90. Meikle, 'Dialectical Contradiction and Necessity', p.16.
91. K. Marx, *A Contribution to the Critique of Political Economy*, Progress, Moscow, 1977, p.48.
92. Marx, *Theories of Surplus-Value*, vol.III, p.130.
93. Ibid, vol.II, p.512.
94. Engels, *Anti-Dühring*, p.321.
95. Giddens, *Central Problems in Social Theory*, p.136.
96. Marx, *Capital*, vol.III, p.264.
97. See Engels, *Anti-Dühring*, p.321.
98. See Magaline, *Lutte de classes et dévalorisation du capital*, p.65. Both Engels and Magaline consider a further contradiction between the organisation of production in separate production units and the social anarchy in production as a whole, as complementary to the capital–labour contradiction.

99. Marx, *Capital*, vol.I, p.542.
100. Ibid, pp.541–2.
101. Ibid, p.542. See also Marx, *Un chapitre inédit du Capital*, p.263: 'The perpetual renewal of the purchase-sale relationship does nothing but mediate the continuity of the specific relation of dependency, by giving to it the *mystified* appearance of a transaction, a contract between *commodity* owners endowed with equal rights and seemingly free one in the face of the other.'
102. See Giddens, *Central Problems in Social Theory*, p.138.
103. Marx, *Capital*, vol.III, p.249.
104. Marx, *Theories of Surplus-Value*, vol.II, pp.500, 510.
105. See L. Althusser, *For Marx*, New Left Books, London, 1977, p.99.
106. Marx, *Theories of Surplus-Value*, vol.II, pp.507–9.
107. Marx, *Capital*, vol.III, pp.247–59.
108. Marx, *Theories of Surplus-Value*, vol.II, p.513.
109. Marx, 'Afterword' to *Capital*, vol.I, p.25.
110. Ibid, pp.24–5; see also Marx and Engels, *Manifesto*, p.36: 'oppressor and oppressed stood in constant opposition to one another, carried on an uninterrupted, now hidden, now open fight'.
111. Marx and Engels, *Manifesto*, p.60.
112. Ibid, p.43.
113. See on this F. Engels, *The Peasant War in Germany*, Lawrence & Wishart, London, 1969.
114. See R. Hilton (ed.), *The Transition from Feudalism to Capitalism*, New Left Books, London, 1976, particularly contributions by Takahashi and Dobb, who believe that the dissolution of feudalism was due mainly to the work of internal contradictions. This viewpoint is opposed by Sweezy, who suggests that 'the root cause of the decline of feudalism was the growth of trade' (see p.41).
115. As Dobb has put it, 'no one is suggesting that class struggle of peasants against lords give rise, in a simple and direct way, to capitalism. What this does is to modify the dependence of the petty mode of production upon feudal overlordship and eventually to shake loose the small producer from feudal exploitation. It is then from the petty mode of production (in the degree to which it secures independence of action, and social differentiation in turn develops within it) that capitalism is born' (see Hilton, *The Transition from Feudalism to Capitalism*, p.59).
116. Marx and Engels, *The German Ideology*, p.53.
117. K. Marx, *The Eighteenth Brumaire of Louis Bonaparte*, in *Selected Works*, pp.116–17.
118. Giddens, *Central Problems in Social Theory*, p.144.
119. Marx, *The Eighteenth Brumaire of Louis Bonaparte*, p.96.120. K. Marx, *The Poverty of Philosophy*, M. Lawrence, London, n.d., pp.159–60.
121. E. Laclau, *Politics and Ideology in Marxist Theory*, New Left Books, London, 1977, pp.104, 106.
122. Ibid, pp.106–7.

Chapter 5

1. L. Althusser, *La Filosofía como arma de la revolución*, Cuadernos de Pasado y Presente, Cordoba, 1970, p.47.
2. K. Marx and F. Engels, *The German Ideology* (unabridged version), in *Collected Works*, Lawrence & Wishart, London, 1976, vol.V, pp.372–3.
3. Ibid, p.89.
4. F. Engels, *Anti-Dühring*, Lawrence & Wishart, London, 1969, p.109.
5. F. Engels, Letter to C. Schmidt, 27 October 1890, in *Selected Correspondence*, Progress, Moscow, 1975, p.393.
6. See, for instance, S. Timpanaro, 'Considerations on Materialism', *New Left Review*, no.85, 1974, p.17. The exclusion of science from the 'ideological superstructure' is also implicit in Althusser. See *La Filosofía como arma de la revolución*, pp.47–9.
7. See Chapter 1. In the particular case of Engels's own writings, this is shown in Chapter 2 (pp.49–54).
8. Marx and Engels, *The German Ideology*, p.37.
9. K. Marx, *The Eighteenth Brumaire of Louis Bonaparte*, in *Selected Works in One Volume*, Lawrence & Wishart, London, 1970, p.117.
10. K. Marx, 'Preface' to *A Contribution to the Critique of Political Economy*, in *Selected Works*, p.181.
11. Ibid, p.182.
12. M. Marković, *The Contemporary Marx*, Spokesman Books, Nottingham, 1974, p.61.
13. Marx, 'Preface', p.182.
14. This solution modifies my views held in *The Concept of Ideology*, Hutchinson, London, 1979. Because I assumed, a bit too hastily, that in English the term 'idealistic' could refer to ideas in general, I thought that the expression 'idealistic superstructure' provided a solution advanced by Marx himself. However, as the term 'idealistic' really means 'pertaining to or characteristic of an idealist; belonging to or having the character of idealism' (*Oxford English Dictionary*), a negative connotation is inevitably attached to it – at least in the context of Marx's thought. Hence the expression 'idealistic superstructure' does not appropriately signify the superstructure of ideas, which, at any rate, has been my intended meaning all along. I think this meaning can also be well represented by the expression 'ideational superstructure' inasmuch as 'ideational' means 'of or pertaining to ideation or the formation of ideas' (*Oxford English Dictionary*).
15. K.Marx, *Theories of Surplus-Value*, Lawrence & Wishart, London, 1969, vol.II, p.106.
16. Ibid, vol.I, p.164.
17. Ibid, p.285 (my emphasis).
18. Max Adler, 'Ideology as Appearance', in T. Bottomore and P. Goode (eds), *Austro-Marxism*, Clarendon Press, Oxford, 1978, pp.254–5.
19. V. I. Lenin, *What the 'Friends of the People' are and how they fight the Social-Democrats*, in *Collected Works*, Foreign Languages Publishing House, Moscow, 1960, vol.I, p.141.

20. B. Hindess, 'The Concept of Class in Marxist Theory and Marxist Politics', in J. Bloomfield (ed.), *Class, Hegemony and Party*, Lawrence & Wishart, London, 1977, p.104.
21. See on this K. Kosik, *Dialéctica de lo concreto*, Ed. Grijalbo, Mexico, 1967, p.126.
22. P. Bourdieu, 'Intellectual Field and Creative Project', in M. Young (ed.), *Knowledge and Control*, Collier-Macmillan, London, 1971, pp.162–3.
23. See K. Mannheim, 'Competition as a Cultural Phenomenon', in *Essays on the Sociology of Knowledge*, Routledge & Kegan Paul, London, 1968.
24. R. Williams, *Culture and Society 1780–1950*, Penguin, Harmondsworth, 1977, pp.49–50.
25. Bourdieu, 'Intellectual Field and Creative Project', pp.174–5.
26. See J. Habermas, 'The Public Sphere: An Encyclopedia Article', *New German Critique*, no.3, Autumn 1974.
27. K. Marx, *Capital*, Lawrence & Wishart, London, 1974, vol.I, p.86.
28. See L. Althusser, *For Marx*, New Left Books, London, 1977, p.213; N. Poulantzas, *Political Power and Social classes*, New Left Books, London, 1973, p.14; and E. Balibar, 'On the Basic Concepts of Historical Materialism', in L. Althusser and E. Balibar, *Reading 'Capital'*, New Left Books, London, 1970, p.220.
29. J. Texier, 'Sur la détermination en dernière instance', in E. Balibar *et al.*, *Sur la dialectique*, Editions Sociales, Paris, 1977, p.266.
30. Ibid, p.270.
31. F. Engels, Letter to F. Mehring, 14 July 1893, in *Selected Correspondence*, p.435.
32. F. Engels, Letter to J. Bloch, 21–22 September 1890, in *Selected Correspondence*, p.394.
33. Althusser, *For Marx*, p.118.
34. Ibid, p.213.
35. See on this Texier, 'Sur la détermination en dernière instance', p.258.
36. Althusser and Balibar, *Reading Capital*, pp.186–7.
37. Ibid, p.189.
38. Ibid, p.97.
39. Althusser, *For Marx*, p.213.
40. B. Hindess and P. Hirst, *Pre-Capitalist Modes of Production*, Routledge & Kegan Paul, London, 1975, p.314.
41. Ibid, pp.316–7.
42. Hindess, 'The Concept of Class', p.97.
43. Ibid, p.104.
44. In A. Cutler, B. Hindess *et al., Marx's 'Capital' and Capitalism Today*, Routledge & Kegan Paul, London, 1977, vol.I, p.206.
45. Ibid, p.216.
46. It can be counter-argued that things are more complicated than this and that there is indeed a general movement of modern philosophy away from epistemology towards ontology. This may be so, but such an argument misses my point. I am not propounding the idea that

philosophy must come back to epistemology as its main concern. All I am saying is that, whether or not epistemological concerns are at the centre of philosophy today, there are still epistemological issues necessarily involved in all positions which posit a claim to validity and that the pretension to having definitively surpassed them is contradictory.

47. Marx, *Capital*, vol.III, pp.791–2.
48. Cutler, Hindess *et al., Marx's 'Capital' and Capitalism Today*, p.219.
49. K. Marx, Letter to Annenkov, 28 December 1846, in *Selected Correspondence*, p.30.
50. Marx, *Theories of Surplus-Value*, vol.I, p.285.
51. F. Rossi-Landi, *Linguistics and Economics*, Mouton, The Hague, 1975, p.5.
52. Ibid, pp.72–5. Rossi-Landi's views on ideology are described in Chapter 6 (pp.212–16).
53. See on this J. J. Brunner, 'La cultura en una Sociedad Autoritaria', *Documento de Trabajo*, Flacso, Santiago, 1979.
54. W. Benjamin, *Understanding Brecht*, New Left Books, London, 1977, p.94.
55. Ibid, p.97.
56. K. Marx, 'Introduction to a Critique of Political Economy', in *Grundrisse*, Penguin, Harmondsworth, 1973, p.111.
57. Kosik, *Dialéctica de lo concreto*, p.153.
58. Marx, *Theories of Surplus-Value*, vol.III, p.261.
59. Marx, Letter to Annenkov, 28 December 1846, p.31.
60. Kosik, *Dialéctica de lo concreto*, p.157.
61. N. Hadjinicolaou, *Histoire de l'art et lutte des classes*, Maspero, Paris, 1978, pp.194–5.
62. Kosik, *Dialéctica de lo concreto*, p.159.
63. Marx, *The Eighteenth Brumaire of Louis Bonaparte*, p.96.
64. See on this P. L. Assoun, *Marx et la répétition historique*, Presses Universitaires de France, Paris, 1978.
65. See E. Laclau, *Politics and Ideology in Marxist Theory*, New Left Books, London, 1977, pp.92–100, 158–63.
66. Ibid, p.160.
67. Ibid.
68. N. Mouzelis, 'Ideology and Class Politics: A Critique of Ernesto Laclau', *New Left Review*, no. 112, November–December 1978, p.53.

Chapter 6

1. See, for instance, A. Schaff, 'Marxisme et sociologie de la connaissance', *L'Homme et la société*, no.10, October–December 1968, p.141. However, Schaff seems to change his position in *Structuralisme et Marxisme*, Anthropos, Paris, 1974, where he maintains that the scientificity of ideology does not only depend upon the class interests it serves but also depends upon the intellectual materials with which it

is constructed. Daniel Bell identifies the first version with the true position of Marxism and argues that for Marxism truth is 'class truth' and that 'the "test of truth" of a doctrine is to see what class interests it serves'. See *The End of Ideology*, Free Press, New York, 1965, p.397. Although Bell's criticism of this version is adequate, its identification with Marxism in general is mistaken.

2. See on this Chapter 2 (pp.63-9). For a discussion of the science-ideology relationship see J. Larrain, *The Concept of Ideology*, Hutchinson, London, 1979, ch.6.
3. See K. Marx, Letter to Kugelmann, 11 July 1868, in Marx–Engels, *Selected Correspondence*, Progress, Moscow, 1975, p.197: 'once the interconnection is grasped, all theoretical belief in the permanent necessity of existing conditions collapses before their collapse in practice'.
4. See K. Marx, *Capital*, Lawrence & Wishart, London, 1974, vol.I, pp.24–5: 'Afterword to the Second German Edition'.
5. K. Marx, *The Poverty of Philosophy*, Progress, Moscow, 1975, p.117.
6. K. Marx, *Theories of Surplus-Value*, Lawrence & Wishart, London, 1972, vol.III, p.56.
7. Ibid, p.239.
8. Ibid, p.261.
9. See K. Marx and F. Engels, *The German Ideology*, Part I, Lawrence & Wishart, London, 1970, p.65, and also *The Eighteenth Brumaire of Louis Bonaparte*, in *Selected Works in One Volume*, Lawrence & Wishart, London, 1970, p.120. Marx asserts the specific role of intellectuals in relation to the bourgeoisie, the petty-bourgeoisie and the proletariat.
10. K. Marx and F. Engels, *Manifesto of the Communist Party*, in *Selected Works*, p.44.
11. K. Mannheim, *Ideology and Utopia*, Routledge & Kegan Paul, London, 1972, p.66.
12. The 'total conception' of ideology is that which discredits the total world-view of the opponent. It challenges the whole outlook of a class and not only individual ideas. The partial falsification of the opponent's thought is typical of a 'particular conception' of ideology. See Mannheim, *Ideology and Utopia*, pp.49–50.
13. Ibid, p.69.
14. See M. Seliger, *The Marxist Conception of Ideology*, Cambridge University Press, Cambridge, 1977, pp.10, 30–45. Seliger's objection is merely a more crude repetition, and lacks the penetration and refinement of Mannheim's approach.
15. See on this Larrain, *The Concept of Ideology*, ch.4.
16. R. Williams, *Marxism and Literature*, Oxford University Press, Oxford, 1977, p.62.
17. Marx and Engels, *The German Ideology*, p.48.
18. Williams, *Marxism and Literature*, p.64.
19. See on this R. Echeverría, 'Marx's Concept of Science', doctoral thesis, Birkbeck College, London, 1978.

20. See D. Lazar, review of J. Larrain, *The Concept of Ideology*, in *Sociology*, vol.14, no.2, May 1980, p.318.
21. See on this T. Kuhn, *The Structure of Scientific Revolutions*, University of Chicago Press, Chicago, 1970; and P. Feyerabend, *Against Method*, New Left Books, London, 1975.
22. See E. Grunwald, 'The Sociology of Knowledge and Epistemology', in J. E. Curtis and J. W. Petras (eds), *The Sociology of Knowledge: A Reader*, Duckworth, London, 1970. A sophisticated argument against this position can be found in B. Barnes, *Scientific Knowledge and Sociological Theory*, Routledge & Kegan Paul, London, 1974. Barnes readily admits that 'the epistemological message of [his] work could be said to be sceptical or relativistic' (p.154). However, it does not seem to me that he successfully escapes from implicitly claiming the validity of his own analysis.
23. F. Rossi-Landi, *Ideologia*, Isedi, Milan, 1978, p.97.
24. Ibid, p.28.
25. Ibid, pp.113–14.
26. Ibid, p.71.
27. Marx, 'Theses on Feuerbach', in *The German Ideology*, thesis II, p.121.
28. Ibid, thesis VIII.
29. G. W. F. Hegel, *Logic*, Clarendon Press, Oxford, 1975, p.41.
30. Ibid.
31. See on this L. Kolakowski, 'Karl Marx and the Classical Definition of Truth', in *Marxism and Beyond*, Pall Mall Press, London, 1968. For a refutation of Kolakowski's account from the point of view of orthodox Marxism see A. Schaff, 'Studies of the Young Marx: A Rejoinder', in L. Labedz (ed.), *Revisionism*, Praeger, New York, 1962. A polemic between opposite interpretations of Marx's concept of truth can be found in *Radical Philosophy*, no.4, Spring 1973, and no.5, Summer 1973: articles by P. Binns, 'The Marxist Theory of Truth', and A. Collier, 'Truth and Practice', respectively. See also S. Lukes, 'On the Social Determination of Truth', in *Essays in Social Theory*, Macmillan, London, 1977.
32. T. Adorno, 'Introduction' to T. Adorno *et al.*, *The Positivist Dispute in German Sociology*, Heinemann, London, 1976, p.27.
33. Mannheim, *Ideology and Utopia*, p.87.
34. Some interesting remarks on the importance of the future for the definition of the present can be found in A. Danto, *Analytical Philosophy of History*, Cambridge University Press, Cambridge, 1965, pp.150–70.
35. J. Habermas, *Legitimation Crisis*, Heinemann, London, 1976, p.113. For a discussion of Habermas's theory of ideology see Chapter 3 (pp.104–9).
36. G. Lukács, *History and Class Consciousness*, Merlin Press, London, 1971, p.51.
37. Habermas, *Legitimation Crisis*, p.113.
38. D. Held, *Introduction to Critical Theory*, Hutchinson, London, 1980,

p.398.
39. Rossi-Landi, *Ideologia*, p.239.
40. A. Gramsci, *Selections from the 'Prison Notebooks'*, Lawrence & Wishart, London, 1971, p.405.
41. L. Goldmann, *The Hidden God*, Routledge & Kegan Paul, London, 1964, ch.5.
42. A. Schmidt, *The Concept of Nature in Marx*, New Left Books, London, 1971, p.160.
43. E. Bloch, *A Philosophy of the Future*, Herder & Herder, New York, 1970, p.91.
44. Schmidt, *The Concept of Nature in Marx*, p.142.
45. Marx, *The Civil War in France*, in *Selected Works*, p.291.
46. K. Marx and F. Engels, *The Holy Family*, Progress, Moscow, 1975, pp.93–4.
47. In this sense Bell is mistaken when he affirms that 'history for Marx as for Hegel, is a progressive unfolding reason, in which society, through man's conquest of nature and the destruction of all mythologies and superstitions, moves on to "higher stages"'. See Bell, *The End of Ideology*, p.397.
48. K. Marx, Letter to the Editorial Board of the *Otechestvenniye Zapiski*, London, November 1877, in *Selected Correspondence*, pp.293–4.
49. K. Marx, *Grundrisse*, Penguin, Harmondsworth, 1973, p.159.
50. Ibid, pp.248–9.
51. Bell, *The End of Ideology*, pp.367–8.
52. Ibid, p.17: 'I am aware, as Fritz Stern has noted in his book, *The Politics of Cultural Despair*, that I have applied the term largely to left-wing thought, and so restrict its scope. This is true. Yet, while there are "ideologies" of the right as well as of the "left" – as there are now "ideologies" of economic development – one's historical context defines one's usage; and the word *ideology* was a product of the "left" and gained a distinctive resonance in that context.'
53. Ibid, p.16.
54. Ibid, p.401.
55. Ibid, p.285.
56. See note 47.
57. Bell, *The End of Ideology*, p.404.
58. Quoted by Bell, *The End of Ideology*, p.407.
59. Ibid, pp.279–80.
60. D. Bell, *The Cultural Contradictions of Capitalism*, Heinemann, London, 1976, pp.60–1.
61. Ibid, p.42.
62. L. Althusser, *For Marx*, New Left Books, London, 1977, p.232.
63. L. Althusser, *La Filosofía como arma de la revolución*, Cuadernos de Pasado y Presente, Cordoba, 1970, p.55.
64. For a critique of Althusser's concept of ideology see Chapter 3 (pp.91–102). See also Larrain, *The Concept of Ideology*, ch.5.
65. Schmidt, *The Concept of Nature in Marx*, p.142.

66. K. Marx, *Economic and Philosophical Manuscripts*, in *Early Writings*, Penguin, Harmondsworth, 1975, p.348.
67. Marx and Engels, *The German Ideology*, p.93.
68. Marx, *Capital*, vol.III, p.820.
69. Schmidt, *The Concept of Nature in Marx*, p.149.
70. Gramsci, *Selections from the 'Prison Notebooks'*, p.405.
71. Marx and Engels, *The German Ideology*, p.61.
72. Ibid, p.95.
73. Marx and Engels, *Manifesto of the Communist Party*, p.53.
74. Marx, *The Poverty of Philosophy*, p.161. See also *The Holy Family*, p.43: 'The proletariat, on the contrary, is compelled as proletariat to abolish itself and thereby its opposite.'
75. Marx and Engels, *Manifesto of the Communist Party*, p.53.
76. Marx and Engels, *The German Ideology*, p.86.
77. K. Marx, 'Critique of the Gotha Programme', in *Selected Works*, p.327.
78. O. Kuusinen (ed.), *Fundamental Problems of Marxism-Leninism*, Foreign Languages Publishing House, Moscow, 1961, p.695.
79. For a description of the Soviet official doctrine about Soviet society, see D. Lane, *The Socialist Industrial State*, Allen & Unwin, London, 1976.
80. See on this E. Balibar, *On the Dictatorship of the Proletariat*, New Left Books, London, 1977.
81. For a discussion of legal and economic forms of property in socialism see C. Bettelheim, *Economic Calculation and Forms of Property*, Routledge & Kegan Paul, London, 1976.
82. Balibar, *On the Dictatorship of the Proletariat*, p.50.
83. This statement is limited to a negative concept of ideology. It is of course possible to put forward the hypothesis that ideology in a positive sense, for instance ideology as 'Marxism-Leninism', is no longer appealing within the Soviet Union. This idea has been put forward by Bell as a sort of extension to his thesis of the end of ideology in the West. The idea is basically the same: ideology as Marxism-Leninism is 'losing its full coercive and even persuasive power', it is no longer dynamic enough as a convincing theory in the socialist societies. See 'The "End of Ideology" in the Soviet Union?', in M. M. Drachkovitch (ed.), *Marxist Ideology in the Contemporary World*, Praeger, New York, 1966. It seems to me that Bell's thesis may have certain elements of truth in so far as the Soviet Union and East European countries are concerned. Even though it is doubtful that Marxism has lost all its power in socialist societies, it is certainly true that its transformation into the schematic and rigid orthodoxy of an 'official ideology' has very much contributed to its lack of creativity and imagination and, in sum, to its general loss of appeal.
84. F. Hinkelammert, *Ideologías del Desarrollo y Dialéctica de la Historia*, Editorial Nueva Universidad, Santiago, 1970, pp.288–93.

Index